Street Football, Gender and Muslim Youth in the Netherlands

Bloomsbury Studies in Religion, Gender, and Sexuality

Series Editors:
Dawn Llewellyn, Sonya Sharma and Sîan Hawthorne

This interdisciplinary series explores the intersections of religions, genders, and sexualities. It promotes the dynamic connections between gender and sexuality across a diverse range of religious and spiritual lives, cultures, histories, and geographical locations, as well as contemporary discourses around secularism and non-religion. The series publishes cutting-edge research that considers religious experiences, communities, institutions, and discourses in global and transnational contexts, and examines the fluid and intersecting features of identity and social positioning.

Using theoretical and methodological approaches from inter/transdisciplinary perspectives, *Bloomsbury Studies in Religion, Gender, and Sexuality* addresses the neglect of religious studies perspectives in gender, queer, and feminist studies. It offers a space where gender can critically engage with religion, and for exploring questions of intersectionality, particularly with respect to critical race, disability, post-colonial and decolonial theories.

Becoming Queer and Religious in Malaysia and Singapore
Sharon A. Bong

Beyond Religion in India and Pakistan
Navtej K. Purewal and Virinder S. Kalra

Experience, Identity & Epistemic Injustice within Ireland's Magdalene Laundries
Chloe K. Gott

Narrative, Identity and Ethics in Postcolonial Kenya
Eleanor Tiplady Higgs

Street Football, Gender and Muslim Youth in the Netherlands

Girls Who Kick Back

Kathrine van den Bogert

BLOOMSBURY ACADEMIC
LONDON · NEW YORK · OXFORD · NEW DELHI · SYDNEY

BLOOMSBURY ACADEMIC
Bloomsbury Publishing Plc
50 Bedford Square, London, WC1B 3DP, UK
1385 Broadway, New York, NY 10018, USA
29 Earlsfort Terrace, Dublin 2, Ireland

BLOOMSBURY, BLOOMSBURY ACADEMIC and the Diana logo are
trademarks of Bloomsbury Publishing Plc

First published in Great Britain 2023
This paperback edition published 2024

Copyright © Catharina Elizabeth van den Bogert, 2023, 2024

Catharina Elizabeth van den Bogert has asserted her right under the Copyright, Designs and Patents Act, 1988, to be identified as Author of this work.

This work is published subject to a Creative Commons Attribution Non-commercial No Derivatives Licence. You may share this work for non-commercial purposes only, provided you give attribution to the copyright holder and the publisher.

For legal purposes the Acknowledgements on p. viii constitute an extension of this copyright page.

Cover image © wundervisuals / Getty Images

Bloomsbury Publishing Plc does not have any control over, or responsibility for, any third-party websites referred to or in this book. All internet addresses given in this book were correct at the time of going to press. The author and publisher regret any inconvenience caused if addresses have changed or sites have ceased to exist, but can accept no responsibility for any such changes.

A catalogue record for this book is available from the British Library.

Library of Congress Control Number: 2022933169

ISBN: HB: 978-1-3502-0504-8
PB: 978-1-3502-0508-6
ePDF: 978-1-3502-0505-5
eBook: 978-1-3502-0506-2

Series: Bloomsbury Studies in Religion, Gender, and Sexuality

Typeset by Newgen KnowledgeWorks Pvt. Ltd., Chennai, India

To find out more about our authors and books visit www.bloomsbury.com
and sign up for our newsletters

To all children and youth in the world out there. Let your play and creativity be an example for all of us.

And to my own children, Jorg and René, the best in the world is playing with you.

Contents

Acknowledgements   viii

1	Introduction	1
2	An ethnography of Muslim girls' street football	19
3	Histories of Moroccan-Dutch youth: Migration, politics and street football	37
4	Being young in a contested neighbourhood	47
5	Invading the public football playground	69
6	The street football competition: Girls only?	101
7	Playing religion, gender and citizenship	125
8	Girls who kick back	153

Notes	161
References	173
Index	193

Acknowledgements

I'm most grateful for all the girls and boys, women and men from the Schilderswijk. You have welcomed me, and you continue to welcome me in your community and in your neighbourhood. This is one of the biggest gifts that a researcher can receive. I truly enjoy every time I'm with you. You are the future and I believe in you, whatever other people say.

This book has been written over a long period. It started in 2013 at the Utrecht University as my PhD research. I wish to thank all my colleagues at Utrecht University for the years we have worked together: my PhD supervisors, the PhD candidates, the international religion and gender network, and the colleagues I taught courses with. A special thanks goes to Gerdien Steenbeek for always being there for me.

The book as it lies in front of you now had been written during my postdoctoral research position at the Radboud University Nijmegen. I thank my supervisors and colleagues for providing me the time and facilities to write this book. I've really missed your presence during the pandemic; no online gathering can make up for the lunches we used to have pre-Covid.

Over these years, I am also indebted to many scholars whom I consider my academic friends, the Feminist Fellowship and the Scuola di Torino, RUNOMI and countless others. A special thanks to Natashe Lemos Dekker for becoming my academic soulmate.

My family, parents, brothers and sister, have always been there for me. And my grandmother, who passed away during the writing of this book. There was also the birth of our children, Jorg, our eldest, and René, who will arrive when this book is being produced. Ivo, I'm proud of how we manage everything together. Thank you all for being with me.

The research for and publication of this book has been financed by NWO, the Dutch Research Council (project number 328-98-006) and by the NWO Open Access Books fund. This research has also been awarded with the *Boymansprijs*, the Dutch national prize for best PhD research on sport, physical education and leisure.

1

Introduction

There is a large parade of orange-dressed football fans walking to the football stadium in Enschede, in the east of the Netherlands. Before the Women's European Championship started that summer in 2017 in the Netherlands, no one had expected that women's football would become so popular in the country. But this is the final, and against expectations, the Dutch Orange Lionesses had placed themselves for the final against Denmark. The players are strengthened by the orange football fans from all over the country, and even when in the fifth minute they are 1–0 behind, they feel they are winning this championship. The match is exciting, and the Danish players do not give it easily away. In half-time, it is 2–2, but shortly after, Sherida Spitse makes it 3–2, and a few minutes before the end of the game, top scorer Vivianne Miedema shoots her team to the championship (Postma 2019, 72–6). For the first time in history, the Dutch women's football players had won the UEFA Women's Euro. Later that year, they received the Joke Smit encouragement prize, a biannual Dutch government prize for emancipation in the Netherlands. The Orange Lionesses received the most votes out of forty nominees in an online election. The prize is named after Joke Smit (1933–1981), a famous Dutch feminist who played a prominent role in the women's emancipation movement. Two years later, in 2019, the Orange players impressively made it to the final of the World Championship in France and in 2021 to the quarter finals of the Tokyo Olympic Games, which they both lost from the United States, historically the leading women's football country.

Despite not managing to beat the United States, the Orange Lionesses became and stayed important role models for girls and boys in the Netherlands, as the jury of the Joke Smit prize stated.[1] Since the European Championship in 2017, they even became real celebrities. However, the striking absence of Moroccan-Dutch football players in the Orange Lionesses team brings to the fore the question whether they are actually a role model for *all* Dutch girls and boys. Most players have white Dutch ethnic backgrounds, two players have

Surinamese-Dutch ethnic backgrounds and one is Colombian-Dutch. None of the players is known to be Muslim. Over the years, the team has professionalized and has been conquering the international sport arena, but there is still little racial/ethnic and religious diversity in the national team, contrary to the Dutch men's football team, which has historically and currently many players with Moroccan-Dutch backgrounds.

Many of these male footballers started playing street football as children, often in urban and multicultural 'disadvantaged' neighbourhoods. Street football is an important starting point for the development of professional football in the Netherlands, although for women's teams this is less the case. Since the 1990s, the Netherlands knows a lively urban street football culture, consisting of mostly men but increasingly also women (de Ruiter 2013; Romijn and Elling 2017, 24). The Amsterdam-based Moluccan-Dutch street football player Rocky became the first and only female member of Street Legends, an international street football team lead by Surinamese-Dutch former professional football player Edgar Davids; and she became the first female character in the street football game Volta Fifa 20. Furthermore, urban football playgrounds named after the famous Dutch football player Johan Cruyff – the Cruyff Courts – are to be found throughout the whole country and also globally. Around the world, every year street football competitions are being played by girls and boys on those Cruyff Courts.

Street football continues to be a popular sport in the Netherlands, and it is gaining more popularity among girls with Moroccan-Dutch, Turkish-Dutch and Muslim backgrounds (Elling 2004, 50; 2015; Elling and Knoppers 2005, 262), who, relatively, are less often members of formal sport clubs (Hoekman et al. 2011b). Although the national team does not have any Moroccan-Dutch or Turkish-Dutch players, Moroccan-Dutch and Turkish-Dutch girls with Muslim backgrounds increasingly occupy urban public playgrounds in Dutch cities by playing street football. At the same time, the increasing visibility of Muslim and ethnic-minority citizens in Dutch cities and public spaces, of which the football playgrounds in this book are an example, feeds anxieties about the supposed 'invasion' of Muslims and migrants in the Netherlands, and in Europe more broadly (Modest and A. de Koning 2016; Oosterbaan 2014). In Dutch public and political debates, ethnic and religious minorities and migrants are seen as 'other', and in need of 'integration', because they, presumably, do not embrace the values of gender and sexual equality (Mepschen, Duyvendak and Tonkens 2010). Moroccan-Dutch and Muslim girls, in particular, are cast as in need of liberation and emancipation, not in the least to be achieved through sport participation.[2] These contestations over ethnic diversity, migration, gender and Islam are often spatialized into specific urban multicultural neighbourhoods that become the iconic sites for racialized politics of integration, emancipation and control (Modest and A. de Koning 2016), such as the Schilderswijk in this research. How do girls in the Schilderswijk deal with and challenge these discourses by playing football in the public playgrounds in their neighbourhood?

Based on ethnographic fieldwork in the Schilderswijk, an urban multicultural neighbourhood of The Hague, this book discusses Moroccan-Dutch and Muslim girls' experiences of playing street football, and it shows how they negotiate their access to and position in both street football and wider Dutch society. The book takes an ethnography of girls' football as its focal point to critically shed light on contemporary dynamics and intersections of gender, race/ethnicity, religion and citizenship in Dutch society. The book focuses on public football playgrounds as well as on a grassroots girls' football competition in the Schilderswijk, Football Girls United, where Moroccan-Dutch Muslim girls between twelve and twenty years old play.[3] The Schilderswijk is one of the most ethnically and religiously diverse neighbourhoods in the Netherlands, and it has a relatively high percentage of young residents. It is also a very well-known place, as it is often portrayed in media, politics and public debates as the most 'disadvantaged' and poorest neighbourhood of the country. Over the years, the neighbourhood became a symbol for all that supposedly went wrong in the Netherlands when it comes to multiculturalism, migrants, Islam, youth and urban public space. This book analyses the experiences of its young residents as they, through playing street football, rework and challenge the categories of difference that are at the core of those discourses on Muslim youth and 'disadvantaged neighbourhoods' in the Netherlands. It emphasizes girls' embodied agency primarily through their sportive (rather than religious) activities, and this is a relevant and new addition to research on Muslim women in sport and research on religion, gender and intersectionality more broadly, in which sport has been indeed a marginal topic.

Muslim youth and sport in the Netherlands

In the Netherlands, the degree of sport participation among various demographic groups is mostly measured in terms of club membership. Thus, groups who play sports mostly outside official club contexts, such as girls with migrant backgrounds, are, in official statistical reports, said to 'lag behind' in sport participation compared with migrant boys and white Dutch boys and girls (Elling and Cremers 2021). Starting from this assumption, various policies and sport programmes for Muslim and migrant girls are developed to enhance their sport participation.[4] For example, the Dutch Royal Football Association (KNVB) engaged in such a project, *Time for Sport: Recruit and Retain Migrant Girls* (KNVB 2009). A few years ago, they broadened the project to 'recruit and retain girls' in general, but they still give specific attention to groups of migrant and religious-minority girls (KNVB 2014; Siebelink 2016b). The assumption by the KNVB that migrant and Muslim girls lag behind in football is striking since other sociological research has pointed out that football is the most popular team sport activity in the Netherlands, amongst all groups: women, men, girls and boys, including ethnic-minority girls living in urban neighbourhoods (Elling and Knoppers 2005; Romijn and Elling 2017, 19–24). This popularity, however, does not always translate into girls' membership of football clubs, especially not in urban neighbourhoods where girls with migrant backgrounds mostly play 'unorganized' football in urban playgrounds and in the streets (Hoekman et al. 2011b).

In Dutch youth sports policies, official participation in sports clubs is seen as 'real' sports participation and 'unorganized' sports in playgrounds merely as a step towards that. The aim of the national *Participation Migrant Youth through Sports* programme initiated by the Ministry of Health, Welfare and Sport and the Ministry of Integration and Housing in 2008, for example, was to increase youths with migrant backgrounds' official sports club membership (Hoekman et al. 2011a). In the Schilderswijk, too, several organizations organize sports hours in playgrounds as a bridge to the ultimate goal: membership of official sports clubs. In practice, this narrative means that 'informal' forms of sports participation, mainly street football, by minoritized groups are valued less than institutionalized forms of sports participation by societies' dominant groups. Framing Muslim and ethnic-minority girls as lagging behind in football and sport fits precisely in the dominant narrative of Muslim girls as oppressed and unemancipated, hence as not truly participating in Dutch society; while their football participation in urban playgrounds is actually high and vastly increasing (Elling and Knoppers 2005; Romijn and Elling 2017). These numbers, however, often do not make it into official statistics.

It is no coincidence that Dutch policies and sport organizations are so preoccupied with Muslim youth' sport participation. Youth sports, and parents' involvement in youth sports through volunteering, are seen as the pre-eminent space for civic engagement and as the main, 'proper' way of participation and inclusion in Dutch society (Rana 2014, 36).[5] Moreover, youth sports is a central element of urban regeneration policies to 'improve' disadvantaged neighbourhoods and its supposed problematic urban racialized youths. Sports is a main instrument through which young citizens in diverse urban spaces can be disciplined, integrated or assimilated into dominant national norms and values (Besnier and Brownell 2012, 453; Gagen 2000; Jaffe-Walter 2016, 64; Silverstein 2000; 2002; Spaaij 2009; Toffoletti and Palmer 2017), and the sphere where the supposed gap between white Dutch and racialized migrant youngsters can be bridged (Krouwel et al. 2006; Rana 2014; van Sterkenburg 2011). Football is especially popular in youth and neighbourhood sports programmes, because of its popularity amongst youths of all backgrounds, but also because of its important role in Dutch nationalism. In Dutch national identity, men's football figures highly and it is, next to King's Day, the biggest space of embodying Dutch nationalist 'orange' pride (Elling, van Hilvoorde and van den Dool 2014). It is telling that at the cover of the yearly report on integration by the national organization of statistics (CBS 2016), there is a picture of a young woman with a headscarf playing football, as if a Muslim 'migrant' girl playing football is the summum of integration in the Netherlands. The racialization of Muslims, and the framing of them as 'other' who still need to be integrated into the Dutch nation (Bracke 2011; El-Tayeb 2011; M. de Koning 2016; Wekker 2016), is thus also very apparent in the Dutch sport landscape, not in the least through urban regeneration and neighbourhood football programmes.

These neighbourhood sport projects are strongly gendered: 'Moroccan' and Muslim boys are framed in public and political discourses as the ultimate embodiment of the 'problematic other' and are seen as a threat or danger, for example, related to crime, radicalization or nuisance (A. de Koning 2013; 2016; Masquelier and Soares 2016, 17). Muslim girls, on the other hand, are mostly framed as 'in danger': they are seen as oppressed, victims of their supposedly backward Islamic and/or ethnic background, and in need of emancipation (Abu-Lughod 2002; 2013; Masquelier and Soares 2016, 17; Ramji 2007). Thus, participation in neighbourhood sports is used as a tool for Muslim girls' emancipation and empowerment, and, for Muslim and racialized boys, as a form of regulating aggression, radicalization and criminal behaviour (Rana 2014). Sports programmes that aim at social cohesion and integration in ethnically mixed neighbourhoods in practice thus often reinforce gendered and ethnic differences and social divisions (Krouwel et al. 2006, 167; Rana 2014; Spaaij 2009; van Sterkenburg 2011; Vermeulen and Verweel 2009). This book takes the public playgrounds and the girls' football competition in the Schilderswijk as starting points to investigate how the 'targeted' youths of urban regeneration and sports policies themselves engage with differences of gender, race/ethnicity and religion in urban public space and in Dutch society more broadly, through playing football.

Women's football and women's sport: Intersectional perspectives

Women's football is one of the fastest growing sports, both in the Netherlands and globally. This is part of a larger development of the feminization of sport, in which women participate in a wider range of sports than in generations past, and have been more often covered in sports media (Toffoletti, Thorpe and Francombe-Webb 2018). Nevertheless, women's participation in traditionally male sports such as football still give rise to experiences of great inequality, as has been well documented by feminist scholars of sport (e.g. Aitchison 2004; Woodward 2009) and football in specific (e.g. Caudwell 2011; Jeanes 2011). They have shown how the organization of football, as most other sports, is built on the premise of sexed and gender-segregated bodies, resulting in a nearly universal separation of men's and women's competitions (Alpert 2015, 30; Anderson 2008; Caudwell 2003). In football, men are the 'default', illustrated by the case that the general term 'football' usually refers to *men* playing the sport, while for women playing football apparently a gender marker is needed and the term 'women's football' is used (Caudwell 2011; Williams 2007).[6] Despite the growing participation of girls and women, football is still very much constructed around traditional gender norms, in which the sport is normatively valued against hegemonic 'masculine' ideals of competition, physicality, aggression, strength and musculairty, and men's football is thereby by default valued higher than women's football (Elling and Knoppers 2005; Jeanes 2011; Williams 2003).

What is considered as an acceptable form of femininity in football is, however, changing. Women's football was traditionally described by referring to the 'butch *lesbian*' image (Caudwell 1999), while its popularity nowadays seems to exist on the premise of *hetero*sexual attraction of the women players for its (mainly) heterosexual male audience. Hence the (hetero)sexualizing of female athletes in sports media seems to be the norm (Caudwell 2003, 380; Elling, Peeters and Stentler 2017; van den Heuvel 2017). Women's and girls' participation in football is often 'accepted' only on the basis of precisely embodying 'feminine' ideals of fitness, sexiness and slimness (Azzarito 2010; Jeanes 2011; Samie 2013), for example, avoiding growing muscles (van den Heuvel 2017, 163; Jeanes 2011). Scholars have also shown that whiteness is central in this construction of normative athletic femininity, as non-white athletic bodies are dominantly considered as less feminine (Azzarito 2010; 2018; Adjepong and Carrington 2014) and hence normative athletic femininity discursively excludes racialized and Muslim athletes. Racialized Muslim women are often stereotypically portrayed as oppressed, passive and inactive, and therefore athletic femininity is seen as 'alien' to them (Ahmad 2011; Ratna 2011; Samie 2013). So, while ideas and ideals of 'accepted' femininities in sport change, bodies, gender, femininity, sexuality and race stay important fault lines in defining the norms and inclusion in football (Scraton et al. 1999).

The regulation, classification, organization and adaptation of sporting bodies in order to fit gender, sexuality and racial norms (such as sex testing and the control and regulation of hormones; think of the case of Caster Semenya) is a central task of national and international sport governing bodies, and those regulations are further enacted in the normative sporting practices on local levels (Besnier, Brownell and Carter 2018; Butler 1998; Caudwell 2003; Woodward 2009). As Judith Butler states, gendered and sexed bodies are socially constructed and naturalized through sport, although she also mentions the opportunity to challenge traditional ideas of femininity in and through women's sport (Butler 1998; Caudwell 2003).

Indeed, sport in general and football in particular are also eminent domains for resistance, empowerment, contestation and transgression of hegemonic gender, sexual and racial norms and for the reworking of dominant power relations (Carrington 2010; Thangaraj 2015). Sport is an embodied domain in which the negotiations of inclusion and exclusion within the national fabric are central (Carrington 2010; Thangaraj 2015). Racialized minorities can portray their athletic bodies in such a way that it goes against dominant stereotypes – of passive South-East-Asian masculinity in the United States (Thangaraj 2015, 4) or 'dangerous' Muslim boyhood in the UK (Farooq 2011), for example. As I will show, for the girls in this book, football is also an important domain in which they could go against stereotypes of them as passive and inactive Moroccan-Dutch Muslim women. It is this contradictory nature of sport that feminist scholars of sport have focused on: sport as dominating *and* empowering, as reproducing *and* resisting gender, sexual and racial norms (Scraton et al. 1999), and this will also be demonstrated in this book.

However, Toffoletti, Thorpe and Francombe-Webb (2018, 7) indicate a recent development in sport that is built on Western neoliberal ideologies and that places an emphasis on self-discipline and 'individual empowerment, personal responsibility and entrepreneurial subjecthood'. Women especially are expected to embody ideals of fit and autonomous subjects that are personally responsible for their own successes or failures. This is even more the case when it concerns women with racialized Muslim backgrounds, as Samie and Toffoletti (2018) show in their discussion of the media representation of American Muslim sportswomen Ibtihaj Muhammad and Dalilah Muhammad. Their sportive success and agency is read in mainstream media as sign of 'overcoming' sexism, racism and Islamophobia, thereby ignoring structural inequalities of class, race and religion in sport and society more broadly.[7] Such a limited conceptualization of agency is also found in much sociological research on Muslim women and sport, as Ratna and Samie (2018, 16) state: 'When attention turned to the agentic capacity of women from these communities, researchers were preoccupied with defining their resistance, not necessarily to overturn racist, Eurocentric structures within sport, but on fighting discriminatory "backward" traditions within their own culture and against their own men.'

Women, and especially racialized women, are dichotomously understood in sports media, dominant Western sociological research and wider public discourses to either be 'emancipated' and equal participants in a sport world in which inequality does not exist anymore, or cast as 'victims' of patriarchal sports industry and racialized culture (Toffoletti, Thorpe and Francombe-Webb 2018, 3). This obscures the complex and continuous negotiations with racial, gendered and sexual norms that athletes are facing in their sport participation and practices, as well as in the larger society.

It is clear that an intersectional perspective, centred on the gendered, sexual and racial structural power relations and inequalities, in women's football and women's sport is necessary and needed. Such a critical perspective in sport studies is growing, albeit still limited (Ifekwunigwe 2017; Ratna and Samie 2018). There is also a gap between studies on sport that take intersections of gender, race, ethnicity and nationality into account, and studies that focus on religion, most notably Muslim women, gender and sport.[8] For example, Adjepong and Carrington (2014), Carrington (2010), McDonald (2014), Ratna (2014), Scraton, Caudwell and Holland (2005), and Watson and Ratna (2011) focus on the intersections of race/ethnicity, gender and sexuality in sport. They discuss the dominant whiteness of women's football and women's sports, the racializing and sexualizing of Black sportswomen and the strategies of non-white players in dealing with racism and sexism. Some of them mention 'Muslim' as part of the category race but do not explicitly conceptualize how the category 'Muslim' is racialized and gendered in sport and how 'secular' assumptions in sport play a role in the racialization of religion and specifically Islam. In most collections, there are separate chapters on Muslim women and sport, taking it slightly separate from discussions of race and gender in sport. With a few exceptions (Rana 2018; Ratna 2011; Ratna and Samie 2018; Samie 2013), intersectional scholars of sport generally do not take racialized and gendered *religious* 'othering' in sport central.

On the other hand, the large body of (mostly sociological) scholarship on Muslim women and sport have not taken a critical intersectional perspective but reproduce 'essentialist representations about "sporting Muslim women" in hierarchical and binary juxtapositions that ultimately position Muslim women as regulated subjects that are "less than" and "inferior" to their western counterparts' (Ratna and Samie 2018, 53). Most research on Muslim women and sport (e.g. Benn and Pfister 2013; Benn, Pfister and Jawad 2011; Kay 2006) has largely been from a problematic perspective centring on the *hijab* and gender segregation without paying attention to intersecting structural power relations, let alone racism.[9] These scholars simply respond to, and thereby reproduce, the assumption of a low participation of Muslim women in sport, especially in Western contexts, and they generally aim to indicate and remove the factors that limit Muslim women's participation, both through proposed adaptations of sports spaces and through providing positive interpretations of Islamic teachings on sports (e.g. Benn, Pfister and Jawad 2011; Dagkas, Benn and Knez 2014; Hargreaves and Vertinsky 2007; Pfister 2010; Walseth and Fasting 2003). Thereby they describe an essentialized picture of Islam and create a duality between 'Western' individual sports cultures, identities and practices and 'Islamic' collective identities, cultures and religious practices. Those 'two sides' are seen as incompatible with each other, and sporting Muslim women are framed as 'caught in between'.

Even studies that critique the narrative that links modern sport only with 'Western' and secular culture build on this dichotomy in their aim to prove that Islamic cultures also engage with sport. These studies keep the 'Western'/secular sport versus Islamic sport dichotomy in place because they merely focus on Muslims who play sports from a religious point of view as different from non-Muslim secular players (e.g. Burrmann and Mutz 2016; Jiwani and Rail 2010; Testa and Amara 2016). As such, these authors single out the *religious* aspects in their analysis, while many sporters who feature in their publications also mention other aspects as central for their sporting practices, such as being fit and healthy, losing weight and having an active and consumer lifestyle. These aspects are now simply overlooked. While these critical studies give important insights into how religious women experience sporting spaces and practices, it has the unintended consequence that Muslim women in sport are seen as constituted *only* or *primarily* by their religious backgrounds and communities, and not *also* by the dichotomous gendered and sexualized organization of sports and the gender and sexual norms in broader society (Samie 2013, 257–8). In line with Samie (2013), this book emphasizes that it is not the girls' Muslim backgrounds but rather the gendered organization of football, the male dominance in football playgrounds and the lack of female role models that form potential barriers for Muslim girls in sport and that made the girls organize their own girls' football competition in the Schilderswijk. Furthermore, the conceptualization of agency in most research on Muslim women and sport as resting on a still secular notion of agency as liberating itself from Islamic men's patriarchy (Ratna and Samie 2018, 51) is highly problematic and limited. It is this question of agency that has also been explored in feminist and anthropological studies of Muslim women, gender and the secular, which I will turn to now.

Muslim women, agency and the secular: Anthropological perspectives

Anthropologist Saba Mahmood's work on the Muslim women's piety movement in Cairo, Egypt, has stimulated a new turn in feminist and anthropological work on women's agency, one that critiques dominant conceptualizations of agency in feminist scholarship that are based on secular neoliberal frameworks. Mahmood (2005) and other feminist scholars of religion and the post-secular (e.g. Bracke 2008; Braidotti 2008) have conceptualized religious women's agency *beyond* resistance and liberation, also accounting for the embodiment and cultivation of gendered and religious conservative norms as a form of agency, for example, by studying pious (mainly Muslim and Christian) women in religious movements. Recent critiques, however, have discussed the prevalence of *piety* in these conceptualizations of agency. Studies of religious women's agency foreground experiences and perspectives from very pious women in explicitly religious settings, in which their *religious* subjectivity and agency is foregrounded (Liberatore 2017; Schielke 2009, 24; 2010, 2; Sehlikoglu 2018, 82).

This is also visible in works that focus on Muslim youth, gender and leisure; for example, Fernando (2016) studied *pious* Muslim French youths, Ryan and Vacchelli (2013) interviewed *observant* Muslim mothers in London about the upbringing of their children, and Amir-Moazami (2010) focused on young *pious* women in Islamic organizations in France and Germany. The single focus on pious youths and mothers results in a rather limited perspective on young Muslims' urban, leisure and sports activities. For example, they emphasize the need for gender-segregated leisure spaces (Amir-Moazami 2010; Fernando 2016; Ryan and Vacchelli 2013), while this is not for all Muslims a key religious issue (Rana 2018). Because of the religious setting as context for the research and the focus on pious or observant Muslim women and youth, these authors mainly explore Muslim women's actions, subjectivity and agency through the lens of piety or religiousness.

Although this work on religious women's agency remains an important counterpart to the implicit secular assumptions in much feminist scholarship on agency, as well as to the secular assumptions in sport sociological research on Muslim women and sport, I agree with Lara Deeb that 'the "pious Muslim" became *the only visible* Muslim' (Deeb 2015, 95, emphasis original). The large attention to piety in studies of Muslim women's agency does not correspond with the experiences and practices of the young Muslim football players in this book. They, like many other religious young women and men, do not necessarily aspire to live a very pious, observant life or engage with explicit Islamic or religious (sport) organizations. And even if they do, many religious young women and men also engage with organizations that are not explicitly religious or find themselves in secular or not explicitly religious spaces, such as fashion, work, sports, leisure or online spaces (Liberatore 2017; Piela 2017; Schielke 2009; 2010; Sehlikoglu 2018). Religious women's subjectivity or agency is not necessarily always primarily constructed through a pious or religious lens, especially not when it concerns young people (Masquelier and Soares 2016, 27; Schielke 2009).

The single focus on pious and observant women and the overemphasis on religion when studying Muslim women overlooks other sources and practices of agency that are not directly related to being Muslim or being pious (Liberatore 2017; Sehlikoglu 2018) or forms of agency that take place in and through non-religious or secular spaces such as sport and leisure. This book, rather, will precisely emphasize those other sources and practices of agency, by studying football as primary domain of agency for Dutch Muslim girls. Indeed, as also Deeb and Harb (2013, 17) state for their Muslim research participants, becoming a more pious person is only 'one goal among many, and not necessarily the dominant one at any given time'. Furthermore, the large focus on piety reinforces the notion of Muslim youth as 'different' or 'other' and unintentionally sets them apart from supposed 'Western' secular or Christian white youth, while they actually share many of their 'ordinary' aspirations with non-Muslim fellow citizens (Masquelier and Soares 2016, 24) or, in the case of this book, with non-Muslim fellow football players.

The girls who participated in my research almost all identify as Muslim, yet most of them were not explicitly observant or pious in the sportive spaces in which the research took place. Furthermore, they were not selected for the research because they are Muslim but because they play football. They could fall in the category that Masquelier and Soares (2016, 25) and Sehlikoglu (2018, 84) have described as 'youth who happen to be Muslim'. It is this group that has, until now, been virtually invisible in feminist and anthropological research on Muslim women, agency and gender. In addition to making the lives of 'girls who happen to be Muslim' invisible, the emphasis on piety unintentionally reinforces the notion of Muslims as 'different' or 'other' in presumably secular European societies.

While the acknowledgement that being Muslim entails more than only being pious has now gained recognition in recent scholarship, as the discussion until now has shown, I contend that there is still a problem with terminology and the framing of those 'other practices', such as sport. For example, some sport sociologists have called for a focus on 'other' practices of Muslim women in sport, such as Muslim women as spectators, as coaches or in leadership positions (Toffoletti and Palmer 2017). Although an important call, this also leads me to ask, what, then, is the added value of the label 'Muslim' here? What is 'Muslim' about being a sport coach, or a spectator or a player for that matter? Can we not simply study them as sport coaches and not as 'Muslims'? Anthropologists Deeb and Harb (2013) and Schielke and Debevec (2012) still approach leisure through the lens of Muslimness, Islam or religion and not as a priori through the lens of leisure or sport in itself, as becomes visible in the titles of their work: *Leisurely Islam* and *An Anthropology of Everyday Religion*. Deeb and Harb (2013), and Masquelier and Soares (2016), also, in the end, look at leisure to explore 'Muslimness', 'ways of being Muslim', or look at combinations of leisure with piety, although they recognize that Islam is not for all Muslim youth 'the most important element in their modes of self-identification' (Masquelier and Soares 2016, 10). In this book, to the contrary, I will not explore what sports participation means for ways of being Muslim or for Muslim identities, but how sport participation in and of itself is a domain in which Muslim youth negotiate intersecting issues of gender, religion, race/ethnicity and citizenship.

This is not to say that religion or a Muslim identity is not important for the girls in my research, but for them it is not the primary concern whilst playing football. For example, they more than once mentioned that, on the field, they do not necessarily identify as Muslim but as football player. Hence, I do not look at what their football practices *say* or *do* for their Muslim identity or belief but rather study their football practices first and foremost as an embodied domain in itself. Inevitably, this brings up the question of whether the girls I studied on the football fields should be described as 'Muslim' girls at all, rather than, for example, as 'football' girls. Building on the work of some anthropologists of Islam who have started deconstructing the label 'Muslim' (e.g. Fernando 2014; Sehlikoglu 2018), I indeed question the attachment of the label 'Muslim' to everything that 'girls who happen to be Muslim' do, such as sport. In this book, therefore, the girls will primarily be described as football players, and where relevant I will discuss how being Muslim comes into their experiences and practices as football players, especially in how they are continuously seen as Muslims by dominant white Dutch society and how they negotiate that stereotypical framing through playing football.

The argument I make to focus on 'Muslim' lives beyond piety, and to question the relevance of the categories 'Muslim' and 'Islam' in sports spaces, is not to reinstall a separation between religion/piety and 'everyday' practices such as football, as religion and piety are of course also lived every day (Fadil and Fernando 2015). It is to question the easy attachment of the labels 'Muslim' or 'Islam' to everything that Muslims do every day, simply because they supposedly embody religious difference and religious otherness in European or Dutch sports spaces.

This also brings up the question of the secular in relation to Islam, religion and football, especially because football and sports spaces in Western societies are often perceived as secular spaces. Anthropologists of the secular have argued that the secular and religion are not opposites but produce each other, and that secular practices, spaces and bodies are also produced through negotiations with ideologies, norms and expectations in particular contexts (Asad 2003; Fadil 2011; Hirschkind 2011), such as the gendered heteronormativity in sports spaces. Thus, the perspective I propose is not a matter of conceptualizing football as religious *or* as secular, but a question of how playing football is informed by intersecting religious *and* secular ideologies, practices and norms, and how and when football spaces acquire religious and secular meanings. For example, this book shows that when Muslim girls play football in public spaces, these spaces are often immediately perceived by white Dutch sports professionals as 'Islamic' spaces that 'clash' with the supposed secular nature of Dutch public sports spaces. Yet, the girls themselves do not necessarily construct their football spaces as religious or Islamic. Rather, by playing football, they resist the dominant construction of their footballing bodies as religious 'others' in Dutch public football playgrounds. Football spaces and practices are thus not fixed as secular or religious but gain meaning through both the dominant discourses about Muslims and Islam in the Netherlands and through the football practices of girls themselves (see also M. de Koning 2008).

The girls in this book are not so much occupied with religious or pious Islamic practices, but primarily with playing football and, as turns out, with their contested belonging to Dutch public football spaces as Muslim girls. By focusing on playing football as a source of their agency, I do not want to go 'back' to a normative idea of agency as resistance based on secular liberal assumptions, as Mahmood (2005) and Samie (2018), among others, have successfully criticized. But I also do not want to limit Muslim girls' agency to their 'Muslim' identity, an agency solely stemming from religious and pious embodied practices. In order to account for the experiences of Muslim girls beyond, on the one hand, as merely enmeshed in oppressive patriarchal power structures, and, on the other hand, as primarily constituted by piety, I develop the concept 'kicking back', based on theories of performance and play and the concept 'talking back'.

Kicking back: The play and performativity of street football

'Talking back', as elaborated on by hooks (1989; 2015) and for the Dutch context by Bracke (2011), Van den Brandt (2019) and Van Es (2016; 2019), refers to minoritized women and girls engaging with and critiquing dominant societal discourses and stereotypes, thereby emphasizing their empowerment and agency. At the same time, this concept acknowledges that in order to talk back at these discourses, one cannot escape, to some extent, to draw on the (stigmatizing) terminologies and categories *of* those discourses (Bracke 2011; van den Brandt 2019, 308). hooks (1989, 22), from her own experiences as a child, defined talking back as 'speaking as an equal to an authority figure', 'daring to disagree', 'just having an opinion' and 'to make oneself heard'. In her childhood, talking back was often seen as negative, especially for girls, but in her writing, hooks has reappropriated talking back as an empowering and agentive act. She suggests that writing and speaking for individuals from oppressed, colonized groups 'is not solely an expression of creative power; it is an act of resistance, a political gesture that challenges politics of domination that would render us nameless and voiceless. As such, it is a courageous act – as such, it represents a threat' (hooks 2015, 27). Talking back represents a threat to the existing discourses on difference and Muslim women in the Netherlands, because it precisely relies on and uses those discourses (Bracke 2011; M. de Koning 2016), and thereby meticulously reshape and transform them.

Talking back, furthermore, is a powerful act because it is a multilayered response, often directed at multiple audiences. Dutch Muslims talk back not only to dominant Dutch discourses that portray them in stereotypical and reductive ways, but also to specific ethnic or Muslim communities, for example, when it comes to gender equality or denouncing (domestic) violence (van den Brandt 2019, 302–3; van Es 2019, 153). Through talking back, Dutch Muslim citizens present themselves as rightful members of the Dutch nation and thereby claim to speak as an equal (van den Brandt 2019, 296, 306; van Es 2019, 154).

Talking back, however, as the term already suggests, emphasizes discursive and linguistic practices of engagement and critiquing dominant discourses. This book shows that there are also other forms that are relevant and worth exploring, forms that draw less on language, writing and speech (or silence) but more on embodiment and movement, playing and performing. Playing football, as has already been suggested in previous sections, is an eminent domain in which dominant discourses and discrimination, racism and sexism can be negotiated and challenged. Anthropologists of play have conceptualized play as a creative force that marks agency, novelty and improvising (Besnier, Brownell and Carter 2018, 28–9), characteristics that are especially visible in children's play (Sawyer 2002). Sport and children's sport, in specific, combines both play and competition, and playfulness and seriousness (Besnier, Brownell and Carter 2018, 1; Dyck 2012). In the case of this book, playing football is a serious attempt to critique and negotiate dominant discourses on Muslim women in a playful manner on the football field.

If play refers to creativity, agency, novelty and improvising, I suggest that informal sports such as street football are in particular a *playful* domain. As will be discussed in more detail in Chapter 3, street football is primarily about creativity, developing tricks, the absence of rules and structures, and the creation of new youth' street cultures. A focus on girls' street football is an important addition to current research on women's football, as that focuses almost exclusively on formal club football. There is little to no research that explicitly addresses contemporary girls' and women's experiences in informal sport spaces such as street football, and this book thus aims to fill that gap.

Furthermore, next to bringing in the realm of informal sports and street football, this book also contributes to existing feminist scholarship by specifically focusing on children's creative practices and experiences. There is little feminist and anthropological research on gender, race/ethnicity, Muslim women, religion and the secular that focuses on children or teenagers.[10] A focus on children allows me to see playing football as a specific form of children's embodied and performative engagement, with gender, race/ethnicity and religion as categories of difference in Dutch society. Feminist scholars have contended that (children's) play is intimately connected to agency and gender performativity (Butler 1990; 1993): Gagen (2000) shows how gender identities and performances were an important aspect of the American playground movement and children's play in those playgrounds, and Thorne (1993) analyses children's play as performance and as a form of 'doing gender' (West and Zimmermann 1987).

Play is also an important component of Butler's conceptualization of gender performativity, the idea that gender comes into being through reiterative acts or performances that are recognized as masculine or feminine and hence become 'naturalized' but also transgressed or critiqued (Butler 1990; 1993). Butler's well-known example of a performative act is drag or cross-dressing, which is according to her the 'parodic proliferation and subversive *play* of gendered meanings' (Butler 1990, 33, emphasis added). Likewise, McClintock (1995) and Smith (2014, 220–1, 233) discuss cross-dressing and play as performative moments that can both affirm and subvert racial and ethnic roles, cultural traditions, social norms and national identity and belonging (see also Hall 2017, 72–3). Play, like performativity, thus points to both inhabiting gender, racial/ethnic and sexual norms and discourses, and to possibilities to transgress these norms. Specifically, women's athletic performances provide alternative meanings of athletic bodies, gender ideals, femininity and masculinity (Butler 1998; Thorne 1993, 5). Going back to children's sports, thus, it is not only about leisure or recreation but also about playful and performative acts of gender, race/ethnicity, religion and national belonging. In the Netherlands, it is especially through the national sport football where women's and girls' athletic performances can create new meanings of gendered and racialized national belonging, as the football players in this book will show.

Integrating insights from 'talking back' and performative play into the concept of 'kicking back' then makes this concept not only about the practice of kicking a ball in the football game but also about playful and performative acts of gender, race/ethnicity, religion and national belonging in which those categories are at the same time critiqued and reappropriated. Kicking back captures girls' politics, resistances and agencies in sport; it is an embodied creative play of minoritized and racialized girls as a way of 'talking back' to dominant societal discourses and categories. In this book, it is the space of street football in which Muslim girls 'kick back' not only at dominant Dutch discourses and assumptions about them but also at gender inequalities within football and within their neighbourhood. Kicking back allows me to emphasize girls' embodied agency primarily through their sportive (rather than religious) activities and this is a relevant and new addition to research on Muslim women in sport and research on religion, gender and intersectionality more broadly, in which sport has been indeed a marginal topic.

Importantly, as also Liberatore (2017) has suggested in her research on Somali Muslim women's aspirations, individuals not only challenge and deconstruct categories of difference and identities but also imagine and reconstruct them in novel ways: 'Aspirational projects are always more than reactive responses, or coping tools in contexts of discrimination and alienation. They are imaginative possibilities that emerge in particular situations, and in response to given circumstances, but are never fully determined by them, as they creatively challenge these circumstances offering new possibilities for the future' (Liberatore, 2017, 19). Kicking back, just like aspirations, emphasizes the creative and embodied practices of resisting dominant norms, restrictive categories and oppressive power structures in society, in and through a newly created space, in the case of this research, the space of girls' street football.

Broader speaking, feminist scholarship should not only be about deconstructing categories; it is also about reconstructing categories more equally, as several scholars have argued: 'To agree that differences – of gender, sexuality, and disability as much as race or culture – have been constructed in oppressive ways that delimit human freedom is to take a stance in which the whole point of *de*constructing such iniquitous structures is to create alternatives in which it becomes possible to *re*articulate difference equitably' (Mercer 2017, 12; see also Collins 2000, 269; Haraway 1988, 585; Liberatore 2017, 3, 17). The girls in this book are the ones who provide the creative lens not only for deconstructing categories of difference but also for rearticulating difference differently through their performative football play.

Overview of the book

The empirical chapters in this book are all dedicated to the different football spaces that are central in the lives of the football players: from a general discussion of the Schilderswijk to the smaller public playgrounds within the neighbourhood, to the girls football competition indoors, and then again to the broader discursive spaces of culturalized citizenship in Dutch society.

First, Chapters 2 and 3 provide the methodological and historical backbone of this research. The feminist ethnographic methods used for this research, as well as its related epistemological and ethical reflections, are presented in Chapter 2. Chapter 3 takes you briefly to the history of Moroccan migration to the Netherlands, the political responses that followed and the emergence of the street football culture in the Netherlands. Chapter 4 functions as a context chapter, in which the Schilderswijk neighbourhood in The Hague is introduced. It shows how public representations of the Schilderswijk are constructed through intersecting classed, racialized and gendered discourses, and critically analyses the role of neighbourhood sports programmes. Last but not least, this chapter discusses how young residents in the Schilderswijk themselves perceive their neighbourhood and how they experience living and playing there.

In Chapter 5, the experiences of girls who play football in the public playgrounds in the Schilderswijk are central. Using Nirmal Puwar's concept 'space invaders' (2004), it shows how public sports spaces are gendered, racialized and based on a secular norm, and how Moroccan-Dutch Muslim girls navigate these spaces. Chapter 6 focuses on playing football indoors, in the gym hall where the grassroots football competition Football Girls United takes place. The chapter discusses the motivations of girls to play football in this specific *girls'* football competition; yet, contrary to what its name might suggest, it also analyses the involvement of *boys* in Football Girls United. Thereby, it critically reflects on constructions of masculinity, femininity and heteronormativity in sport. Chapter 7 zooms out on discourses of culturalized citizenship in the Netherlands and the place of Muslim girls and football within those discourses. The chapter shows how football girls in the Schilderswijk incorporate the categories of gender, Islam and ethnicity in their football strategies, and how they create alternative citizenship practices by playing football. In the final chapter, I discuss the ways in which the football girls in this research are kicking back at multiple discourses and audiences through their football play. I conclude by arguing that feminist and anthropological research should attend to the experiences of Muslim girls not only from a religious point of view but also by taking into account practices that are not explicitly religious, such as playing football. Those practices are important for studying the performative and agentive possibilities of Muslim women and girls in its full scope, rather than only from a religious agency perspective.

2

An ethnography of Muslim girls' street football

This book is primarily based on ten months of ethnographic research in the Schilderswijk in the The Hague between 2014 and 2015, as part of a broader research on women's football in the Netherlands.[1] Between 2015 and 2021, I continued to engage with the football players of Football Girls United (FGU), and those follow-up visits also informed the ethnographic material and analysis in this book. In this chapter, I discuss the specific methods, locations, ethical considerations and the politicized nature of doing research with Dutch Muslim teenagers. The research is based on a feminist epistemological approach (Abu-Lughod 1990; Brooks and Hesse-Biber 2007; Collins 2000; Fonow and Cook 2005), seeing knowledge and data not as objective facts but as constructed through situated and reflexive research interactions with the young football players from the Schilderswijk (Haraway 1988; Narayan 1993). The book also relates to the core feminist principle of social justice (Davis and Craven 2016, 9–11), as it focuses on a grassroots girls' football initiative that is itself committed to this principle and to the empowerment and inclusion of Moroccan-Dutch and Muslim girls in the Schilderswijk and in broader Dutch society.

Feminist ethnography: Fieldwork, methods and ethics

The ethnographic fieldwork for this study started in 2014 in several cities in the Netherlands: The Hague, Maastricht, Arnhem, Utrecht, Amsterdam and Kampen. For four months, I visited Cruyff Court playgrounds in these cities during organized football activities, mostly 6 vs 6 Cruyff Court competitions,[2] and I focused on the experiences of girls in street football. After this initial fieldwork phase, I decided for an in-depth case study of one specific urban neighbourhood and its different street football spaces, namely the Schilderswijk in The Hague, where I conducted fieldwork for eight months in 2014 and 2015. Since 2015, I have stayed closely in touch with Hanan, the coordinator of FGU and my key research participant, and until now I continue to visit the football and youth activities she organizes in the neighbourhood, some periods quite intensively and some periods less.

There were different reasons why I chose the Schilderswijk for my in-depth case study. First, there are many different (girls') football activities taking place: the Cruyff Court 6 vs 6 competitions, playgrounds with organized football activities by the municipality, football in community centres and, especially interesting for my research, a large girls' football competition organized by women and girls from the Schilderswijk themselves: FGU. Second, the Schilderswijk is one of the most ethnically and religiously diverse neighbourhoods in the Netherlands, and its young inhabitants often figure in public debates about integration, urban regeneration, Islam and gender. The grassroots organization of a girls' football competition in a neighbourhood where gender, race/ethnicity, Islam and urban regeneration were perceived to be so urgent proved an interesting case study to see how girls themselves deal with issues of gender, race/ethnicity and religion in a Dutch multicultural neighbourhood.

Hanan, the coordinator of FGU, was very much in favour of more research on girls' football and she was interested in cooperating in this research, so she granted me access to the football trainings and competitions FGU organized and introduced me to the volunteers and the football players. So while the football girls from the Schilderswijk are central in this book, the analysis of girls' football in this neighbourhood is supplemented with research and data from urban diverse neighbourhoods in Utrecht, Amsterdam, Arnhem, Maastricht and Kampen. This is an insightful addition, as it shows that the Schilderswijk is not an isolated or exceptional neighbourhood in the Netherlands – contrary to how it is often represented in media – and that similar experiences and dynamics of girls' football, gender, religion and structural discrimination also play a role in other neighbourhoods.

During the fieldwork, the main methods were participant observation, 'hanging out' and informal talks (Buch and Staller 2007), taking place at public sports playgrounds in the neighbourhood and at street football competitions in sports centres and in public playgrounds. During the fieldwork periods, I travelled about two to three times a week from Utrecht (where I worked and lived) to the Schilderswijk to visit girls' football activities, usually on afternoons after school, evenings or on the weekend. I also participated in other activities FGU organized, such as youth debates and network meetings. In the last four months of my fieldwork, I also lived in The Hague, at the border of the Schilderswijk and an adjacent neighbourhood. In this way, I came to know the neighbourhood better, beyond the football activities I visited.

The football players I engaged with were between ten and twenty years old, and the volunteers of FGU, who were my key research participants, were between fourteen and twenty years old, except for the coordinator Hanan, who was in her early thirties. Often, in ethnographic sports research, the researchers are full participants in the sport they study (Bolin and Granskog 2003). In my research, however, this was less the case. Because of the age differences and, importantly, my lack of football skills, I mostly participated along the sidelines of the football field. I helped with organizing the FGU competition, coaching the teams, keeping track of the scores, preparing food and drinks, and participating in the meetings with the FGU volunteers. This provided ample space for small talks with football players about their experiences and about developments on the football field or in the competition, and to follow the talks the football players had amongst themselves. During other football activities and competitions in the Schilderswijk, such as the 6 vs 6 Cruyff Court competition, I also participated along the sidelines: chatting with substitute players, teachers and trainers. During the course of the research, I found that informal talks were the best method for this study with young football players. I could immediately follow up on their experiences when the players ran off the field, and when they were agitated about the match or the organization of a competition (e.g. the lack of attention for girls in the street football competitions), they were happy they could rant about it to someone who was interested in their story. The number of girls present at the football activities varied from five to eighty, and I usually engaged with one football team of about five to ten girls per research visit.

I took extensive field notes during and after participant observations. Usually when in the field, I took small notes in my notebook or on my phone, writing elaborate field notes on my laptop on the train or when back home. Although I was always open about my role as researcher in the field, I increasingly used my phone to take notes, since that felt less invasive in the research context than a notebook: most of the football players were busy with their phones off (and sometimes on) the field as well.

In addition to participant observations and informal talks, I conducted twenty-one semi-structured in-depth interviews with football players and sports professionals. Ten interviews were with (mainly white) professionals from the municipality and health and welfare organizations in the Schilderswijk, of which two were with Hanan, the coordinator of FGU. Nine interviews were with football girls and two with football boys. Of the interviews with the girls, two were focus groups with a whole football team and two were interviews with a duo, as they preferred an interview together with a fellow football player. Most interviews were conducted on-site near the playgrounds or in a locker room, and some in a community centre, restaurant or at the home of the girls. Also, I walked with some research participants to different football and leisure locations, thus in that way participating in how the girls navigated through their neighbourhood.

All the data that I collected through observations, talks and interviews are in Dutch, and I have performed my analysis based on the Dutch transcripts and observation notes. I have only translated quotes into English when selecting them for inclusion in the chapters; in these translations, I have tried to attend as much as possible to original style and not polish language. I organized and coded my data following the qualitative data analysis approach developed by Boeije (2010), starting with open coding to identify themes and topics in the research data, and then using axial and thematic coding for the analysis.

As part of the reflexive character of feminist ethnography, and as a modest attempt to 'give back' to the research participants (Davis and Craven 2016, 114), I discussed my analysis and findings with some of my research participants after having written the first draft. In March 2018, I attended a network meeting of FGU, where girls and boys from the Schilderswijk are given the opportunity to enlarge their network with potential employers or internship opportunities by playing football together. I was also invited, and, in between the football matches, I informally discussed the chapters and content of the book with the FGU volunteers I worked with most. Although most of them were enthusiastic to hear that my research was almost finished, they were not overly interested in the results; they rather wanted to go back as soon as possible to the football field to play. One participant even said,

> Listen, I've already talked to you in the interviews, I trust that you write about us in a sound way as you've been around for so long, but really, writing this book is your job, not mine.

Although I acknowledge the importance of not only 'using' research participants for the data that they help to produce but also by engaging with them in building the results and conclusions, my research also shows that this might not always be of interest to the research participants themselves, as Davis and Craven also recognize (2016, 114). This was also the case with the women and girls from FGU: they saw my book and conclusions above all as my responsibility; their interest was, and still is, playing football.

As I have described, a considerable part of my research participants were under eighteen years old, the legal age in the Netherlands when someone is considered an adult. Especially in research with minors, ethical issues are necessary to take into account, and I did so during the whole course of the research. I was always open about my role as researcher to the people I encountered during my research. Mostly, I introduced myself as a researcher with an interest in girls' football and in football being played in ethnically and religiously diverse neighbourhoods. However, 'researcher' was a very abstract concept for most of the young research participants, as this is not a role or job they often come across in their daily lives or amongst acquaintances. They could relate to the role of journalists, however, as, at the time of research, many journalists were visiting the Schilderswijk and were interviewing people, similarly to what I was doing. As a result, my research participants sometimes called me 'house journalist' (*huisjournalist*) and I accepted that position; it made it easier for the children and youths in my research to understand what I was doing – namely, interviewing and writing about them – and it therefore enabled them to make a more well-formed decision about whether they wanted to take part in the research or not. I liked the 'house' in 'house journalist', because it suggested that I was not just another researcher or journalist visiting the neighbourhood, but that I was, in a way, attached to the girls' football competition, which I will come back to later in this chapter.

In addition to having informed consent from minor research participants themselves, it is common in social scientific research to also ask the parents or caregivers for informed consent, yet this is not the only way (ERIC 2013). I chose not to ask consent from my research participants' parents or caregivers directly: in the first place, I asked consent from the research participants themselves and the adult who was responsible for the specific youth activity I participated in, usually a sports professional, team coach or a teacher. In addition to that, Hanan, the coordinator of FGU, included a message about my research in a newsletter she sent to the girls' parents. I chose not to ask for direct informed consent from the parents since I considered the spaces where my research participants played football with their friends precisely as spaces where they could play without supervision from their parents, as part of adolescence and the process of growing up. Furthermore, in this way, I could acknowledge children's agency as young citizens in football spaces rather than seeing them as dependent on adults. However, I did engage with parents when they were present during some of the football competitions, talked with them about my research and asked them about their thoughts on girls' football. The parents

I have encountered were all enthusiastic about their daughters' participation in football and stimulated me to conduct research on that topic, as they endorsed the importance to generate more attention for girls' football.

My main concern was thus that the children and young football players themselves gave informed consent for their participation in my study, that they understood that I was going to write about them – without using their real names – based on the talks and interviews. There was always the option for them to decline participation in the research when they did not feel like it, although this only happened a few times. To prevent recognition, I anonymized the specific locations (playgrounds) and organizations where I conducted fieldwork. All names of persons and organizations in this book are pseudonyms, and I removed connections between persons and specific locations to prevent recognition as much as possible. Yet, I cannot avoid the possibility that people from the Schilderswijk might recognize their fellow football players or trainers.

Researching Muslim youth in the Netherlands

This research cannot be seen separate from the tradition of research on Islam and Muslims in Europe and the Netherlands that has proliferated especially since the 1980s. In social research, the category 'Muslim' has become increasingly used as a category of difference and identification that is, presumably, of high importance (Brubaker 2013; M. de Koning 2012; Sunier 2012). The growing amount of research about 'Muslims' resembles what Essed and Nimako (2006, 284) have previously described as the 'Dutch minority research industry': the prolific subsidized production of reports and research, almost exclusively by white scholars, about 'ethnic minorities and their cultures'. Currently, this has shifted to a 'Muslim' or 'Islam research industry' (Abbas 2010, 133), with the result of a fatigue amongst many Muslims for being asked to participate in research because of their religious identification and their 'otherness', especially in neighbourhoods where many Muslim citizens live (Abbas 2010, 132–3) and since 9/11 (M. de Koning 2008, 41). The growing visibility and categorization of 'Muslims' in social research is also visible in sports research, which has seen a growing body of literature on Muslim women and sports, as discussed in the introduction chapter. The following sections, therefore, reflect on the politicized nature of researching Muslim girls in the Netherlands – a group that can be considered an 'over-researched' group (Brubaker 2013; M. de Koning 2012) – as a white non-Muslim Dutch scholar.

I use the terms 'Muslim' and 'Muslim background' in this book while acknowledging that they are container concepts that may include a diverse array of identifications, religions, backgrounds and belongings. Most of the girls in my research, however, are born Sunni Muslims and have Moroccan-Dutch ethnic backgrounds. Because the focus of this research is not on diversity and belonging within Islamic faith but on how Muslim girls are dominantly perceived in Dutch society and in public (football) spaces as 'others', and how they deal with that, I simply use this category of 'Muslim'. However, I acknowledge that the use of this term comes with the risk of reinforcing the category of 'Muslim' as a homogeneous essentialist category and with privileging a faith-based identification above other social identifications (van Es 2016, 7), which will be precisely the subject of this book's Chapters 5–7. I consider that Muslims and Muslim youths are not merely Muslims but also teenagers, girls, boys and football players. Choosing one's research group and participants and categorizing them as 'Muslims' is therefore not an innocent practice, as it can indeed reproduce existing inequalities and representations of this group as 'other' in the Netherlands, especially since Islam is still considered as a migrant religion (M. de Koning 2012). Furthermore, the representation and categorization of 'Muslims' in the Netherlands is strongly related to (negative) stereotypes of ethnic-minority youths, especially 'Moroccans'. In this study, I therefore did not approach the young research participants primarily as Muslims or as 'Moroccans', although I sometimes do use these terms in this book, but as football players. This was also the way in which I introduced my research to the girls and boys of FGU, as a research on girls' football; only later in the fieldwork, I carefully considered questions of religion, race/ethnicity and being Muslim in relation to girls' football.

As the relationship between identifying as Muslim and playing football is not self-evident, this approach had some limitations. I was hesitant, especially in the beginning of my research, to ask football players about their religious belonging and how that mattered on the football field. I was granted access to FGU based on my research topic of girls' football, and not of Islam, and I felt that the girls and boys of FGU accepted me as a researcher within their midst *precisely because* my research was about girls' football and not about Islam or Muslim youths. Taking the problematic 'Islam research industry' into mind, it felt morally slippery to ask football players about Islam and about their experiences of being Muslim. At the same time, asking about Islam was inevitable to be able to critically relate my research to existing research on 'Muslims', race/ethnicity and gender in sports and in the Netherlands. Also, as will become clear in the coming chapters, religion and race/ethnicity did matter on the football field in relation to dominant white constructions of Dutch identity and citizenship and experiences of racism and Islamophobia. As such, the question of how to relate to my research participants – as Muslims, as football players, as girls and so forth – is a main topic in the chapters of this book.

Taking these thoughts about the categorization and identification of research participants in mind, I describe the girls and boys in my research variously as football players, as Moroccan-Dutch and as Muslims, depending on which identifications they placed at the foreground in the different contexts. This practice highlights the fluidity of identifications and intersectional differences in different social contexts (McCall 2005, 1781–2). It corresponds to my research participants' own practice of identification, which alternates between Moroccan, Dutch, Muslim, girl and football player, depending on the context. Sometimes, when paraphrasing or quoting voices of my research participants, I use the term 'Moroccan', as the football players amongst themselves often used this term. When talking to me or to other white Dutch people, the football players rather emphasized being Dutch with a Moroccan background. When I want to highlight ethnic identifications, I thus usually describe my research participants as Moroccan-Dutch, stressing both their identification as Dutch and as Moroccan. This runs against the problematic practice of much research on Dutch multicultural neighbourhoods and sports (e.g. Cevaal and Romijn 2011; Franke, Overmaat and Reijndorp 2014; Smit 2014; van der Wilk 2016), in which young residents, most of them born and raised in the Netherlands, are framed as 'Moroccan', 'Turkish', 'Somali' and so on, thereby reproducing the idea that these residents are not full Dutch citizens, but always 'other'.

When I decided to focus on the Schilderswijk as the main location of my fieldwork, this was not without hesitation. Taking critical discussions of the problematic aspects of feminists and anthropologists studying ethnic, racial, religious, cultural or colonial 'others' seriously (Abu-Lughod 2002; 2013; Mohanty 1988; Wekker 2016, 62–3), researching the Schilderswijk was both a reproduction and a departure of this practice. The Schilderswijk, as part of the Netherlands, and therefore of my 'own' social and cultural environment, is still one of the most 'othered' places in the country. By taking this process of 'othering' – of both the Muslim research participants and the neighbourhood itself – into account in this research, and studying how young residents critically deal with stereotypical representations, it is my goal to represent this neighbourhood differently (Jaffe and A. de Koning 2015, 34). Specifically, this is possible since my research focuses on girls' football, something that is generally regarded as positive by both people from and outside of the Schilderswijk, compared with the often negative representations of the Schilderswijk that focus on radicalization, crime and women's oppression. By focusing on a girls' football competition that aims at the empowerment and inclusion of girls in public spaces and in sports, it is possible to provide different representations of youths from the Schilderswijk, thereby contesting their supposed 'otherness'.

First encounters: Positionality and power

The young women and men in my research were very much aware of this politicized context of Muslim youth in the Netherlands and thus critically engaged with me as a white non-Muslim Dutch researcher from outside the Schilderswijk in their football competition. My positionality formed an integral part of the talks and encounters with my research participants, often implicitly and sometimes explicitly. As a white researcher from a different part of the Netherlands, my involvement and acceptance within FGU was at first quite limited. After I met Hanan, the coordinator of FGU, she quickly saw the potential of having a researcher at the girls' football competition who would, hopefully, represent a more positive story of the Schilderswijk, and she granted me access to all activities of FGU. The football girls themselves, however, had a wait-and-see attitude towards me. Many Dutch Muslim youths, and especially youths from the Schilderswijk, experience fatigue about being a research subject all the time. Much research, both journalistic and from (applied) universities, is conducted in the Schilderswijk, most often in the form of incidental visits by researchers or journalists. At first, the girls and boys from FGU perceived me as 'another one' and paid little attention to me. Talks and interviews were rather short and superficial, and not many in-depth experiences were shared. Later, in the informal talks we had, my research participants criticized the stereotypical images that journalists create and reproduce of the Schilderswijk without seriously engaging with them, the young inhabitants. This specifically became clear in two events, of which the first took place on a Saturday in November 2014:

> I am visiting FGU for a few months already, but I am increasing my visits as I just decided to focus on the Schilderswijk as an in-depth case study. I hang around with some volunteers and football players of FGU in a public playground that is often used for outdoor sports activities by different organizations in the neighbourhood. One of the FGU boys tells about his experiences with the police and ethnic profiling in the Schilderswijk. Then, a group of five white, middle-aged

people, four men and one woman, appear around the corner of the school next to the playground. One of them points towards the playground and starts to talk. The others observe us while we hang around and sit on the benches, but they stay at a distance and do not come closer. When it begins to feel like a weird situation, one of the football players, who is running on the field, shouts: 'Yes, indeed, this is the Schilderswijk!' The other footballers on the benches next to me mumble and laugh a bit, but quickly go on with their talks without paying any more attention to the group of adults. After a few minutes, the group leaves. I feel that the footballers were ridiculing their white adult observers, and it gives me an uncomfortable feeling. It seems to me that what I am doing is not that different after all. I am also a white adult outsider who is studying and observing the football players of the Schilderswijk. My discomfort makes that I am not asking the girls and boys about this incident; I do not want to put any attention on myself being present in the playground, and I silently remain seated with the football players on the benches, until I feel it is time to leave.

During the second event, a few days later, the reaction of my research participants, and their thoughts about researchers and observers, became clearer:

This evening, I am attending a debate between youths and the police at the multicultural youth centre in the Schilderswijk. The evening is organized to improve the relation between youths and the police, which has been disturbed by incidents of discrimination, racial/ethnic profiling, and violence by the police. Many FGU volunteers join the event, and Hanan has invited me to come along. When I arrive at the youth centre, one of the Moroccan-Dutch organizers of the debate is very surprised to hear that it is the first time that I visit the centre: 'Oh, you have not been here before? Your colleagues … they … are you from the police?' I explain to him that I belong to the girls from FGU and that I am conducting a research on girls' football in the Schilderswijk, and then he warmly welcomes me. The debate starts with several discussion points about prejudices about the police and about youths. One discussion point is about the high level of crime amongst Moroccan youths. A Moroccan-Dutch youth leader refers to research that concludes that the majority of youths in Dutch prisons is Moroccan, and he argues that the Moroccan community should take its responsibility for this situation. A young man in the audience becomes agitated and interrupts him: 'But what *is* a Moroccan? I'm not a Moroccan! I'm Dutch! I'm born here.' Ilias (twenty years old), a trainer at Football Girls United, agrees with him: 'What research is this? Then show me. Because I saw it myself, the term Moroccan is often really used too easily, while sometimes it's a Tunisian or a Turk or somebody else. I'd really like to know where those researchers get their data from!' Upon Ilias's statement, the FGU girls in the audience start to chuckle and look at me. Some of them giggle loudly, and I start to feel uncomfortable again. The girls know that I am also one of those researchers. But, this time, I decide that I must face it, and when the evening has ended, I approach Ilias and I ask him: 'You don't like researchers here, do you?' Ilias is still a bit agitated, and replies: 'No, really not! I really wonder where they get their data from.' I ask, a bit insecure: 'Do you then think it's okay that I am a researcher at Football Girls United?' Ilias, in turn, looks a bit surprised by my question and responds: 'Yes, yes, of course, but you are really *here*, and you see what is happening with your own eyes, so that is different.'

I was relieved by his answer and his agreement of my participation in FGU. Later in my research, I also asked some football girls about their thoughts about my presence as a researcher in FGU, and they responded in similar ways. What was a crucial difference, I think, is that, for the girls and boys in FGU, I was not a distant and disembodied researcher, producing data about 'Muslims', 'Moroccans' or Schilderswijk youths out of sight, but a human being of flesh and blood who was approachable and really present in their midst. My relatively long-term engagement with FGU as a researcher made me different from researchers and journalists who only incidentally visit the neighbourhood and then disappear again. It was important for my research participants that I would not exclusively write about negative issues in the Schilderswijk. Because I was so often present at the FGU activities, they could make sure that I also came to know the positive sides and experiences of living in the Schilderswijk, of which girls' football was an important aspect. Furthermore, my regular presence at FGU meant that research participants could ask me questions about my research, my findings or about my own life, which they did now and then. These questions were eventually not so much related to my research but more to concerns in their daily lives that they could not as easily discuss with other adults, such as questions about menstruation or about suitable girls' sports clothing, but it generated a mutual feeling of trust, respect and accountability.

For Hanan, there were more concrete stakes in my presence as university researcher within FGU: this could contribute to a positive outreach of the FGU organization towards the municipality, stakeholders or other potential funders. Indeed, I wrote multiple reference letters and evaluation reports based on my research which FGU successfully used to raise more funding. For me, this is a crucial part of feminist ethnography as in this way, I could make my research not only academically relevant but also concretely for the young residents in the Schilderswijk and their own football organization.

As becomes clear in both vignettes, the relation between me as researcher and the youth in the Schilderswijk was a racialized one. Most professionals who work in the neighbourhood and who hold positions of power – whether sports trainers, researchers, police officers, policy makers or social workers – are white and are not from the neighbourhood themselves, while most residents are non-white. These racialized power relations also played out in my fieldwork. The position of white researchers, including myself, was problematized by young football players, whether implicitly by yelling something at their adult observers while running in the football field or explicitly in a debate, as Ilias did. Furthermore, my presence in the neighbourhood was immediately assumed as belonging to the people who do not live but work in the neighbourhood, be it a police officer, researcher, or policy maker. This created specific relationships not only with my research participants from FGU but also with the sports professionals who were part of my research. With the two following vignettes, I will reflect on how these racialized relationships took form.

The first was on a Sunday in December 2014:

> After the football trainings in a sports hall, the FGU football players are leaving the building to go home. Sarah (fifteen years old) and Aliya (eighteen years old), two FGU volunteers, call everyone together because they have a plan. They want to buy a present for Hanan, to thank her for all the work she is doing for FGU. They ask the football players to bring five euros with them the next training, so that they can buy a wellness retreat in a hammam for Hanan. I really like this initiative and I ask Sarah and Aliya: 'How nice! Can I also participate in the present? Then I'll also bring money with me next time.' Sarah responds: 'Yes, of course, you belong here too, you are just a Moroccan too.' Many of the girls laugh and look at me amused. Hafsa (sixteen years old), another volunteer, approaches me and asks: 'Can I ask you something? Some time ago, you said 'hamdulillah',[3] but are you Muslim?' I explain to her that I learned this in Egypt, where I have lived for a few months, and where everyone, also Christians, say 'hamdulillah'. Some girls nod and Hafsa says: 'Ah okay, yes, for us that's a bit weird you know, that eh, a Dutch person says this. We're not used to that.'

Interestingly, at first, my belonging to FGU is articulated through using the ethnic identity marker of 'Moroccan'. Although this does not mean that girls and boys from FGU really identify me as Moroccan – a few minutes later, I was again a 'Dutch person' – their use of this identity marker can be interpreted as a funny sign of their acceptance of me in the football competition, similar to the label 'house journalist' that I received. Precisely because of my racial/ethnic, locational and religious difference in FGU, the football players needed a symbolic way to articulate my 'inclusion' – girls who are already included because of similar religious, ethnic and location backgrounds do not need such symbolic marker. It is not only religious or racial/ethnic identification that matter in fieldwork but also a classed and locational/geographical identification (Carrington 2008). My affiliation with a university, educational background, and geographical and classed background of not being from the working-class Schilderswijk thus also contributed to my position as 'different' in FGU.

When FGU played against other girls' teams in the Schilderswijk, girls whom I had not met before would sometimes ask the FGU volunteers who I was, and they responded by saying that 'she belongs with us' or 'she belongs with Hanan', or calling me their 'house journalist'. The use of funny nicknames for anthropologists to emphasize inclusion and exclusion is not an uncommon practice. Martijn de Koning (2008, 65) argued that, by using humour or humorous nicknames, it is possible to temporarily exceed existing ethnic, religious or locational boundaries, without affecting the boundary itself, which is also an adequate description of my position within FGU.

My position as a white non-Muslim researcher did evoke different responses from white sports and health professionals in the Schilderswijk, which became clear, for example, during an interview I conducted with Peter, one of the coordinators of the municipal sports activities in the neighbourhood, in his office in the school next to one of the playgrounds in January 2015:

> After I have finished the interview with Peter, Mo (twenty years old), a volunteer at both FGU and at Peter's playground, comes into the office to get some sports equipment. I had already met Mo before at FGU, and after we have greeted each other, I tell Peter that I know Mo from FGU and we will also do an interview together. Peter then says to Mo: 'Yes, you should do the interview with her, it's important, about girls' football'. Mo nods and, when he leaves the office to go to his football training, Peter says to me: 'I just told Mo that he has to meet with you. Then he has also heard this from a man, then he knows that it's okay. He's still a Moroccan, eh.'[4]

I was too perplexed to further inquire what Peter meant by that, yet it is clear that gender and race/ethnicity both play a role in Peter's interaction with me and with Mo. It seems that he believes that Mo adheres to conservative gender relations because of his Moroccan-Dutch and Muslim background, and therefore would not be willing to do an interview with a woman if not told to do so by another man, and that I, as a female researcher, need Peter's help to find 'Moroccan' male interviewees. This is even more ironic considering that

Mo volunteers at several girls' football activities that aim to stimulate gender equality and the empowerment of girls and women in football. It is precisely improving gender equality that is Mo's main motivation for spending so much of his time volunteering at girls' football, as I later learned during the interview with him. Yet, in the interactions I had with Peter, or with some of the other white sports and health professionals in the Schilderswijk, a kind of implicit 'us' – white professionals (gender and sexually emancipated, understand the value of sports) – versus 'them' – ethnic- and religious-minority residents (gender and sexually conservative, still need to be educated on the value of sports) – is created. This was expressed by utterances such as 'eh' or 'you know ...' when talking about sports, gender and girls' football in the Schilderswijk. It implies a common positionality and an opinion about the Schilderswijk and its ethnic and religious 'other' inhabitants, which these professionals assumed I shared with them. Despite my discomfort in these situations, I regard these instances as highly valuable in my research, as it gave me insights in the underlying assumptions of white sports and health professionals in the Schilderswijk, and how these affect the organization of girls' football in the neighbourhood, as will become clear in the chapters that follow.

Football and research locations

There are many different locations where football is being played in the Schilderswijk. This section gives an overview of the football locations that were part of this research, whilst Chapter 4 provides a more in-depth discussion of the Schilderswijk in general. Important to mention here is that almost all formal sports clubs have moved out of the neighbourhood, and few young residents of the Schilderswijk are a member of those sports clubs.[5] Often, these clubs are located too far away to go to on their own, are too expensive or are not known amongst young residents. There are, however, several local neighbourhood sports organizations in the Schilderswijk.[6] These organizations can easily adapt to the wishes and needs of the residents in the way they organize sport, because they are not reliant on a national sports federation. They ask a small financial contribution and are generally very popular in the Schilderswijk amongst youth and increasingly also adults (Houdijk and Ekelschot 2014). Almost all the participants in my research played football in one or more of those local neighbourhood sport organizations, in addition to their participation in FGU and to 'unregulated' playing at public playgrounds. I will discuss these different neighbourhood sports organizations together under the umbrella pseudonym of Sportteam, to prevent recognition and to protect the anonymity of my research participants. Almost all sports organizations in the Schilderswijk have football as their most important activity, yet basketball and kickboxing are also popular (see Rana 2014).

Sportteam is an organization attached to and funded by the municipality of The Hague to support and organize sports for youths in the city, including the Schilderswijk. They organize after-school sports hours in playgrounds, where a sports professional gives training, and they organize the local rounds of some national street football competitions discussed below. For a large part, my participant observations took place during these after-school activities in the playgrounds in the Schilderswijk. Peter, Frank and Joost are coordinators of Sportteam for the Schilderswijk, and Jimmy, Ibrahim and Kayleigh are Sportteam's trainers who work in the Schilderswijk and whom I have interviewed. Sportteam also works together with other initiatives in the neighbourhood, such as youth and community centres, FGU and ADO Den Haag, the professional football club of The Hague. Since 2015, Sportteam's aim is to attract more girls to their sports activities in the playgrounds, as they observed that girls participated less than boys. To achieve this aim, Sportteam appointed two female sports professionals, Kayleigh and Chaimae, and, as Kayleigh explained to me, they started organizing sports for girls in more 'shielded' spaces. Before Chaimae became a trainer at Sportteam, she volunteered at FGU and now and then she still joins the FGU trainings and competitions to catch up with her friends. Sportteam also takes care of the management of the playgrounds, some of which are closed with a fence at night to prevent them from being used by 'hang-around youths'.

The 6 vs 6 Cruyff Court competition is a nationwide competition for street football teams of local Cruyff Courts, for pupils in the final two years of primary school (between ten and twelve years old). Cruyff Courts are football playgrounds with artificial grass that are built and sponsored by the Cruyff Foundation (named after the famous Dutch footballer Johan Cruyff), in cooperation with schools and local sports organizations. These local partners organize the local 6 vs 6 competitions, of which the winners go to the next round on city level, and then to the regional, national or international finals. In The Hague, the local Cruyff Courts are exploited and managed by Sportteam; the trainers of Sportteam organize weekly activities on the Cruyff Courts and also organize the yearly 6 vs 6 competitions, which have a separate girls' and boys' competition. The Cruyff Foundation regards gender equality as very important, and therefore as a rule, local Cruyff Court teams may only participate in the competition if they also put forward a girls' team, so local organizers are forced to compile girls' teams as well. In most places, including the Schilderswijk, there are indeed local girls' teams in the 6 vs 6 competition, but in some places, I observed only boys' teams despite the official rule on gender equality. During my fieldwork, I followed one girls' team from the Schilderswijk in the several matches they played in the 6 vs 6 competition, and I conducted a focus group interview with its team members. Most of these girls I also encountered in the other football locations I studied, such as FGU and the community centres.

Besides the 6 vs 6 Cruyff Court competitions, other street football competitions are organized in playgrounds in the Schilderswijk as well, such as the Danone Nations Cup and the Schilderswijk Street League, but these do not have a specific policy on the participation of girls' teams. Therefore, much fewer girls participate in these competitions, or sometimes even none. The Danone Nations Cup is also a nationwide street football competition, and Sportteam is the local partner of the Cup in The Hague. The Schilderswijk Street League is a local competition, organized by the professional football club ADO. In 2015, nine boys' teams participated while only one girls' team did, and I followed this girls' team in the Schilderswijk Street League competition as well.

Several community and youth centres organize girls' football hours in the Schilderswijk next to their more general social work. These girls' football hours are mostly indoor and are usually attended by six to fifteen teenage girls. During these football hours, I also participated and interviewed some of the girls and volunteers. Most of the times, these community centres ask a female volunteer or intern to organize the football trainings for the girls, and this makes for an unsustainable practice. When a volunteer or intern leaves, the girls' football hours usually also disappear, until a new female volunteer restarts it. The boys' sports hours that are offered at community centres are incorporated better in the standard programmes and are organized by more permanent employees of the centres. Because the girls' football trainings are indoor, not many girls are actually aware of these football opportunities; contrary to football in public playgrounds, it is invisible when walking through the neighbourhood. Participation usually goes via the snowball method: girls bring friends, sisters or neighbours with them to the trainings. Nisa and Hamza are two social workers and sports trainers who organize football at youth and community centres in the Schilderswijk, and who have participated in my research.

Last but not least, FGU is a collective of girls and boys who organize a weekly girls' football competition and football trainings for girls in the Schilderswijk. It is not a traditional football club with an official membership but a 'looser' organization where football players organize their own trainings, teams and activities in public playgrounds and sports halls, and only pay a modest contribution of twenty euros a year. Hanan is the coordinator and initiator of FGU and started with organizing girls' football in the Schilderswijk in 2008. She manages the competition with the help of a group of nine volunteers, who are all between fourteen and twenty years old: Nina, Noor, Hafsa, Sarah, Ilias, Aliya, Mansour, Nora and Mo. They give most of the trainings to the younger girls but also play football themselves in the competition. Sometimes, former volunteers, such as Siham, Chaimae and Khalid, still help out on busy competition days. In the competition, football teams from different community centres and playgrounds in the Schilderswijk play against each other, with a final match every year in May. At the peak of the FGU competition, about eighty girls between ten and twenty years old participate in the different teams. The competition is divided into one for girls under thirteen and one for those over thirteen. Some boys have also joined FGU as volunteers, and boys actually are highly welcomed in the competition as long as they subscribe to FGU's main aim: organizing football primarily for girls. I will discuss boys' participation in FGU extensively in Chapter 6. Most girls and boys in FGU are from the Moroccan-Dutch community in the Schilderswijk, but not exclusively. Some Pakistani-Dutch, Turkish-Dutch, Surinamese-Dutch and white Dutch girls also participate in the competition. A nickname the girls from FGU sometimes use for their football competition is 'The Familia', to underscore the feeling that they are like family to each other.

FGU uses different existing sports spaces in the neighbourhood for their activities, both indoors in the sports hall and outdoors in public playgrounds in the Schilderswijk. Irregularly, FGU also organizes other sports, such as volleyball, Thai boxing and kickboxing. In 2015, the subsidy for FGU was stopped, which meant the end of the weekly competition. The trainings continued on a more informal basis, with about fifteen to twenty-five girls participating. The football players of FGU also take part in and volunteer at several other initiatives in the neighbourhood, such as helping out in an elderly home or assisting at the activities from the youth centre in the Schilderswijk. FGU became the most important organization in my fieldwork, since the FGU's girls' football activities are organized by girls from the neighbourhood themselves and not by social workers or sports trainers from more official neighbourhood sports organizations or from outside the neighbourhood. FGU is different from the other sports organizations in the Schilderswijk, as it does not have its own location or organizational structure with paid employees; it is a real grassroots initiative with almost only volunteers. When there is funding, this is used to rent sports locations and to compensate Hanan for the hours she puts into coordinating the competition. The organizers and volunteers at FGU belong to the same group they want to reach with their activities, which is different than most of the initiatives I described above, of which the paid coordinators and decision makers on the football activities are mostly white Dutch men from outside the neighbourhood. The ethnographic data on FGU thus show how girls themselves organize and play football in the Schilderswijk, and how this differs from the more established sports or football organizations. The experiences of the girls – and some of the boys – who play football in and volunteer for the FGU football competition form the core of this ethnography.

3

Histories of Moroccan-Dutch youth: Migration, politics and street football

At the time of the research, in 2015, 385,700 persons with a Moroccan background lived in the Netherlands, that is 2.3 per cent of the total population. This includes migrants themselves (first generation) and their children who were born in the Netherlands (second generation).[1] In 2015, there were also 14,846 'third-generation' Moroccan-Dutch in the Netherlands, 90 per cent of them below the age of twelve (CBS 2016, 27). This corresponds with the youth in my research who were mostly above twelve years old and from the second-generation Moroccan-Dutch. In total, currently, 24.8 per cent of Dutch citizens has a migration background (first or second generation), and after Turkey, Morocco is the second-largest country of origin or descent (CBS 2021). Although there were also some football players with other backgrounds involved in my research, I do provide a brief history of Moroccan migration to the Netherlands in the first part of this chapter, and in the second part I sketch the background of today's political framing of migrant and 'Moroccan' youth as urban 'problem youth', increasingly framed through the lens of Islam as 'Muslim' youth. Third, I describe the little-known history of street football, an informal urban form of football that has developed for a large part in urban parts of the Netherlands among youth with Moroccan-Dutch or other racialized migrant backgrounds. As such, this chapter connects the social-political context of 'Moroccan' and Muslim youth in the Netherlands with a discussion of the history and development of street football in the Netherlands as an urban and migrant youth sport.

Moroccan migration to the Netherlands

Due to rapid economic growth and a shortage of low-skilled labour in the Netherlands in the 1960s and 1970s, young Moroccan men were recruited as labour migrants, or so-called guest workers.² Besides Moroccan migrants, there were also labour migrants recruited from Yugoslavia, Spain, Portugal and Turkey to work in heavy industries such as steel and shipbuilding. As these sectors were mostly populated with male workers, the recruitment of guest workers focused on young men who were, due to housing shortages, placed in (overcrowded) pensions for labour migrants and were not allowed to bring their families (Bouras 2012; Geense 2004, 13). Besides the 'official' recruitment through agencies, a large part of Moroccan migrants in the Netherlands arrived through own channels, often via other European countries such as France, and also looking for better work opportunities. Most of them came from the north of Morocco, the Rif, a rural Berber region that knows a long tradition of emigration (Bouras 2012, 55).

Moroccan migrants arrived slightly later than migrants from the other countries and thus, more than the others, came to work in sectors that were then already known to disappear in the future, such as the mines. The idea was that Moroccan guest workers would then go back to their home country, but many of them stayed in the Netherlands and opted for family reunification from the 1970 onwards. The main reasons for the permanent residence in the Netherlands were the economic and political instability in Morocco and the Dutch restrictive migration policy which made migrants fear that they could not return to the Netherlands in the future (Bouras 2012, 56).³ Many of the Moroccan migrants then moved to the larger cities Amsterdam, Rotterdam, The Hague and Utrecht, after the industries in the rural areas where they worked had closed down. The urban residential pattern largely reflected the region of origin; migrants from Al Hoceima, in the north of Morocco, for example, tended to settle in The Hague and more specifically the Schilderswijk.

In the 1970s and 1980s, many women and children of the Moroccan migrants came to the Netherlands in the context of family reunification policies, which made women dependent on their husbands for their residency status. In case of a divorce within three years, the woman had to go back to Morocco (Bouras 2012, 57). Subsequently, in the 1980s, many Moroccan men became unemployed and did not manage to find new jobs because the sectors they worked in had closed down or moved to low-wage countries. In these years, more Moroccan women got informal jobs as cleaners and some became breadwinners. This resulted in a stronger orientation of Moroccan women towards the Netherlands, at a moment when many men due to their unemployment started to feel more connected towards Morocco (Bouras 2012). This gender balance is interesting, given the dominant narrative about Moroccan-Dutch Muslim women who are seen as inactive and unemancipated, while they actually tended to participate more in Dutch society via work and children, than many of their husbands who were simply set aside after years of hard manual labour (Bouras 2012).

Political responses to 'Moroccan' and Muslim youth

When, in this history of Moroccan migration to the Netherlands, did 'Moroccan' youth begin to be perceived as a problem? And when did they become framed as 'Muslim' youth? During the 1970s, Dutch migration policy was focused on migrants' country of origin, because the idea was that guest workers would eventually return, for example, by giving subsidies through Moroccan organizations and through stimulating (children of) migrants' own language and cultural education (Bouras 2012; Prins 2002). In the 1980s, the idea that return was a false assumption slowly emerged, and the Dutch 'ethnic minority and integration' policy was drafted, of which the direct causes were the violent protests of young Moluccan-Dutch citizens, the Dutch-born children of Indonesian postcolonial migrants, at the end of the 1970s (Wekker 2016, 53).[4] The first policy document on ethnic minorities in 1983 was the direct result of these Moluccan-Dutch protests, not in the least because they concerned *Dutch-born* youth with migrant backgrounds, making politicians realize that migration and integration were not a 'temporary' issue (Essed and Nimako 2006, 287). The policy, however, included not only Moluccan migrants and youth but also a 'strange amalgam' of different (ethnic) groups: Surinamese, Antilleans, Moroccans, Turks, Southern Europeans, Moluccans, Roma and people who permanently lived in mobile homes, and it was aimed at the adjustment of 'backward' ethnic-minority groups into the Dutch social norm (Wekker 2016, 54). In the 1980s, the focus was still on holding on to one's own ethnic and cultural identity, but after 1990, because of the economic recession and cutbacks in social welfare, this policy altered.

Since the 1990s, migrants' orientation towards their country of origin and cultural background was seen as radically *against* their integration in Dutch society. Migrants were individually held responsible and blamed for their supposed lack of integration in Dutch society, thereby neglecting the decade-long policies that precisely stimulated this orientation towards countries of origin (Bouras 2012; Prins 2002). Furthermore, socio-economic factors, such as the unemployment of many Moroccan migrant men due to the closing of industrial sectors, were overlooked in favour of a focus on the supposed problematic 'cultural' and 'religious' backgrounds of migrants, suggesting that Moroccan culture and Islam is a threat for 'Western' secular society. This was expressed, for example, not only by VVD (Conservative Liberals) politician Bolkestein in the early 1990s, who specifically pointed out the oppression of women in Islam, but also by journalists, other public opinion makers (e.g. Scheffer 2000) and feminists (Berg and Schinkel 2009, 398–9; Bracke 2011), resulting in a 'national minorities debate' (Prins 2002, 367).

This debate signified, Dutch philosopher Baukje Prins (2002) argues, the emergence of a specific genre of 'new realism' to talk about multiculturalism and Islam. This 'new realism' genre claimed that now it finally 'could be said what could never be said' about migrants and Islam, and it has a strong essentialist focus on the cultural backwardness of migrants, specifically Muslim migrants, that was seen as a cause for their socio-economic deprivation (Berg and Schinkel 2009, 397; Prins 2002). Prins (2002) emphasizes that this genre of new realism is not a description of an existing reality, but rather that it produces a new reality on multicultural society and Islam, in which migrant and Muslim citizens are increasingly cast as problematic.

Since the new millennium, the focus on migrant *youth* in migration and integration policies became stronger, with an emphasis on their proper participation in Dutch society, on educating them Dutch values and norms, and setting boundaries and disciplining ethnic-minority youths (Wekker 2016, 55). Gender and sexuality continued to be important elements in those supposedly Dutch values, emphasized, for example, by right-wing politicians Pim Fortuyn and Ayaan Hirsi Ali in the early 2000s. Both expressed strong anti-immigration and anti-Islam sentiments, linking this explicitly to gender and sexuality and women's and gays' freedom (Berg and Schinkel 2009; Bracke 2011; Mepschen, Duyvendak and Tonkens 2010; Prins 2002). But politicians from other parties across the political spectrum also blame 'Moroccan youth', implying often Moroccan boys, for problems in urban neighbourhoods. For example, on the evening of the municipal elections in Amsterdam in 2002, Labour politician Oudkerk talked about '*kutmarokkanen*' being the reason for the rise of the political right in the Netherlands, a slur literally translated as 'Moroccan cunts' (A. de Koning 2016, 111). It was, and still is, not uncommon among politicians and journalists to talk about a 'Moroccan problem' or 'Moroccan street terrorists' when talking about problems with criminal youth in urban neighbourhoods (de Jong 2007, 11; A. de Koning 2013). Sometimes it is even explicitly suggested that Moroccan boys have an 'ethnic monopoly' on urban nuisance in the Netherlands, as Labour politician Samson did in a newspaper in 2011 and in a television talk show in 2014.⁵ 'Moroccan' boys, as anthropologist De Koning argues, became 'the nation's foremost abject figure' (A. de Koning 2013, 15; see also 2016). 'Moroccan' is not a self-explanatory ethnic category but is, in public discourses, a racialized ethnic category (Hall 2017, 62; Silverstein 2005, 364; Stolcke 1993, 27), based on physical appearances of brown skin and hair colour that look 'North-African'. Everyone who looks this way can then be called a 'Moroccan', making it a derogatory term for racialized difference rather than for ethnic belonging. One of my research participants, discussed in Chapter 2, rightly questioned the racialized use of that term by journalists and researchers by asking 'What is a Moroccan?', for he recognized that the term is often used for everyone who looks 'different'.

'Moroccan' boys, thus, are cast as the troublemakers in Dutch society and 'Moroccan' Muslim girls as the victims of their cultural and religious background. Moroccan and Muslim, in these public debates, are often used interchangeably (A. de Koning 2016, 112), although in recent years more focus has been put on Islam and Muslim migrants as threats. In the context of the parliamentary elections in 2017, for example, women's rights and feminism, both portrayed as the results of secular modernity, were taken up to 'warn' against Islamization and 'newcomers'. In a public speech, Edith Schippers (2016), then minister of Public Health, Welfare and Sports, argued that Dutch culture is superior to immigrant and Islamic cultures, especially when it comes to girls', women's and LGBTQ's freedom in the Netherlands. Other examples of an implied troubled relationship between Islam and migrants, on the one hand, and feminism, women's and sexual rights, on the other, are the open letter from Prime Minister Mark Rutte (2017) to all Dutch citizens, in which he calls groups of people, for example, 'people who hang around in the streets' and who behave 'poorly', to 'act normal' or otherwise 'leave the country':

> People who abuse our freedom to ruin things here, when it's those very freedoms that actually brought them here. People who do not want to adapt, who criticize our customs and reject our values. Who harass gays, catcall women in short skirts or call ordinary Dutch people racists.⁶

In this letter, Prime Minister Rutte thus implies that migrants or urban migrant youth who hang around in the streets are those who reject the supposed Dutch norms and values of sexual freedom and women's equality. He does not explicitly mention Islam, but the examples he gives of Dutch norms and values, such as shaking hands and freedom and equality, suggests that he is pitting this against the group that supposedly does not embrace these values: Muslim youth and migrants. Sybrand Buma (2017), leader of the Christian Democrat Party (CDA), delivered a similar public lecture as Schippers, in which he also called for migrants to adapt to Dutch traditional norms and values, which, according to him, encompass 'enlightened' Jewish-Christian traditions but not 'backward' Islam.

Currently, Geert Wilders, the leader of the right-wing and populist Party for Freedom (PVV), and other right-wing parties such as *Forum voor Democratie* are known for their xenophobic, Islamophobic and anti-immigration standpoints, but historically and today, this is a much wider shared idea among Dutch politicians, also among those who are considered not to be from the political right. Muslim and 'Moroccan' youths are framed as 'foreigners', 'newcomers' and 'immigrants', as fundamentally 'from elsewhere', even generations who are born and raised in the Netherlands, and who want to profit from the Dutch welfare system, cause nuisance and are a threat to Dutch society (El-Tayeb 2011; Modest and A. de Koning 2016; Wekker 2016). Furthermore, the socio-economic marginalized positions of many Moroccan-Dutch youth 'seemingly becomes a logical outcome of his imagined ethnic habitus' (A. de Koning 2016, 112), thereby ignoring the economic history that was behind the labour migration of Moroccans to the Netherlands in the first place.

I would like to stress that the political responses to Moroccan migrants and Muslim youth have not only originated from the migration history with which I started this chapter but should also be located in the gendered and sexualized construction of racial and Muslim 'others' in Dutch colonialism (Stoler 2002; 2016; Wekker 2016). Part of the dominant framing of Muslims as 'other' to Dutch society and culture is the idea that they are a 'new' migrant group in the Netherlands, ignoring the fact that Islam has been part of the Netherlands for a long time, through the colonization of Indonesia (van der Veer 2002). The Netherlands is imagined as a racial and culturally homogeneous space that is now 'invaded' by strangers, while, in fact, there has never been something such as a homogeneous country or identity (Modest and A. de Koning 2016, 99). Especially when Muslims became more visible in Dutch public spaces through labour and family migration from Morocco (and Turkey), colonial ideas of Islam as backward and unemancipated were taken off the discursive shelves of the Dutch colonial 'cultural archive' (Wekker 2016, 2–3).

The use of sports in integration, minority and urban regeneration policies is also not new: historically, sports have been an important domain through which national citizenship and belonging is produced. Sports were an essential part of colonization processes to discipline and civilize the colonized into modern and moral subjects (Bale and Cronin 2003; Besnier and Brownell 2012). This makes sports, Bale and Cronin (2003, 5) argue, a 'legacy of colonization', one that is continued today in sports global governing bodies that are still 'on a colonising mission' (Bale and Cronin 2003, 3). Locally, a 'colonizing mission' could be observed in the implementation and promotion of youth sports in 'disadvantaged' neighbourhoods, including the Schilderswijk, for the social and cultural integration and civilization of its racialized Muslim residents. Sports were, and are, seen as a meaningful leisure activity for urban young residents, which will keep them away from hanging around in the streets and which will make them familiar with what are seen as 'Dutch norms and values' (Rana 2014, 35). In Chapter 7, I will discuss these neighbourhood youth sports programmes in more detail and how the football players in the Schilderswijk critically engage with such programmes. In the remainder of this chapter, I will discuss the emergence of a related but different form of sports, namely the informal sport street football.

Street football and urban superdiversity

As a result of the migration and residential pattern of the labour migrants in the 1960s and 1970s, many youth with Moroccan backgrounds grew up in so-called urban 'disadvantaged' neighbourhoods in the Netherlands: densely populated working-class areas with a low average income and high unemployment rates. Starting in the capital Amsterdam in the early 1990s, in those neighbourhoods a specific youth culture around street football emerged among teenagers and youth. They often spent much of their time on the streets, because they had not much to do: there was no organized leisure, their homes had no balconies or gardens and their parents were busy with smaller siblings and work to make ends meet (Smit 2014). On public playgrounds or squares, designed on not more than a concrete surface, youth gathered and played street football with and against each other.

Street football is characterized by an absence of formal rules and structures; there are no clubs or training. The rules are made as the game progresses on the field and players learn by imitating and improving tricks from others. The game can be played with any number of players, so you can come and go whenever you want to play. Some street football players characterize street football as 'playing in complete freedom, without instructions and commands' (Willemse

2013, 115, translation mine). Specifically, the street football culture was not only about winning the game but also about developing new street football tricks and styles to impress the opponents and the audiences. So, the location of the football playgrounds are important: ideally, they are placed in the centre of the neighbourhoods and surrounded by flats and balconies, so that there's a large audience (de Ruiter 2013). Street football playgrounds became places of football innovation: new tricks and styles were shared on YouTube and often adopted by famous international football players such as Ibrahimovic and Ronaldo.[7] For some famous street football players, indeed, it proved to be an opportunity to make a living off playing football because they became (semi-)professional players or were approached by companies such as Nike for sponsoring and advertising.

In the early 2000s, large street football tournaments in arenas were organized and cast online by multinational corporations such as Nike and Burger King, who saw this as an opportunity for a new form of advertising. Amsterdam-based street football became famous internationally, not in the least through their collaborations with commercial parties, and players travelled around the world to give skills workshops and to play against local teams, for example, in the Dutch Caribbean islands (de Ruiter 2013). The development of this urban street football scene is often compared with hip hop: 'What hip hop is for New York, is street football for Amsterdam' (Boussaid, in Echo 2013, translation mine). Both are the result of multicultural minority communities that share precarious living conditions and are economically and discursively excluded from the society they live and grew up in (El-Tayeb 2011, xii). Both share the neighbourhood as primary location of belonging and identification in a society that continues to define them as foreigners. Hip hop and street football provide the means for marginalized youth to claim the streets of their cities and neighbourhoods (El-Tayeb 2011, 28, 35).

Street football was innovative not only with football tricks but also with regard to multicultural society and innovative forms of living together in marginalized neighbourhoods and in poor socio-economic circumstances. Street football was for many an escape from the hard reality of growing up in poor migrant communities with stigmatization and societal exclusion. Dutch anthropologist Francio Guadeloupe mentions that youth with different ethnic and religious backgrounds and different languages come together in street football, and that it therefore is primarily an expression of urban superdiversity, referring to the increasing urban diversity based on not only migration or ethnicity but also class, religion, gender and language: 'Amidst those differences, youth were looking for something that they shared and where they could derive an identity from. This became street football' (cited in Water 2013, translation mine; see also El-Tayeb 2011, xl, 29). In this light, Amsterdam-based heritage organization Imagine IC sees street football as youths' contemporary superdiverse heritage that goes beyond the known patterns of ethnic, cultural, classed, religious or language differences. 'Street football is not about who you are, but what you are able to do.'[8]

In a few meetings on street football that Imagine IC organized in 2013, and that I attended in light of my research, a famous Moroccan-Dutch male street football player also emphasized: 'It's only about your skills!' Other players characterized the street football culture as a space without racism, one with respect for each other and where everyone was equal.[9] The anthropologists affiliated to Imagine IC described the street football youth culture as a domain that transcends differences in religion, class, ethnicity and language, emphasizing skills as most important and as the basis for respect (de Ruiter 2013; Water 2013).[10] Although this is not necessarily a false claim, as indeed in many cases differences did not matter anymore on the football playground, this book also shows that the situation is often much more nuanced. Differences do matter on the football playground, for example, in the unwritten rules of who belongs most on the playgrounds (boys and men) and how audiences react to the different racialized and gendered bodies in the football playground. Differences matter in particular when it comes to gender, as the street football culture is characterized by a male and masculine norm, as the subsequent chapters will show in detail. Also on this matter, it indeed shares an important characteristic with the hip hop youth culture that also tended to be exclusionary when it comes to non-normative expressions of gender and sexuality and towards feminist voices within the hip hop community (El Tayeb 2011, 41).

Female street football players from the early street football scene in Amsterdam all mention that their participation was seen as exceptional and special; for example, everyone *knew* the female players *because* they were women. Male street football players were even more afraid to lose to women than to other men. Two Surinamese-Dutch sisters recalled: 'We were the only girls here on this playground, and together we played against the boys who were afraid of us. Lovely!' (cited in Willemse 2013, 116, translation mine). So while the street football youth culture was not male-only, and actually quite some young women with Moroccan-Dutch, Surinamese-Dutch and Moluccan-Dutch backgrounds participated, their presence on the street football playgrounds was not 'natural'. They, more than boys, had to prove their skills, and the spaces were nevertheless characterized by a male and masculine normativity. These women players functioned as role models and they inspired many other girls to play street football,[11] including the women and girls in The Hague. Hanan, the coordinator of Football Girls United (FGU), came in touch with street football by playing with many of the 'founders' of the street football scene in Amsterdam, just like players from other Dutch cities.

So, while street football continues to exist in urban neighbourhoods across the country, the street football scene as it existed in Amsterdam in the 1990 and early 2000s, with its large tournaments and corporate sponsoring, disappeared as quickly as it emerged (de Ruiter 2013). Many of these famous street football players from Amsterdam started to play as (semi-)professional futsal players, indoor football, as this has more similarities to street football than the better-known field football. Others have set up their own organizations for giving sport workshops and training for vulnerable communities in the Netherlands and worldwide. Street football nowadays is played often in a more organized form, as is also the case for the FGU competition, but still it shares much of the characteristics of the early street football, especially when compared with 'official' club/field football. It still is a bottom-up sport, with rules not set in stone but rather agreed upon together, the freedom to play when, where and how you feel like, and the popularity among youth with migrant backgrounds. Furthermore, nowadays, the design of urban public space has changed, and it does not stimulate the technical tricks-based football that Amsterdam has become famous for. For example, the Cruyff Court football playgrounds are nice and look attractive, but the artificial grass makes it unsuitable for many tricks, and the field and goals are actually too large to play with a few players; Cruyff Courts are simply too static. Other public squares have been transformed into seating areas, leaving less room for creative football play on its concrete surfaces. Nevertheless, today, young urban citizens with migrant backgrounds manage to claim and transform public spaces for playing street football, also in the Schilderswijk.

4

Being young in a contested neighbourhood

Sunday afternoon, 7 December 2014

In the River Square sports hall, about twenty teenage girls have gathered for the Football Girls United (FGU) football training. Hanan, the coordinator of FGU, is absent today. On one side of the hall, Mo, one of the FGU volunteers, is training the younger girls between ten and thirteen years old. On the other side of the hall, Lamyae, Nora, Mansour and the older girls are kicking balls around. There are also two girls, around six years old, the sisters of one of the football players. Mo gives them a ball and a small trampoline, so that they can play together; they are too young to participate in the football training. Aliya looks at the little girls and jokingly says to her FGU friends: 'So the mother thinks, let's bring the girls here so that I can quietly clean the house!'

I am joining Sarah, Chaimae, Lamyae, Aliya, Hafsa and Siham, all volunteers of FGU. They are sitting on one side of the hall, chatting and catching up with each other. Lamyae talks about her two brothers who live in Morocco but who want to come to the Netherlands.

Chaimae: But then they have to come when they are under eighteen, it's much easier then.
Lamyae: But they already have a Dutch passport, eh.

After Chaimae expressed her surprise, Hafsa says: I don't even have a passport. But I'm born in Morocco, eh. My brothers don't have one either.

Chaimae: But then you should apply before you are eighteen years old, otherwise you don't get the monthly student grant.[1] Oh never mind, that became a loan anyway…

Most girls express their frustration about the abolition of the student grants and the increase in tuition fees.

Aliya: The Netherlands is one of the richest countries and yet tuition fees are much higher here than in Belgium.
Siham: Yes, that's why my neighbour went to Belgium for her master's degree, there the fees are only 500 euro.

The others nod, affirming they can understand this decision. After a while, some of the girls have to leave and the others are joining the game. At 3.00 pm, Mo brings the football match to and end and yells through the hall: 'Hey people, stop please! It's time, we only have the hall till 3 pm today!' The volunteers quickly tidy up the hall and take all the girls outside. Most of the girls go home, while some of them go to one of the outdoor football playgrounds that are near River Square to continue their match. Sarah, Hafsa, Nora, Aliya and Siham linger a bit outside the sports hall and then they decide to go to the newly opened youth centre: 'Because now we just want to sit and chat somewhere together and that's possible there,' Nora (sixteen years old) tells me. I walk with them to the youth centre, which is only five minutes away from River Square. On our way, we pass by another playground, where a few boys are playing football. Whereas River Square is a large open square with multiple sports playgrounds and an indoor sports hall next to the square, most other playgrounds in the neighbourhood are situated in the spaces between the mid-rise flats that are characteristic of the design of the Schilderswijk.

When we arrive at the youth centre, Gamal, the founder, welcomes us. He is still busy with furnishing the centre, and he shows the girls the new couch that he placed in the kitchen next to the bar. He also shares that a new television and cameras will arrive next week: one camera will be placed outside at the door and one in the hallway, and the television will be put in the corner of the kitchen. The girls quickly mention that they do not want any cameras there:

Aliya: No, there should be no cameras here, only in the hallway. Because sometimes we're here amongst girls ourselves, and then we take off our headscarves, for example.
Hafsa: But in any case, one doesn't want cameras here, right …
Gamal: No, only in the hallway there will be a camera.

Then Gamal leaves us alone, and the girls make sweet Moroccan mint tea and continue their chat. They show each other pictures on their smartphones of a wedding they attended, and of their holidays to London and Morocco. They impress each other with the Arabic and Berber words they have learned, and talk about the Arabic and homework classes they take at the youth centre. I realize that this is one of the few places in the Schilderswijk where teenage girls can be free amongst themselves without adults supervising them. Suddenly, I am very aware of my presence as an adult researcher who is there to observe the teenage girls, and I decide to leave them some time together for the rest of the afternoon, and I go home.

The myth of the problem neighbourhood

This vignette illustrates a typical Sunday afternoon for the girls who participate in FGU in the Schilderswijk. Since 2008, the River Square sports hall has been the place where they gather to play their football matches. River Square is situated on the border of the Schilderswijk, next to one of the biggest squares in the neighbourhood which has the same name. Typically, on Wednesday afternoons the girls' teams practice their street football skills on the public playgrounds in their local area within the neighbourhood, and on Sundays they play matches against the other street football teams. Although these matches are played indoors, because there is space for multiple matches to be played simultaneously, it is still the kind of street football characterized by small teams of about five to six girls. FGU, however, is not only a place where the girls play football together but, equally important, where they can catch up with each other and exchange experiences of weddings, family issues, education, holidays and citizenship matters. Their exchanges illustrate the diverse backgrounds of the girls when it comes to citizenship and migration status: from Hafsa and Sarah, who are born in Morocco, to the other girls, who are second generation, and to family members who move back and forth between the Netherlands and Morocco. The girls also have diverse educational backgrounds, from (pre-)vocational schools to higher education at (applied) universities.

The youth centre is a popular place where the teenage girls come together after the football trainings. Before the youth centre opened, and after the public library in the neighbourhood closed down, FGU was the only place in the Schilderswijk where teenage girls could hang out together. Most other leisure places, such as cafés, public squares and sport playgrounds, are targeted more at boys and/or adults (Franke, Overmaat and Reijndorp 2014, 29). Nevertheless, most girls in my research enjoy living and growing up in the Schilderswijk very much, as will become clear in this book. Their positive experiences of FGU, the youth centre and the neighbourhood in general do not correspond with the often negative ways in which the Schilderswijk is represented in media and political debates as the most 'disadvantaged' and poorest neighbourhood of the country. Dutch urban scholars Franke, Overmaat and Reijndorp (2014) argue that these negative representations of the Schilderswijk in media and politics install and reproduce a 'myth of the problem neighbourhood'. This myth keeps the attention away from residents' (including youths') lived experiences, which cannot be reduced to problems of ethnic and religious diversity, radicalization or youth nuisance but include much more complex relationships, problems, challenges and solutions (Franke, Overmaat, and Reijndorp 2014; Lammers and Reith 2014, 24). Furthermore, popular representations of the Schilderswijk do not pay attention to the broader social history and context of the neighbourhood. When looking at this history, however, it will become clear that the negative image and the socio-economic situation in the Schilderswijk are not new phenomena that emerged with the arrival of migrants or ethnic and religious minorities, but have a longer trajectory.

This chapter debunks the 'myth of the problem neighbourhood' by presenting a brief social history of the neighbourhood, with specific attention for the role of youth; and it discusses how public (media) representations of the Schilderswijk as a 'problem neighbourhood' are constructed through racialized, gendered, classed and religionized discourses, in particular about its young Muslim residents. It thus shows how the social-political context of the Netherlands, described in the previous chapter, plays out in this urban working-class neighbourhood in relation to the local (sport) policies designed for its racialized youth. In the second part of the chapter, I present young residents' gendered experiences of living and playing in the Schilderswijk. It also shows how young residents in turn deal with negative representations and urban policies and how these inform the activities they undertake and organize themselves.

The Schilderswijk is a residential neighbourhood next to the city centre of The Hague. It has 31,000 inhabitants and is one of the most densely populated areas in the city and in the Netherlands. The name of the neighbourhood, the Schilderswijk, literally means the 'painters' neighbourhood', since the streets in this neighbourhood are named after famous Dutch painters such as Van Campen, Van Ostade, Vaillant and Rubens. In addition to being framed as a 'problem' neighbourhood (*probleemwijk*) or 'disadvantaged' neighbourhood (*achterstandswijk*), it is sometimes also referred to as a 'no-go area' for native (white) Dutch people in public debates (Franke, Overmaat and Reijndorp 2014, 36). This is fundamentally related to the composition of the population in terms of ethnicity, religion, class and age, making the neighbourhood the ultimate 'other' to Dutch society (Franke, Overmaat and Reijndorp 2014; Rana 2014). The

Schilderswijk has an ethnically and religiously diverse population: 91.5 per cent of the inhabitants have a migration background, of which the four largest ethnic groups are Turkish-Dutch, Moroccan-Dutch, Surinamese-Dutch and Antillean-Dutch; 8.5 per cent identify as native Dutch. Almost a quarter of the inhabitants (22.9 per cent) have a (first or second) Moroccan background ('Buurtmonitor Den Haag' 2017).[2] The neighbourhood is also diverse in religious terms: after non-religious people (50.8 per cent), Christians (23 percent), Muslims (14.1 per cent) and Hindus (5.5 per cent) form the biggest religious groups of The Hague (Schmeets 2014; 2016), of which many live in the Schilderswijk. In addition, the neighbourhood is a 'young' neighbourhood in terms of the age of its residents: 29.1 per cent of the inhabitants is below twenty years old and 46 per cent below thirty, which are much higher numbers compared with The Hague as a whole, respectively 23 and 38 per cent ('Buurtmonitor Den Haag' 2017).

The Schilderswijk is listed every year as the poorest neighbourhood in the Netherlands (Hoff et al. 2016; SCP and CBS 2014). This position as poorest neighbourhood in the Netherlands needs a critical note, as differences with other neighbourhoods are very small and negligible, and socio-economic differences within the neighbourhood are more significant (Klein Kranenburg 2013, 264). Yet, it is notably the last place on the socio-economic list that the Schilderswijk has been associated with. This image of poorest neighbourhood in the Netherlands was strengthened when the Schilderswijk became one of the forty 'Vogelaar' urban regeneration neighbourhoods in 2007 (Franke, Overmaat and Reijndorp 2014; Rana 2014, 37). These were 'disadvantaged' neighbourhoods that needed special attention and special policies to improve social and economic conditions, and they were named after Minister Vogelaar of Integration and Housing.

The marking of the neighbourhood as a 'Vogelaar' neighbourhood, combined with its densely populated multi-ethnic and multireligious composition and poor living circumstances, fed the stereotyped and negative images of the Schilderswijk in public and political debates and media. The Schilderswijk is framed as the example par excellence of the failure of multiculturalism and the failed integration of ethnic minorities, and is, supposedly, a breeding ground for Islamic radicalism. Over the past years, numerous articles in newspapers have been written about the Schilderswijk, almost all of them about social problems such as unemployment, police violence, youths, riots, radical Islam and integration.[3] In addition, three books and a theatre play about the Schilderswijk have recently been produced around similar topics: radical Muslims, multiculturalism, criminal youths and terrorism.[4] Interestingly, this negative image of the neighbourhood is not new. A short social-historical overview of the Schilderswijk, mainly based on a PhD dissertation by historian Klein Kranenburg (2013) and a chapter by Geense (2004), will show that the Schilderswijk has figured as the poor, problematic and uncivilized 'other' in Dutch society since its emergence.

A social history the Schilderswijk

From the second half of the nineteenth century, the residential area that is now known as the Schilderswijk was constructed, with houses mostly for the middle and working classes. It was especially built for workers who moved from the province to the city, making the Schilderswijk a migration neighbourhood from its inception (van der Leun 2005, 307). Since there was no official policy on housing, architecture and urban space, it became a densely populated area with small and crowded houses, often in a dire state. From the end of the nineteenth century until the Second World War, the middle class moved out of the neighbourhood, and the Schilderswijk became known as a real working-class area with little prestige. At the beginning of the twentieth century, official social housing was added to the neighbourhood (Geense 2004, 9–10). Despite the neighbourhood being known as a working-class neighbourhood, there were significant differences in wealth and welfare amongst its inhabitants, combined with differences in social, cultural and sexual norms and contacts in the neighbourhood. Roughly, the Schilderswijk could be spatially divided into a poorer and richer area in the period up until the Second World War (Klein Kranenburg 2013).

After the Second World War, richer people continued to move out of the neighbourhood to the newly built houses in neighbourhoods with better reputation and better housing (Geense 2004; Lammers and Reith 2014, 24). New groups, mainly poor people from the city centre of The Hague, consequently moved into the Schilderswijk (Klein Kranenburg 2013; Lammers and Reith 2014, 24). The Schilderswijk thus continued to be a poor, working-class neighbourhood, with quite a closed social structure. There was a rather strong feeling of 'us' and 'them' in the Schilderswijk, which was the result of the bad image people outside the neighbourhood had of the Schilderswijk. Vice versa, the feeling of 'us Schilderswijk' against 'them outside' in turn strengthened that negative image (Geense 2004). Already in the 1950s, people from outside were warned not to go to the Schilderswijk because of the supposed danger (Klein Kranenburg 2013, 189). This partially resulted in a process of socio-economic homogenization of the neighbourhood in the post-Second World War years, in which the inhabitants constructed their own set of norms and values to 'rebel' against the outside. Yet, also in these years, the Schilderswijk, with its internal migration processes, was a patchwork of relatively separated quarters and streets (Klein Kranenburg 2013). Already in the 1950s, there was discussion about restructuring the overcrowded neighbourhood, but it took until the beginning of the 1980s for this to become materialized. In the decades in between, hardly any investments were made in the Schilderswijk, which resulted in a poor state of housing and which attracted criminal transactions, illegal sex work and drug trafficking (Geense 2004, 13; Klein Kranenburg 2013).

In the 1960s, the Schilderswijk became nationally known as a problem neighbourhood, nourished by a 1969 documentary about a poor family in the Schilderswijk. This documentary geared a lot of protest, as residents were upset about the negative portrayal of their neighbourhood. In these years, the strong sentiments and distrust against national and local institutions resulted in riots and actions of especially young residents against authorities, such as the police, the municipality and the church (Klein Kranenburg 2013). Instead of a sense of national belonging, there was a strong sense of local belonging in the Schilderswijk in the 1950s, 1960s and 1970s. This was not so much a strong overarching 'Schilderswijk identity' – except in response to outsiders and outsiders' portrayal of the neighbourhood – since it was attached to the streets in which families lived. Inhabitants identified especially with micro-local spaces such as streets, local pubs (for men) and local stores (for women), which formed the core of the social design of the public space in the Schilderswijk (Klein Kranenburg 2013). Furthermore, there was a strong social control by powerful families in local communities, who defined 'normal' behaviour in the neighbourhood and excluded those from other local areas and families. This became especially visible when (transnational) migrants entered the neighbourhood, who did not conform to and did not 'fit' in micro-local norms, behaviours and belongings (Klein Kranenburg 2013).

From the 1960s, the ethnic composition of the neighbourhood diversified, when many labour migrants from Spain, Portugal, the former Yugoslavia and, later, Morocco and Turkey moved in (the 'guest workers' discussed in the previous chapter). Most of these (mostly male) labour migrants lived in overcrowded pensions. In the same period, postcolonial migrants from the (former) Dutch colonies Suriname and the Dutch Antilles arrived in the Schilderswijk (Geense 2004, 13). While the early migrants were mainly single men, in the 1970s and 1980s, migrant families established themselves in the neighbourhood, which made the presence of transnational migrants in public spaces more visible. Especially once migrants no longer restricted themselves to their pensions or workplaces but increasingly occupied public spaces in the neighbourhood as well, it generated tensions between local powerful families and the new residents of the Schilderswijk (Geense 2004, 13; Klein Kranenburg 2013, 248).

In 1977, 15 per cent of the inhabitants were from the Mediterranean and 15 per cent from Suriname and the Dutch Antilles (Geense 2004, 13). These numbers increased during the urban renewal of the Schilderswijk, which took place from the early 1980s until 2002. Almost one-third of the houses in the neighbourhood were demolished and replaced. In this process, inhabitants temporarily had to move out of the neighbourhood, yet most of them did not return and they stayed in the newer suburban neighbourhoods of The Hague. In this way, the urban renewal process demolished not only houses but also the local family and street belonging in the Schilderswijk. New, cheap social housing was built during the urban renewal process, precisely according to the demands and needs that were put forward by the residents. However, since many of these residents did not return in the end, more migrant families moved in after the urban renewal was completed because they suited the profile for the new houses: big families with low, working-class incomes (Geense 2004; Klein Kranenburg 2013, 348). In 1995, 80 per cent of the inhabitants were migrants or second-generation migrants, and, in 2001, the number had risen to 86 per cent. This included not only the migrants formerly known as 'guest workers' from Morocco and Turkey and their children, but also people from or with roots in the former colonies of the Netherlands: Suriname and the Dutch Antilles (Geense 2004).

The Schilderswijk now: Public and political responses

Since finishing the urban renewal in the new millennium, there has been lots of attention for the improvement of public space and social problems related to drug nuisance, crime and illegal sex work in the Schilderswijk. Nowadays, many public squares and playgrounds in the neighbourhood are much safer and more attractive for children and youths to play in, as was expressed by many sports and youth professionals in my research (see also Franke, Overmaat and Reijndorp 2014). Still, even after the process of urban renewal, the neighbourhood is very densely populated and consists mostly of social housing and flats (Geense 2004, 16; Smit 2014, 40). The urban renewal did not always result in better living conditions, as there are still many undefined public spaces in the neighbourhood, and some districts are rather isolated, which can attract nuisance or crime. Neither did the public image of the neighbourhood improve, which had been one of the aims of the urban renewal as well.

According to Franke, Overmaat and Reijndorp (2014), it is not surprising that the Schilderswijk continues to have a bad public image, as hardly any people from outside the neighbourhood visit the Schilderswijk, with the exception of the daily market (*de Haagse Markt*). This large market lies at the border of the Schilderswijk and is a major attraction for residents from The Hague and beyond, but not many visitors know that it is actually part of the Schilderswijk. The public image of the neighbourhood is therefore mainly produced and reproduced through the media, in which the neighbourhood is portrayed as the ultimate problem neighbourhood of the Netherlands, with Islamic radicalism, problematic 'Moroccan' youth, crime and failed integration (Franke, Overmaat, and Reijndorp 2014), often through images of non-white youths 'hanging around' in the streets. Moreover, the criminalization and radicalization of young residents are highlighted in the media (El-Tayeb 2011; Puwar 2004, 31). In these representations, there is little attention for nuances, internal differences and the lived experiences of residents themselves. Furthermore, often white residents of the Schilderswijk figure as the protagonists in media representations such as the popular television series 'Making Ends Meet in the Schilderswijk' (*Rondkomen in de Schilderswijk*),[5] which makes that white residents are still framed as the 'real' or 'authentic' residents of the Schilderswijk, and ethnic- and religious-minority residents implicitly as 'others'.[6]

In national debates on themes such as integration and Islam, media and politicians often quickly turn to the Schilderswijk. For example, Geert Wilders from the right-wing and populist Party for Freedom (PVV) uses the Schilderswijk in his anti-Islam campaign. He visited the neighbourhood in 2013 to 'support native [meaning white] inhabitants of the neighbourhood',[7] after the publication of an article in Dutch newspaper *Trouw* about a supposed 'Sharia-triangle' in the Schilderswijk. Minister of Social Affairs and Employment Lodewijk Asscher from the Labour Party (PVDA) also visited the Schilderswijk after this publication in *Trouw*, because he wanted to see the neighbourhood that is so often written about with his own eyes.[8] Later, *Trouw* retracted the 'Sharia-triangle' article, as well as 126 other articles of that same journalist, because they were based on unverifiable sources.[9] Yet, the damage of this article and the attention that it generated was already done: a strong association of the Schilderswijk with radical Islam was constructed, and the neighbourhood continues to be seen as the ultimate problematic 'other' to Dutch society (Duijndam and Prins 2017, 13–14).

A second case in which the association with radical Islam was made were two protests in the summer of 2014, which were widely reported in Dutch media. The right-wing group Pro Patria, supported by Wilders, organized a protest in the Schilderswijk 'against ISIS and radical Muslims'. They had banners with slogans such as 'We stay here, we will not be chased away from the Schilderswijk' and 'No Jihad in our street'. The Pro Patria protest was a reaction to a march that was held in the neighbourhood in July 2014 to support Gaza, where some boys and men appeared with flags of the Islamic State (IS). The group of protesters carrying IS flags was small and consisted mostly of people coming from elsewhere in the country (which was, ironically, also the case with the protesters from Pro Patria).[10]

All Schilderswijk residents I spoke with about this so-called IS protest declared that it was by no means supported by most of the inhabitants of the Schilderswijk, and some said that the boys with the IS flags had them pressed into their hands by unknown men without knowing the meaning of the flags. This was indeed the experience of one of those boys who was then fourteen years old: he told me that he thought they were supporting Gaza and had no idea that he was carrying fundamentalist IS flags (see also Duijndam and Prins, 2017, 14). Nevertheless, images from the protest were widely distributed, portraying the Schilderswijk as a breeding ground of jihadism and Islamic extremism. After the Pro Patria protest, the mayor of The Hague forbade future planned demonstrations in the Schilderswijk and in the neighbouring Transvaal, to protect 'most of the citizens of the Schilderswijk that have good intentions' and, especially, to protect the youths of the Schilderswijk from radical influences.[11] Indeed, the Schilderswijk residents I spoke with feel that their neighbourhood, and especially their favourite football squares and playgrounds, are being misused for all kinds of (political) protests and national ideological conflicts.

Not only in media representations, but also in official municipality statistics, the level of 'disadvantage' of neighbourhoods is coupled with migrants and ethnic- and religious-minority residents. The level of 'disadvantage' of a neighbourhood in the 'neighbourhood monitor' database of The Hague is measured in terms of how many people move out, the average economic value of houses, the average income, the percentage of unemployed people and, quite shocking, the percentage of 'non-Western *allochtonen*' – *allochtonen* being the Dutch word for first- and second-generation migrants ('Buurtmonitor Den Haag' 2017; Rana 2014, 36). In other words, places become framed as 'disadvantaged' when they have a low socio-economic status, high unemployment and poverty rates, and relatively many non-Western migrants or ethnic minorities. This assumes a direct relationship between socio-economic and cultural 'disadvantage' of a neighbourhood and a migration or non-white ethnic background of residents (A. de Koning 2013; 2015b; 2016).

Discourses about 'disadvantaged' neighbourhoods are thus often not about the space itself but about its lower-class or ethnic-minority residents (Brah and Phoenix 2004, 81–2); or, in the words of urban anthropologists Jaffe and A. de Koning (2015, 35–6), 'the term is used to map a social category (poor people) onto spatial terrain, and confuses the physical problem of substandard housing with the characteristics of the people who live there'. Because the issues of integration, poverty, problems with multiculturalism, and 'Moroccan' and Muslim youths are so often coupled with the status and development of 'disadvantaged' neighbourhoods, they almost become a 'natural' compound (A. de Koning 2013, 16). 'Disadvantaged neighbourhood' becomes synonymous for problems with ethnic minorities or with Islam (Rana 2014) – the 'myth of the neighbourhood'.

These representations do not account for the historical developments of the Schilderswijk, in which the neighbourhood has always been a place or refuge for lower-class, working-class and poor people and 'outcasts', and not only since the arrival of migrants or ethnic and religious 'others' (Klein Kranenburg 2013). Similarly, the bad reputation of the Schilderswijk is not new, nor are its socio-economic conditions and the attention of researchers, policy makers and journalists for the neighbourhood. In the 1950s, there was an upsurge in research about the 'bad state' and the 'wild youths' of the Schilderswijk, which meant that many researchers visited the neighbourhood to research the neighbourhood and its 'othered' residents. This caused a lot of distrust amongst inhabitants towards institutions and researchers (Klein Kranenburg 2013, 47, 364), something that continues even today, as I have discussed in Chapter 2.

Most young inhabitants of the Schilderswijk I spoke with think that the problems in the Schilderswijk, such as crime and radicalization, are overrepresented and exaggerated in Dutch media. Incidents of nuisance and crime that are not unique or exclusive to the neighbourhood are constantly highlighted in the media when they take place in the Schilderswijk. This overrepresentation of social problems is something that urban anthropologist Anouk de Koning (2013) also observed for the Diamantbuurt in Amsterdam, a neighbourhood similar to the Schilderswijk in terms of ethnic diversity, socio-economic history and public representation. In local and national media, there is often an overrepresentation of reporting on incidents in 'disadvantaged' neighbourhoods, while these incidents are not seen as interesting when they take place in other spaces (A. de Koning 2013, 19). This strengthens the image of the specific 'disadvantaged' neighbourhood and its residents as a locus for social problems. Social problems are in this way constructed 'in' the neighbourhood, while other, positive things are constructed 'out'. For example, the beautifully renovated houses on the border between the Schilderswijk and the Stationsbuurt, a neighbourhood with a slightly better reputation, are deliberately mentioned as belonging to the Stationsbuurt and not to the Schilderswijk. Former drug crime in that same spot on the border is often narrated as belonging to the Schilderswijk only (Franke, Overmaat and Reijndorp 2014, 37). This is also something that A. de Koning (2013, 21) observes for the Diamantbuurt: 'Problems that occur in a larger area are often projected onto the "core Diamantbuurt" and thereby feed into the continuous recitation of its problematic nature and its exceptionality.' She calls this a 'fluid territorialization', which constructs these neighbourhoods as a static and homogeneous problem space with a clear border from neighbouring spaces that are considered unproblematic (A. de Koning 2013, 22). Additionally, the girls in my research feel that the focus in the media on the negative things in the Schilderswijk takes the attention away from the positive things, in particular their FGU football competition, which is famous in the Schilderswijk but hardly known outside of it.

It is also important to mention that The Hague is the most segregated city in the Netherlands (Verweij 2014, 96), and it is – typical for The Hague in comparison with other big cities in the Netherlands – strongly segregated based on income and class (Lindner 2002, 8). As becomes clear from the historical overview discussed above, the Schilderswijk has always been a neighbourhood with a high level of social mobility: when families earn a higher income, they often move to another neighbourhood with better and bigger housing, making space for new families with a low income (Franke, Overmaat and Reijndorp 2014, 55; Lammers and Reith 2014; Smit 2014). The neighbourhood can thus be described as a 'passage neighbourhood' or 'springboard neighbourhood' (Klein Kranenburg 2013; Lammers and Reith 2014, 23). This is inherent to the spatial organization of and housing in the Schilderswijk, which consists mostly of small, cheap apartments, not attractive for families who can afford more space. In this way, the Schilderswijk stays one of the poorest neighbourhoods in the Netherlands, but the people who live there continuously change. This aspect is often ignored in representations of and research on the Schilderswijk, in which the Schilderswijk is presented as if it houses people without any social mobility, while the place is in fact highly dynamic. Jaffe and A. de Koning (2015, 35) call this the 'urban hierarchy of people and places': a hierarchy that frames certain neighbourhoods, such as favelas or ghettos, and its residents as always already deprived and disadvantaged. Even when these spaces and the living conditions improve, it could be the case that their position in relation to other, wealthier neighbourhoods becomes even worse; in other words, the inequality can still increase (Jaffe and A. de Koning 2015, 35). This is also the case for the Schilderswijk, which stands out next to the adjacent affluent neighbourhoods in the segregated city of The Hague.

Spatial segregation based on income and class in The Hague is also related to ethnic segregation. Families who move into the Schilderswijk are often families with an ethnic-minority or migrant background. For the Netherlands, and specifically The Hague, ethnic segregation is caused mostly by education level, the relatively bad position of ethnic minorities on the labour market and thus income level, the allocation of social housing and white people moving out of neighbourhoods with lots of ethnic-minority residents (Lindner 2002; Verweij 2014, 96–7). Lindner (2002) concludes that, in the Netherlands and in The Hague, there is no preference of the vast majority of people with migrant backgrounds to live in ethnically segregated or concentrated neighbourhoods; rather, the native (white) Dutch people are the ones who segregate, because young residents with a native Dutch background have most social encounters within their own ethnic group (Crul, Schneider and Lelie 2013, 76). Yet, the role of white citizens in ethnic spatial segregation in cities is often not recognized. Rather, in public and political discourses about integration, the responsibility for 'ethnic segregation' is 'transferred onto racialized communities through the trope of "self-segregation" and "self-ghettoising", supposedly caused by their fundamentally different and inferior culture, increasingly identified with Islam' (El-Tayeb 2012, 82). The Schilderswijk is seen as a neighbourhood with a 'concentration of ethnic minorities' that is 'segregated' from the rest of The Hague ('Buurtmonitor Den Haag' 2017). In reality, the Schilderswijk consists of a very diverse array of ethnic backgrounds and is highly heterogeneous. In comparison, a neighbourhood with mostly white Dutch people, which is much more ethnically homogeneous than the Schilderswijk, is hardly ever seen as 'ethnically segregated' or 'ethnically concentrated', nor perceived as a problem (Rana 2014, 36). This racialized narrative of problematic 'ethnic segregation' is also used in policy discourses about sports, where the homogeneity of white sports settings is never questioned, while sports clubs with an ethnically diverse and non-white membership are perceived as homogeneous, as segregated and as problematic (A. de Koning 2015b, 1218; Rana 2014, 35–6; Vermeulen and Verweel 2009, 1215).

The Schilderswijk neighbourhood and its residents are thus placed in racialized discourses that project social and urban problems onto migrants, ethnic and religious minorities, and young people of colour: the racialized 'other' of a supposed 'homogeneous and trouble-free white Dutch society' (A. de Koning 2015b, 1220; see also Silverstein 2008). In the Schilderswijk, rather, there was never a homogenized happy neighbourhood without any social problems that is now 'invaded' by ethnic minorities or Muslims. Instead, the neighbourhood has, for a long time, been a place for migrants and citizens who are constructed as the social outcasts of Dutch society (Klein Kranenburg 2013). This idea of a homogeneous neighbourhood is part of a broader nostalgia of white Dutch residents towards a homogeneous and tolerant past in the Netherlands that has actually never existed (Duyvendak 2011; Mepschen 2016; Wekker 2016).

In practice, these public and political discourses translate to security policies in the form of CCTV and intensified police surveillance, and massive police action in response to what are only small incidents, prompted by exaggerated media attention (A. de Koning 2015b; 2016). Furthermore, racial/ethnic profiling and police brutality against non-white residents are an urgent issue in the Schilderswijk (Çankaya 2015; Duijndam and Prins 2017). The relationship between mainly young residents and the local police is a complicated and disturbed one, and it receives attention both nationally and locally and amongst residents who have set up projects to improve this relationship. Young inhabitants, especially boys, experience that they are often asked to show their ID cards without reason or are arrested when they question doubtful police actions they experience as racist (Duijndam and Prins 2017; see also A. de Koning 2016, 122). These experiences were often the talk of the day amongst boys and girls in the public football playgrounds where I conducted my research. Furthermore, there have been major incidents of police violence against racialized minorities in or near the Schilderswijk: the killing of seventeen-year-old Rishi Chandrikasing and Mitch Henriquez (forty-two years old) in 2012 and 2015, respectively, and the violent arrest of fourteen-year-old Oubayda Jab Allah in 2014, which all triggered protests in the Schilderswijk against police brutality and racial/ethnic profiling (Duijndam and Prins 2017, 42–51). What is interesting to note is that the protests against the police in the Schilderswijk are not new, as Klein Kranenburg (2013) also documented: the complicated relationship involving riots between young residents and the police and other authorities have existed since the 1960s.

Young residents are often a specific target group in urban renewal and urban development policies, also in the Schilderswijk. Since 2012, the municipality pays specific attention to the problems with unemployment and poverty amongst young residents in the Schilderswijk. They developed policies to guide youths to paid work, to combat early school dropout, to help socially vulnerable families and to prevent youths from hanging around in public spaces and engaging with criminal activities (Franke, Overmaat and Reijndorp 2014, 8). One of the ways this is done is through organizing youth sports as a way of 'integrating' urban youths into desirable and disciplined citizens and residents. Mariet, who works at the municipality in The Hague, mentions in an interview that Sportteam, the organization that organizes sports for youths in public playgrounds in neighbourhoods in The Hague, is mainly there to prevent youth nuisance and 'hang-around youths' (*hangjongeren*):

Mariet: Sportteam was started about ten years ago to get young people to move and sport, maybe it was even fifteen years ago. But now it is there for totally different reasons, to reduce nuisance by youths, yes, I'll be honest about that.
Kathrine: What kind of nuisance are you talking about then?
Mariet: The uncontrolled hanging around in those playgrounds.

As follows from her statement, young residents who simply hang around in public playgrounds are perceived as undesirable. Public playgrounds and public space, which used to be the domain of young people for unorganized, creative play, are now increasingly under regulation by adults and used for education, integration and discipline purposes (Harris 2004). According to adults and policy makers, youths need to be taught how they should spend their leisure time in a productive manner: 'The notion that young people's unstructured free time is a breeding ground for "social problems" and that they need to be taught to use this time in "constructive" ways lies at the heart of the discourse of education and training' (Griffin, in Harris 2004, 96).

Discipline, education and training are increasingly put into practice via the organization of structured sports activities in public playgrounds in urban spaces (Harris 2004), also in the Schilderswijk. Clubs, companies, municipalities and parents increasingly determine what should happen in the public sports spaces, when and why. There are street football competitions organized by many different organizations, some of which are sponsored by commercial companies such as the Danone or Calvé. Although some of these institutionalized street competitions aim to create a more equal access to public space, they do have their own inclusion and exclusion mechanisms based on gender, race/ethnicity and religion, as will become clear in the next chapters. The girls, for example, are only given access to the playgrounds in a limited number of 'girls' hours', and some Muslim girls are excluded if they wear a headscarf. Public space in the Schilderswijk becomes increasingly 'privatized' and commercialized by companies and organizations (Harris 2004, 116), and freely accessible public spaces become replaced by commercial spaces, such as cafés, terraces or private gyms, which mostly cater to men (Franke, Overmaat and Reijndorp 2014; see also van der Wilk 2016). In the design of public squares and playgrounds, the municipality of The Hague does not sufficiently take residents' experiences, wishes and needs into account (Franke, Overmaat and Reijndorp 2014, 9), and especially not young residents' voices (Lammers and Reith 2014, 24). Although the municipality tries and promises to work from the needs of the youth residents, these, however, do have to 'fit in their plans', as was mentioned by a policy maker from the municipality during a residents' meeting on public space in the Schilderswijk. Let's turn to young residents' own experiences of their neighbourhood, and to what extent this resonates with adults' assumptions and ideas about the design of urban public space, hang-around youths and about the Schilderswijk as 'disadvantaged'.

Being young in the Schilderswijk

Urban public space is not only the domain of local and national urban regeneration policies but also a domain occupied by youths. Youth cultures and lifestyles are often developed in urban public spaces, of which street football and hip hop are good examples. Urban public spaces are spaces for popular culture, creativity, resistance, politics and critiques of dominant, adult or colonial constructions of racialized youths as problematic (El-Tayeb 2011; Jaffe and A. de Koning 2015, 95–6). But first, it is important to look at young residents' daily experiences of their neighbourhood and the public spaces in their neighbourhood. Many young residents are actually very positive about the Schilderswijk, and, contrary to their parents, many want to stay in the neighbourhood. Nisa (twenty-two years old) said:

> I will never leave this neighbourhood, it is so nice here, everyone knows each other, everything is close, and there is always something to do. This really is my neighbourhood.

Other research participants, too, mentioned that they will 'never leave this place'; they feel their neighbourhood to be a real home. Aspects that were mentioned a lot were the proximity of friends and family, the playgrounds at almost every corner and the liveliness of local stores, which are open until late. However, this does not mean that these young residents, who feel at home and familiar in the Schilderswijk, also want to stay when they are older (Lammers and Reith 2014, 28). Franke, Overmaat and Reijndorp (2014, 37) also interviewed young residents in the Schilderswijk, for example, a young Moroccan-Dutch woman, who stated that she never wanted to leave the neighbourhood, but that she, once she has children, might leave, she might want to get rid of the label 'Schilderswijk'. The Schilderswijk is thus a neighbourhood that is differently experienced and perceived with age. The young residents usually have positive experiences of living and growing up in the Schilderswijk, yet they are also very aware of the stigma of the neighbourhood and want their future children not to have that stigma.

The young residents in my research feel the pressure of the negative label attached to the Schilderswijk, and they often tried to debunk it in the interviews. Youssef (twelve years old), for example, said:

> People say a lot of things about this neighbourhood, but really, it's just a super neighbourhood. Maybe not in the past, but now I think it's just the best here. There are so many playgrounds to play football!

Aliya also recognized the negative label that the Schilderswijk has and blamed the media for the bad image:

> The Schilderswijk, really, it's just ... it's the media that makes everything bigger than it is.

At a girls' football hour at a community centre in the Schilderswijk, I talked to a young woman from another city doing her internship at the centre, and I asked her what she thought of the Schilderswijk:

> It's such an exaggeration, like really. Everything is normal here, even boring. When I got my internship here, people at home said: 'Oh scary, there's so much happening there.' Well, there's actually often nothing going on.

Some young residents do not understand the fascination of journalists, researchers and outsiders for their neighbourhood, and describe the Schilderswijk as 'boring', 'nothing happening' and 'nothing special'.[12] This corresponds to young residents' experiences from the Diamantbuurt in the research of A. de Koning (2013,

18): they often only heard about incidents in their neighbourhood through the media and not from their own experiences or observations. Both youths from the Diamantbuurt and the Schilderswijk consider precisely the exaggerated media attention for their neighbourhood as creating a problem that otherwise does not exist.

This negative portrayal of the Schilderswijk also influences the daily lives of some of the young residents. At an evening at the youth centre in the Schilderswijk, I talked to a boy about the Gaza protest where the IS flags were seen, and he said to me:

> Those people with those flags were not even from here, they came here from all over the country to mess around. They don't dare to do that in their own neighbourhood. And now we have the trouble here because of that, a very bad image of our neighbourhood. Personally, I have not had experiences with it, but friends of me did, they were treated negatively because of it.

However, this negative portrayal also creates a high involvement of residents, including many youths, to commit themselves to their neighbourhood: to reduce social problems and to do something positive to counter the bad image of the Schilderswijk. In the Schilderswijk, there are, for example, the 'neighbourhood fathers' (*buurtvaders*), who maintain peace in the streets and mediate between youths and the police, especially around events such as New Year's Eve and during demonstrations. There are also 'neighbourhood mothers' (*buurtmoeders*), who want to reduce loneliness amongst women, and the football players from FGU volunteer at elderly homes and in community centres. Furthermore, FGU football players invite youths from other neighbourhoods in The Hague to the Schilderswijk to play football together with the aim of getting to know each other and of reducing stereotypes about the Schilderswijk and its residents. Hanan, for example, mentioned inviting girls from the rival white neighbourhood Duindorp to the FGU competition:

> The Schilderswijk was recently negatively in the news and we want to show the positive side with our initiatives. And we did this last Sunday: we invited girls from Duindorp, and they came and said afterwards: 'we didn't know foreigners were that nice!'

Although playing football together helped in creating a more positive image of the Schilderswijk, this event also showed that the Schilderswijk and its Moroccan-Dutch young residents are still perceived as 'foreign' by white Dutch youths from another neighbourhood, rehearsing the dominant narrative about 'Moroccan' youths, Muslims and the Schilderswijk as 'other' in media and politics.

In relation to the world 'outside' of the Schilderswijk – other areas in The Hague and Dutch society as a whole – the young residents are concerned about the image and representation of their neighbourhood, but they do not necessarily feel a strong belonging to the Schilderswijk as a whole. Often, more local places, such as the street, squares, football courts or public playgrounds, are more important spaces of belonging in the daily lives of young residents. Gathering and playing in local football playgrounds are important in how young people experience and identify with the neighbourhood. The football teams in the FGU competition are based on local squares and playgrounds, and the names of these squares often also function as the names of the teams. In the competition, the teams thus compete with teams from other playgrounds and squares in the Schilderswijk. Young residents' experiences of living and playing in the Schilderswijk are thus strongly attached to the particular squares and playgrounds that are close to their homes. When I, for example, asked one volunteer at FGU about a specific playground in the Schilderswijk and whether that was also a spot where he sometimes plays football, he said:

> Yes, sometimes I go there because some friends of mine live there, but that's not my area and not my playground, so I cannot just go there and occupy that playground to play football.

The experiences of belonging to smaller local squares and areas in the Schilderswijk is not something new, as this has always been the case in the history and development of the Schilderswijk. The division of the Schilderswijk into smaller local areas of belonging is a character of the social and spatial design of the Schilderswijk (Klein Kranenburg 2013).

However, the local belonging to urban public playgrounds is highly gendered. There are very few public spaces in the Schilderswijk for girls to relax, play or study together. Most shisha lounges and coffeehouses are perceived as male spaces, and girls or women feel like outsiders or do not feel welcomed there. This is often also the case for public sports playgrounds, as I will elaborate on extensively in the next chapter. The FGU competition and a few smaller girls' football initiatives are the only leisure places in the neighbourhood that are explicitly for girls, and these will be discussed more in depth in Chapter 6. There is one other important place for girls in the Schilderswijk – the local library – but it was closed in 2012 due to municipal budget cuts. Franke, Overmaat and Reijndorp, who conducted research on public space in the Schilderswijk and organized tours in the neighbourhood, explained what this meant for the girls in the neighbourhood:

> With every Schilderswijk tour we organized with Zoulikha and Kaoutar, two Moroccan girls of nineteen years old, we stop at the now empty library. Angrily, they tell us how much they miss the library. For years, it was the place where they did their homework and where they met with their friends. And since they do not want to go to the coffeehouses and shisha lounges, it was the only safe place in the neighbourhood where their parents allowed them to go to. And now there is no longer such a meeting place for adolescent girls in the Schilderswijk. (Franke, Overmaat and Reijndorp 2014, 29, translation mine)

After a lot of protest from residents, the library reopened in 2015, and it now also houses social initiatives such as education projects, office hours of social services and media projects for youths and children. The lack of public spaces for girls in the Schilderswijk contributes to the strong attachment many girls feel with FGU. Because this space is specifically created for girls, many girls mention that they feel at home at FGU, and they have even come up with the nickname 'The Familia'. It is through playing with their local teams in FGU that the girls perform their belonging and attachment to the local squares and playgrounds in their area; outside FGU, these are still often the domain of boys.

Another specific gendered experience of the neighbourhood is social control, something that some of the girls I talked to mentioned, especially in relation to playing football. I asked Nisa, who organizes girls' football in a community centre, if there are religious or cultural norms that prevent girls from playing football in public spaces in the Schilderswijk:

> You know what? Here, in the Schilderswijk, social control is huge. Really, wherever you are, the Schilderswijk is one big social control. So, it is not even only your family, but talk goes around the neighbourhood. For example, this is actually not the case with me, or with my family; people can talk, but I am really free, my parents are like that. But, for example, for those who are not that free, and they were to play football in the streets, then people who don't even know them will talk about 'look, that girl is playing football till late, what kind of girl is that? What kind of daughter is that?' You have a social control in the Schilderswijk that makes that many girls don't dare to play football in the streets. So, therefore, there are a lot of community centres that offer girls' football indoors. But yes, culture and religion, not only in the Moroccan community, but yes religion, it does play a role a little bit, because then they look at you.

She continues to explain that, in her view, cultural or religious backgrounds matter because it makes that people belong to the same community, and there are norms and restrictions within communities. If one is from another community, there is, according to Nisa, less talk or social control. Without dismissing Nisa's experiences and explanations, because strict gendered and spatial norms and social control can certainly be exercised within ethnic communities, there are also other factors that contribute to the degree of social control in specific neighbourhoods (Green and Singleton 2007). A strong social control is also related to class and the density of the neighbourhood and the precarious situations of many residents, such as poverty, unemployment, and the stigmatization of their neighbourhood.

For example, according to girls' football trainer Lara, the white working-class neighbourhood Duindorp also has a rather strict social control with gendered norms in public spaces. Furthermore, this kind of social control is not new for the Schilderswijk or limited to migrant communities, as Klein Kranenburg (2013) also described when discussing the existence of self-contained areas within the historical Schilderswijk, where local, powerful families defined the social, cultural and sexual norms that were attached to that local area. It is therefore likely that a strong degree of social control is also related to the socio-economic history of the neighbourhood and the position of the neighbourhood as 'other' in relation to broader Dutch society. Despite the gendered access to public leisure places and some girls' experiences of social control in the neighbourhood, many girls in the Schilderswijk play street football in both public playgrounds and competitions in sports halls, the subject of the following chapters.

5

Invading the public football playground

What stands out while walking through the Schilderswijk is the abundance of public squares and playgrounds filled with young inhabitants. There are at least fourteen of such squares and playgrounds (Franke, Overmaat and Reijndorp 2014, 16), and even more if also counting the smaller public lawns on every street corner. Some of them are specifically designed for sports, such as basketball or football courts. Many are designed for general leisure and play, with children's playground equipment, such as swings and seesaws, benches and grass lawns. Often, squares are a combination of both. They are frequently used by children, youths and adults from the neighbourhood. On a nice spring day, the squares fill quickly with mothers, fathers, children, groups of friends and sports teams. Community centres also organize activities in the public squares and playgrounds: cycling classes, sports hours and football competitions such as the 6 vs 6 Cruyff Court competition and the Danone Nations Cup. At first, the streets and public playgrounds in the Schilderswijk look like spaces where everybody can participate in playing street football. There is no need of a membership, the game can easily be adapted to the amount and wishes of the players, and there is an absence of formal rules and regulations. Yet, while the squares and playgrounds in the Schilderswijk are public and thus, in theory, accessible to everyone, in practice they are not. Girls' football is growing, but, compared with boys, girls are still marginally present in public football spaces.

This chapter discusses the experiences of girls who play street football in the public playgrounds in the Schilderswijk. It analyses how public sports spaces are gendered and racialized, and how Moroccan-Dutch Muslim girls navigate these spaces. While much existing sociological research argues that public football playgrounds are constructed as normative masculine spaces (Elling 2004; Elling and Knoppers 2005; Massey 1994), because boys claim those spaces for themselves (Cevaal and Romijn 2011, 12–13; Christensen and Mikkelsen 2013; Clark and Paechter 2007; Karsten 2003; Swain 2000) and because football is one of the main domains to perform hegemonic or 'idealized' masculinity (Renold 1997; Swain 2000, 96), this chapter explains in detail how the gendering and racializing of public playgrounds comes into being through spatial, embodied and discursive practices and differences on the field. Specifically, it discusses the gendered contestations over football space and time, players' embodied practices in the football playgrounds, and gendered and sexualized discourses about football by players, trainers, parents and teachers. Furthermore, through the lens of intersectionality (Valentine 2007; Watson and Ratna 2011), I also show the gendered construction of public sports spaces intersects with secular norms of public space and with racialized discourses on Muslim girls and boys in the Schilderswijk. I pay specific attention to the paradoxical role of neighbourhood sport organizations: even if they aim to increase the presence of (Muslim) girls on public playgrounds, their practices often result in the opposite.

Throughout the chapter, I use Puwar's (2004) concept of 'space invaders' to describe and analyse how girls' bodies do not 'naturally' belong on public football playgrounds but that through those spaces, they change the status quo and make visible and destabilize the white and male norm of those spaces. They do not readily accept but contest and destabilize the dominant gendered, racialized and secular constructions of the football playgrounds by acting as role models and by winning the match.

Contestations over space and time

The first times that I visit the Schilderswijk for my fieldwork, in March 2014, I attend a 6 vs 6 football competition at the Cruyff Court. There are three girls' teams and four boys' teams from the surrounding schools playing against each other in the competition. I express my interest in girls' football to one of the girls waiting to play the next match and ask about her experiences with the competition and with street football. Quickly, a group of about eight girls and a few boys gather around me, and they are all eager to talk with me about football. I ask the girls questions about football, but, because of their enthusiasm, the conversation proceeds rather chaotically and is difficult to follow. However, one thing that does become very clear to me is that the inequality between boys and girls in the football playground is a very important topic for the girls, as I continue to jot down phrases such as:

'There are many more boys playing football than girls.'

'Some parents do not allow girls to play football, but they do allow boys.'

'You have to be safe as a girl.'

'Boys do not shoot the ball at us, because they think we are bad players.'

'Yes, but in the end, we won, and they didn't!'

Then, one of the boys approaches me and asks: 'Will you also interview me?' I answer him that I first want to talk with the girls and will then come to him. However, he does not leave and asks me a couple of minutes later whether I will interview him now. I do, and I arrange to visit the girls' team at their school the day after to conduct an in-depth group interview in a quieter context, to further talk about the issues they have raised.

This vignette exemplifies what my general impression was of playgrounds in the Schilderswijk and other neighbourhoods in the Netherlands: regularly, girls will be playing football, but boys are often the majority and receive the most attention from trainers, coaches, teachers and spectators. Girls often mentioned that they feel like 'second-class' players on football playgrounds. In this context, it was exceptional that a researcher was particularly and primarily interested in the girls and in girls' football, and, many times, girls were jumping around me to talk about their experiences. It gave me the impression that, for many girls, being interviewed about football was a recognition of their status as a real football player. The boys in the fieldwork encounter above, however, were not used to come 'after' the girls in football spaces: one of them demanded to be interviewed and did not leave before I also asked him some questions. The next day, when I conducted a group interview with the girls at their school, the boys also became annoyed that the girls had the privilege to be in the teachers' room and were allowed to come late to class because of the interview about football. This was opposite to what they were used to: usually, in football contexts, most of the time and attention goes to the boys, and the girls are 'second'.

The boys had to get used to street football spaces and times being increasingly claimed by girls who want to play, and especially since the last decade this change has become clearly visible on the streets. At the start of my research in 2013, I spoke with Aisha, a well-known Moroccan-Dutch Amsterdam-based street footballer in her late twenties. About ten years ago, she was one of the first women who organized girls' football for mainly Moroccan-Dutch girls in Amsterdam. She told me that, nowadays, she sees much more girls playing football in the public playgrounds than when she was a teenager. Jasmine, another street footballer from Amsterdam in her late twenties, told me something similar:

> I think that street football became just much more accessible for girls. I see this, for example, also in Rotterdam South and in other places; a lot of girls just play football in the streets. Also with a headscarf and with different cultural backgrounds. Yes, what I said, it is much more accessible, and I see a lot of opportunities now for girls' and women's football.

Football players Hanan and Nisa from the Schilderswijk also mention this difference. Nisa, who is twenty-two years old, told me that, when she played football in the playgrounds in the Schilderswijk as a teenager, she was always the only girl amongst boys. Now, she sees much more teenage girls playing football, who are all very enthusiastic when she, as a young adult woman, joins them. However, although more girls play football in public playgrounds, this does not mean that they experience equal access to these spaces as compared to boys. Many girls still experience being marginalized in the football playgrounds and their increasing presence in football spaces is contested.

Girls do not always feel welcome when a football playground is occupied by boys. For example, I heard from my research participants that boys make comments such as 'What are you doing here?' or 'Girls cannot play football' when girls enter playgrounds. Girls feel 'out of place' and experience an 'unwelcome and awkward position as footballers', as Clark and Paechter (2007, 264) observed. Skill is often the main criterion in the selection and access of players (Karsten 2003, 269), but skill is differently defined and evaluated for girls than for boys. For boys, skill is assumed, while girls must first prove that they are really good enough to enter the playground. Thus, in these football spaces, boys claim ownership and girls need 'permission' to enter based on their skill and performances (see also Clark and Paechter 2007, 265–6). Often, only the girls who are known to be good players are accepted in the game by boys. During a 6 vs 6 match in the Schilderswijk, I had a short interview with Lily (eleven years old), who often plays football with her female friends after school in a small playground near her house. When I asked her if she prefers playing with boys or with girls, she said:

> Actually, not with boys. But sometimes we have to. If they come to the playground and if they ask to participate then we always let them join, because otherwise they will bully us and take away the ball. But vice versa, if they are already there, then we are not always allowed to participate, actually that is not fair and mean.

Other girls whom I interviewed mentioned the same dynamics and power relations in the playground: they must share the space with the boys, but when boys occupy the football space, girls have to wait and see if the boys allow them to participate. This is also observed by Thorne (1993) in her famous sociological research on gender and children's play in US schools: boys invade girls' games much more often than the other way around, which is, according to her, a sign of the dominant position of boys in the playgrounds.

Contestations over playground spaces also intersect with age. Sahar (eleven years old), whom I met at a community centre, told me that she is sometimes chased away from football playgrounds by older boys and girls of fourteen years or older. For this reason, she likes playing girls' football at the community centre, because the girls are of the same age there. The occupation of playgrounds is formed through the group that is most dominant or powerful when it comes to claiming the space, which are often boys and older boys specifically (see also Franke, Overmaat and Reijndorp 2014, 19–20), but sometimes also older girls.

At times, in extreme cases, girls are aggressively chased away from football courts by boys. Nora said:

> At the football court, girls are chased away. Or once they threw eggs at us. We were with two girls' teams at a street football competition and then the boys of the football court, they immediately called us whores because they think we came to play for the boys. But we just play football where we want, we don't go there to be seen by boys. But there was no one from the organization there, so they just threw eggs at us. Later, when we complained, they were sent away.

Nora's story makes clear that, sometimes, girls who play football are not only chased away but also sexualized. Their presence on the football field is then 'read' by boys not as a wish to just play football, but as a (hetero)sexualized performance – but more on that later in the chapter. The experiences that I have discussed so far show, at first, that girls do not automatically have the right to play football in public playgrounds; it depends on the access that is granted to them by boys.

A second important observation was that, often, boys play football in the official football courts, while girls play in the children's playground or on the lawn next to the football court. In these spaces, girls use children's playground equipment, such as swings, to make goals. Hafsa, a volunteer at FGU, shared how she and her friends deal with the gendered division of football spaces. When they go to a public playground in the Schilderswijk to play football, usually boys already occupy the football court, and they just play next to it:

> It is not a real football field, but if we also want to play, we just create our own field where we can play.

Lily also creates her own football space with her friends in the playground:

> We make a football pitch ourselves, we put the swings aside and we mark the boundaries of the field with the fence and the slide.

When comparing these children's playgrounds with the actual sports playgrounds, the children's playgrounds have a more 'feminine' image, as they are often occupied by mothers and small children. The gendered use of different kinds of spaces is also something Karsten (2003, 466–8) and Clark and Paechter (2007) observed in their research on playgrounds in Amsterdam and London, where the girls often occupied the marginal or hidden spaces at the borders of the playground. As such, although girls' football participation in public playgrounds is growing, boys still dominate the 'real' sports spaces, and girls often use smaller or marginal public spaces that require more adaptation and spatial creativity of the girls.[1]

To my surprise, this was also, or even especially, the case when a sports professional from Sportteam was present in the playground. I often observed that a trainer from Sportteam was having a sports hour after school in which only boys participated. Sometimes, I saw girls hanging around the football court or playing football next to the court on the pavement. During one of these sports hours with only boys, I conducted a short interview with Ibrahim, who works for Sportteam and organizes football in a playground in the Schilderswijk on Wednesday and Saturday afternoons. I asked him whether girls also participated in his football hour, and he responded:

> Yes, they do come, that group of girls for example, always on Mondays. Girls also want to play football. And then usually we go to the small field there in the children's playground, and then here the boys. And then we play handball or something like that, football. Oh, but sometimes also boys and girls together, but that is more difficult. Because what do I do when a mother comes and says, that and that boy assaulted my daughter? I do not want that. I just do not dare to let the boys and girls play together.

Ibrahim talked about a big square in the Schilderswijk that is divided into two parts: one part is a big football and basketball court, the other part is a children's playground with grass. Often, during the football hours organized by Sportteam, the boys play in the real football court and the girls play on the small grass field, like Ibrahim explained. Although it is a tactic to attract more girls, and to avoid problems between girls and boys, it does confirm the idea that 'real' football is for boys, putting girls at the margin of football spaces. It also suggests that boys are still the main target group of Sportteam, which is confirmed by Kayleigh, who also works for Sportteam, with the specific task to attract more girls:

> We now have a new strategy: everywhere we are, we're with two of us. And then, for example, my colleague Jimmy goes to train with the boys who already always come here, and I can then every time try to involve more girls. But if I am on my own, yeah, then I also do the training with these boys, I can't leave them alone. If there are like twenty boys and two girls, yes, then it is difficult to let the girls participate. On some squares, there's the advantage that it's a bit more secluded, so you play a bit out of sight. Then that's nicer for the girls. On other squares, it's different, they are very open, girls are present there only very occasionally. It's difficult then to let them participate structurally.

This new strategy follows from the goal of Sportteam to involve more girls in their activities. However, paradoxically, this does not result in a more equal use of football space, as Sportteam leaves the boys on the football court and directs the girls to the spaces next to the 'real' football court. Sports trainers often find it difficult or too time-consuming to structurally include girls in their sports hours on the 'real' football courts because the boys will clash with the girls or because the trainers are afraid of problems, as Ibrahim mentioned. Even if this strategy increases girls' participation in Sportteam's activities, it also simultaneously confirms the idea of 'real' football spaces as masculine. The increasing participation of girls is not supposed to change anything in boys' dominant access to football spaces, or boys as the main target group of Sportteam. Furthermore, Kayleigh assumes that girls prefer to play in more closed-off spaces (none of the girls in my research themselves expressed this wish), thereby reproducing the traditional association of girls with more private or domestic spaces and boys with public and open spaces (Massey 1994; Rosaldo 1980).

The role of sports organizations is an important addition to existing studies on gender and playgrounds, which focus on the role of schools and teachers in the gendered construction of the playground (Clark and Paechter 2007; Evaldsson 2003; Swain 2000; Thorne 1993) but not on organizations or actors with the specific aim to increase girls' participation. This research shows that, even when organizations specifically focus on girls' participation, they still reproduce the gendered masculine norms of public playgrounds.

Third, when specifically analysing street football competitions, for example, the Danone Nations Cup and the Schilderswijk Street League, it becomes clear that the main focus of these organizations and actors is also on the boys. Often, there is only one girls' team, or none, in the competition.[2] This makes girls the 'exception' in a competition that otherwise consists only of boys and boys' teams. Again, this reinforces the dominant idea of football spaces as masculine spaces, giving girls the idea that football competitions are organized 'more for boys', as they mentioned to me. Sometimes, girls think that football competitions are actually boys' competitions, like Jamila, who plays on the only girls' team in the Schilderswijk Street League:[3]

Kathrine: What do you think about the fact that you are the only girls' team?

Jamila: Yeah, we did not know about that at all, because this competition is actually for boys. You know, that is really strange, because there is never something for girls. So much is only being organized for boys. We also thought that we would play only against girls, and only when we went to the club to sign the contracts, we heard that it was for boys. We really were made to look like a fool, because you have to step onto the stage to sign and it was really so embarrassing. You really saw everybody look like 'oh ... also girls'. And we went to McDonald's afterwards, and we were only with four girls, because the other girls of our team could not come, they had to go to school. And we were with the four of us, sitting at a table, alone.

Jamila expressed a feeling of being 'out of place' when her team stepped onto the stage. The fact that other participants were surprised to see a girls' team meant that the football competition and its spaces were dominantly perceived to be masculine and male spaces by the actors and players involved. This implicit or 'hidden' norm of football space as masculine became uncomfortably visible when the girls stepped onto the stage to present themselves (Puwar 2004). Furthermore, the girls literally occupied a separate space from the boys when they went to eat at McDonald's after the start of the competition. Although it is not exceptional that players sit together with their own team after the match, here, the division also marked a gender division, and Jamila felt 'out of place' and isolated from the other football players, the boys.

During organized street football competitions, social and spatial divisions are visible not only on the official football field itself but also in the 'additional' spaces, such as the table settings at McDonald's described above. Next to the official football fields, there are often also smaller panna courts,[4] grass fields or gym equipment. Whereas during training hours the girls are usually directed to these marginal spaces, during larger competitions, these spaces also become the domain of boys. In between or before the matches, boys are often exercising in the additional sports spaces or already warming up on the field. Girls are usually only on the field during their official playing time and hardly make use of the panna court or gym equipment. I saw girls warming up only a few times, and this was on the sidewalk and not on the field or using the gym equipment. During mixed competitions, I also observed that girls quit the match earlier than boys, for example, when there are too many players, when someone needs to change or when they do not receive the ball in the field (see also Karsten 2003, 466). In other words, even though girls' participation in football competitions is growing, in the spaces and times 'in between' official matches, football spaces are the domain of boys, and this is perceived as a self-evident or 'natural' given by football players, organizers and spectators. The 'somatic norm' in football is still defined by male bodies (Puwar 2004). At the same time, girls are increasingly occupying and invading football spaces, or moving at the borders of these spaces, and thereby also contesting the masculine norms of football spaces by being space invaders, which I will come back to later.

Fourth, the normative ideal of football as masculine is constructed through gendered processes not only of space but also of time. An important way of constructing football space as masculine through gendered time is the 'girls' hour' in football playgrounds. In sports sociological literature, women's or girls' hours in swimming pools (Elling 2005), after-school clubs (Christensen and Mikkelsen 2013) or gyms have been critically discussed. These hours often take place at unpopular times at which no one else is using the sports space. Furthermore, girls' and women's hours often quickly cease to exist, due to practical matters (Christensen and Mikkelsen 2013), or due to resistance in society, especially when mainly Muslim or ethnic-minority women use the women's hours – it is seen as a bad sign of integration (Elling 2005). These examples in the literature emphasize women's or girls' own wishes and needs for a separate space, because they do not want to play a sport with men or boys for various (not only religious!) reasons (Rana 2018). Yet, I found in my research that, also when girls *do* like to play football with boys, sports organizations still find it easier to organize a separate girls' hour. Trainers organize girls' hours not only to increase the participation of girls in their activities but also because they think it is easier to train boys and girls separately, by which they avoid having to deal with gender stereotypes, interactions between boys and girls, and differences in level.

Many neighbourhood sports organizations, including Sportteam in the Schilderswijk, organize a girls' hour once or twice a week, which means that during this designated time, only girls are allowed in the playground. In practice, the existence of girls' hours means that girls are encouraged to *only* come during the girls' hours and not during 'regular' sports activities. Girls, then, are 'forced' to attend the girls' hours, not because they do not want to or are not allowed by their parents to play football with boys, but because they are not welcome during the 'regular' football hours, which are, implicitly, for boys only. Peter is the coordinator of several sports playgrounds in the Schilderswijk, in which trainings for different sports are offered, including some trainings for girls only. After I conducted an interview with Peter, he gave me a tour of the playgrounds and showed me the various sports training sessions. We watched a football training for children of about ten years old, in which only boys participated, and I asked him whether girls can also come to this 'regular' football hour. Peter responded carefully:

> Let's say we do not stimulate that, if one girl shows up, that she participates here.

Officially, Peter cannot prevent girls to participate in the 'regular' football training, but by stimulating girls to *only* come to the girls' football training, the 'regular' football training becomes a boys' training. The organization of separate girls' hours, when football space is temporarily defined as feminine, then only confirms regular sports time and space as masculine.

Furthermore, there is a specific spatial aspect in the organization of girls' hours. Mostly, these girls' hours are organized indoors, in a sports or gym hall, even though most girls in my research do not have a preference themselves to play indoors. At one of the football playgrounds in the Schilderswijk, I talked with Jimmy and Ibrahim, both Sportteam staff members. I asked Jimmy whether any girls play at his football court. He responded:

> No, for the girls we have the gym hall behind the court, so they can play football there. We organize that with the community centre. And with them we agreed that sometimes we reserve the football court here for the girls. Once in a while.

Jimmy then had to return to his training, so I continued the conversation with Ibrahim. I asked when this 'once in a while' took place specifically, but he remained vague:

> When it suits us and the girls. In the beginning, we had some girls, but now they go to the gym hall and that is better, because playing together with the boys doesn't work out. In this way, we don't get any problems and we don't have to explain the parents anything, because sometimes people think that girls play to hit on the boys. And now, in Winter, we don't really have girls, because they need to be home on time and so on.

When I tried one last time to figure out when the outdoor football court is reserved for the girls, Ibrahim said:

> You really have to ask the community centre that, we really left that part to them.

Some community centres indeed organize girls' football indoors, but, here, it seemed that these girls' football hours indoors served as an excuse for Sportteam to not include girls or organize girls' football in their public playgrounds outdoors. Peter, who cooperates with Football Girls United (FGU), also said:

> I think it is ideal that they [FGU] take care of that part [girls' football].

Indeed, the more institutionalized and subsidized sports organizations, such as Sportteam, often leave the organization of girls' football to community centres and grassroots organizations such as FGU, who receive much less and no structural funding. Boys' football is thus the core of Sportteam's activities in public playgrounds, and girls' football is offered when there is time and space (and money) left, often on a less structural basis and often indoors or in more domestic, closed-off spaces. Both the temporal and spatial organization of girls' hours confirm outdoor public football spaces as normatively and implicitly masculine.

The organization of girls' football hours indoors is also related to the emphasis that is put on safe spaces for girls, both by sports organizers and parents. Nisa organizes girls' football in a community centre and sometimes comes across parents who are hesitant at first to send their daughter to girls' football. She said:

> Sometimes, parents or other people in the neighbourhood have conservative ideas that girls should not play football or should not be in the streets but at home.

According to Nisa, this mostly has to do with concerns about safety in public spaces, and organizing girls' football in a safe space indoors therefore makes the threshold for parents and girls lower. Concerns about safety are diverse and include parents' fears of sexual and racial attacks on their daughters in public spaces (Parmar, in Green and Singleton 2007, 111). Nisa told me that after the parents' initial hesitation, they are usually very positive about their daughters' football participation. In the next chapter, I will discuss the girls' own motivations for playing girls' football in the FGU competition indoors in more detail.

The gendering of football space and time is also reflected in the amount of training time that girls and boys receive to prepare for competitions. I asked Jamila what she thought of the Schilderswijk Street League competition:

Jamila: Well, we are the only girls here, so I actually think that is quite embarrassing.
Kathrine: Why do you think so?
Jamila: Well, because we lose all the time, now we just won one time and once we played draw, and the rest we lost. I think we are at the bottom. And people look at you all the time when you are playing, I just don't like that. And I also thought that we would get much more training, that is way too little. Hamza has not enough hours, they say, to give us training. But he also has weekends and leisure time, so he just has to do it then, because we are also here in our leisure time. And he does train the boys. And I want more trainings. Because this *sucks*, we just do something on the field now and we do not train. When I started with this, I expected that we would have trainings. And I said it many times to the community centre, but they do nothing.

Jamila explicitly connects football and training with contestations over time: she and her fellow team members receive less training time from Hamza, who works at the community centre that supports Jamila's team, than the boys' team from the same centre. Swain (2000, 100) also observed that girls receive less training time in football trainings at a UK school. The lack of training that Jamila experiences directly translates to their performances on the field. Because of the limited training time and limited skills that girls practise, their practices and performances on the field are often not as good as those of boys, and girls feel more insecure about their football performances. The differences in girls' and boys' football skills are thus not 'natural' aspects of gender difference but constructed through differences in the access to football space, time and training (Butler 1993; 1998).

This section has shown that girls have to compete with boys over the access to football spaces and times, and boys are still seen as the 'automatic' or 'natural' occupiers of football space both by boys themselves and by sports organizers. Paradoxically, sports organizations that aim to increase the participation of girls reproduce and institutionalize football space and time as normatively masculine by directing girls to separate spaces and special girls' hours. Girls contest and resist those dominant constructions of football space and time precisely by entering and claiming these both. Just by being present in football spaces as football players, girls already act as space invaders who lay bare the masculine norm of these spaces (Puwar 2004). Clark and Paechter (2007, 272) argue: 'In many ways, simply stepping onto the football pitch can be seen as a form of resistance, since embodying the concept of "footballer" represents a challenge to its masculine association.' The gendered bodies that are normally 'constructed out' of football spaces are now visible and active on the inside (Puwar 2004, 1). Yet, being a space invader is not merely a by-product of girls' wishes to play football, or an unwitting practice; sometimes, the girls in my research also deliberately act as space invaders. Hafsa said:

> Except for FGU, I do not know of any girls' competition. Nowhere. But as soon as we see a competition, also with only boys, then we sign up as a girls' team.

She is very aware of the masculine norm of football competitions and tries to challenge this by invading competitions with her girls' team. Nisa also explicitly stimulates girls to claim football spaces, by telling the girls she trains at a community centre:

> If you want to play football, then you go play football! It's none of your business what people say.

Yet, dominant construction of football as masculine are not easily challenged by girls invading football spaces. The presence of girls' bodies in public football playgrounds, 'marked' as gendered bodies 'out of place' (Puwar 2004), generate embodied and discursive practices that reconfirm masculine dominance in football (Swain 2000), for example, through gendered or sexualized comments to girls who play football, or through embodied practices on the field.

Even if girls' street football is growing, the dominant construction of football spaces as 'masculine' goes beyond mere numbers of male or female football players. It is not the actual and growing number of girls' players that determines how a space is gendered, but rather it is through the gendered access to those spaces, the unequal gendered division of those spaces and of trainings times, and the designing of street football competitions as primarily for boys. Despite an increase in girls' participation in street football, the football spaces are thus still perceived to be dominantly masculine, and this is reproduced not only through contestations of space and time but also through embodied practices in the field and gendered and sexualized discourses.

Embodied practices and play

In football trainings and competitions, I observed gendered differences in the embodied practices on the field. First, differences were visible in how the game, the teams and the competitions were managed and divided. Usually, when there is a group of football players in a playground, a few of them alternately choose which players they want on their team. Girls often mentioned that they are the last ones to get picked. For example, Nora told me in an interview about her experiences with street football:

> You were always the last one chosen and so on, because yes you are a girl and you cannot play football, you cannot run, you cannot do anything.

Even if girls are allowed or invited to participate, in the practice of dividing teams, boys are often picked first, and female bodies are perceived as less desirable in the game. Having good football skills that are seen as 'exceptional' for girls can turn around this dynamic, as Noha (ten years old) from Utrecht mentioned:

> Boys like it that I'm good, often they want me on their team. So, if one of them says, 'I choose her', then the others are all like 'Ohhh, I also wanted her!'

In this case, boys find it special that a girl is very good at playing football and want her on their team. The fear of losing from a girl could also contribute to this preference for exceptionally good football girls, as boys usually do not want to lose to girls and therefore pick her for their own teams.

In organized street football competitions, girls also have different experiences of the organization of competition than boys. Zainab tells me about her experiences with a yearly national street football competition. The competition starts locally with group stages and ends with a regional and national final:

> Often, we were the only girls. And then we had to play against the boys. We always made it through the group stage because we were the only girls' team and,

because of that, the organizers wanted our team in the next regional stages. But that's really not nice, you just want to play *real* football.

Because Zainab's team was the only girls' team, it did not matter whether they played well or not, whether they lost or won the matches during the group stage: they always proceeded to the next rounds anyway. In Zainab's experience, this was not 'real' football. The competition element, which is the whole point of a football competition, was lost for the girls. Some sports organizers think that the competition element is more important for boys, and that girls like to play football just to be with their friends. However, most of the girls that I spoke with play football precisely because they enjoy the competition element. This way of organizing also implicitly constructs 'real' competitive football as a boys' matter and girls' football as a practice where 'participation' (in the next rounds) counts as more important than playing 'real' competitive football. Of course, if girls play 'real' competitive football, there is the risk that they lose to boys all the time because of limited training and skills, as Jamila experienced. Yet, in both cases, girls' football is taken less seriously by organizers than boys' football and it is that experience, of being considered 'second-class' players, that bothers girls.

Second, the gendered differences in the ways in which football competitions and teams are organized also translates into the embodied practices and play on the football field itself. In her famous article 'Throwing like a Girl', feminist philosopher Iris Marion Young (2005) argued that girls and women move and use their bodies differently than boys and men. She shows that men are taught to take up more space than women, leading to more free motion in their bodily movements. Women are socialized to use their bodies in a more limited and confined way; their bodily movements are constrained through social norms on what is considered 'feminine' bodily behaviour. To be clear, these different embodied practices are not 'natural' characteristics of male and female bodies but socially constructed norms related to gendered bodies (I. M. Young 2005), and this was visible in my research as well. If the competition element is lacking, it demotivates girls and gives them less challenges on the football field, which, in turn, prevents them from developing new and creative embodied practices and tactics. Girls often mentioned that they have less possession of the ball while playing mixed football; boys rather shoot the ball to other boys or keep the ball themselves than to shoot the ball to the less desired bodies of girls on the field, something I also observed myself (see also Clark and Paechter 2007, 265–6). Boys take up more space by running with the ball through the field instead of passing it to girls, and girls are often positioned in the net (Clark and Paechter 2007, 267–8).

Especially in sports that are perceived to be 'masculine', such as football, gendered norms about the use of the body on the field are reproduced to keep up male dominance, Clark and Paechter (2007, 262) argue: 'Gendered expectations about play and the use of the body serve actively to discourage girls whilst consolidating male dominance in the game.' Boys interact mainly with other boys on the field and remain therefore the central players of the game (Evaldsson 2003, 484). Men's bodily convictions and performances of strength, skill and power in football are especially important to perform hegemonic masculinity (Swain 2000). The embodied practices of football in public playgrounds thus show how gender and space both co-constitute each other (Massey 1994).

Gendered expectations and norms of bodily movements also guide the design of public spaces. I talked with Mariet from the municipality of The Hague about the design of public space in the neighbourhood:

> You only see boys in the public spaces, but it is changing now, more girls come to the public spaces, and we have to adjust the use of public spaces for that. Because, now, there are too few locations for typical girls' things, such as fitness equipment where you can train in not-too-revealing poses.

Besides football courts, Mariet often mentioned seesaws as an example of the design of public playgrounds, and it could well be that she sees seesaws as a 'feminine' counterpart for the 'masculine' football courts. In that way, girls are not only relegated to the marginalized spaces of playgrounds, but different kinds of embodied activities and sports are offered to them. In the choice of sports and play activities that are offered, a gender division is present: often, sports organizers think that if they offer *other* sports or activities than football, more girls will show up. The way in which Mariet and sports organizers think they should adapt the activities to girls' wishes reflects dominant ideas on what is considered feminine bodily movement (confined, not-too-revealing, closed, docile) and masculine bodily movement (loose, open, expressive, capable) (Azzarito 2010; I. M. Young 2005).

Yet, girls' embodied movements on the field cannot only be read as confirming a dichotomous gender division, but football practices are more diffuse. Women's and girls' athletic behaviour in 'masculine' sports can be precisely an important domain where gender and body norms are *altered* (Butler 1998). Girls can be considered as space invaders in football contexts in that they make visible and resist the gendered and masculine norms that underlie football spaces, and, in addition, some of their embodied football practices can be seen as explicit resistance to and as performative play with those gendered body norms

(Butler 1998). For example, Hafsa told me about her experience with gendered expectations in football playgrounds. When she, with her friends from FGU, goes to a playground and asks the boys if they can participate, this is the reaction they often receive:

> Even very small boys then laugh at us, because they think 'Oh girls, they cannot play football'. But only until we play, because then they are shocked, like 'Wow, they can really play football'. And then the story goes like 'Wow, they can really play football, it's better you don't play against them'. Before the match, they are like 'Yes, come on, come on, we can handle you', and that is the fun part. We act as if we cannot play football and then we prove otherwise, and then they get scared.

Here, Hafsa and her friends go along with the gendered expectations that girls cannot play football at first, only to turn it into their football strategy later. Because their opponents do not expect their strong play, they can attack suddenly and win the match. The idea that girls are not good at playing football or move less expressively than boys is incorporated in the girls' tactic to win. The girls invade the sports spaces by performatively using specific bodily expectations, thereby simultaneously challenging the gender and body norms and expectations that underlie embodied football practices and play. They do not merely resist or oppose these norms and expectations but incorporate them into their embodied competitive practices on the field. This is precisely the kicking back that I conceptualized in the introduction: they cannot escape the gender and body norms in football but rather reappropriate them in their football play in order to critique those norms, expectations and dominant discourses, and hereby emphasize their empowerment and agency.

Nora had a similar experience and tactic, but she mentioned that norms and expectations about girls playing football are also related to their racial/ethnic and Muslim backgrounds, something I will come back to later in this chapter. Girls are space invaders not simply by being present on and invading the football space, but also through specific embodied practices and tactics, in which they performatively incorporate gender norms, expectations and stereotypes, thereby altering them (Butler 1993; 1998).[5]

Gendered and sexualized discourses

Gendered and embodied constructions of football spaces, times and practices are maintained through a dominant gendered discourse that is present in street football. I approach discourse not merely as a reflection of the social world but as a system of knowledge that creates that social world (Bucholtz 2003, 45; Hall 1997, 44–7) – in this case, the world of street football. In street football, there is a strong discourse about girls and football skills, to which I already referred earlier. The idea that girls are not good or are not 'real' football players is implicit in much of the competitions and organizations, and within players themselves. I already mentioned that girls often have to prove themselves before they are allowed to participate. Sports professionals and organizations also contribute to the dominant idea that boys are better and more motivated football players than girls through the language they – intentionally or unintentionally – use. Sometimes, girls are blamed for a lack of involvement or motivation by coaches and trainers (see also Clark and Paechter 2007, 272). For example, when Peter was making a short film about his sports playground, he instructed the children who were to figure in it and especially emphasized to the girls that they needed to be active:

> Okay, you start with the warm-up. The girls are in the front, I see, so there's a big chance that you are most prominent in the picture. So, walk a bit active please, can you manage that? Do not just trudge.

During some of the Cruyff Court 6 vs 6 competitions that I attended throughout the country, the organizers also mentioned that boys are a bit more fanatical, or that girls are really not pushing forward. Some sports trainers mentioned to me that there is no real interest amongst girls to play football, and I heard others emphasize to the girls they train that they really need to do their best. For boys, the emphasis was much less on their motivation or on 'being active' but more on the tactics and techniques on the field. Trainers already assume that boys are motivated for football, so they do not need to emphasize that.

For girls, stereotypical feminine descriptions were often used by trainers and bystanders to describe girls' behaviour in the field, such as 'soft', 'little dreamer', 'chit-chatters', 'they're too sweet', or 'they complain' and 'they cry'. Boys' behaviour, in turn, was often described with typical masculine characteristics such as 'rough', 'strong' or 'offensive playing'. The masculine characteristics that are attributed to boys are generally valued higher than those of girls (Ortner 1974; Rosaldo 1980), exemplified by the expression 'you play like a girl', which means poor play (Clark and Paechter 2007, 264). I only heard this expression a few times, probably because people are aware of its sexist meaning, but it is still a lingering example of the gendered hierarchy in football. Another example is the way in which girls' performances are hailed when they do play very well. When girls demonstrate good football skills, this is often firmly articulated by statements such as 'Do you see that girl play! Wow', or 'those girls nowadays, they are real good football players!' or 'They are no less good than the boys'. These expressions frame girls' good performances in football as rather extraordinary. Thus, through the implicit gendered language use of trainers, bystanders and teachers, a dominant position for boys in football is reproduced.

Sometimes, trainers or teachers were more explicit in thinking football is more of a boys' sport. When I was at the 6 vs 6 Cruyff Court competition in the Schilderswijk, I talked with a female school teacher who coached one of the teams from her school. I explained to her that I was conducting research about girls' football and that I was therefore interviewing girls who participate in the competitions. She responded:

> But what do you want with your research? You just see that girls play less football, also I think it is more of a boys' sport. Maybe that's discriminating, but yeah. It also matters what you are used to from the past, I think. You also just see that boys are much better at playing football than girls.

Her observation that less girls play football, and that they are usually not as good as boys, translates into a conclusion that football is more of a boys' sport, although she recognizes that this connection of football and boys is historically formed. Other sports organizers, as I also mentioned before, assume that girls like other sports better than football, such as horse riding. The employee of a neighbourhood sports organization that organizes sports in public playgrounds in Maastricht said:

> *Because* we organized mainly football at the start, the enthusiasm from the boys was significantly bigger. Now we aim to offer more diverse sports.

Instead of investigating why there was a bigger commitment from boys, this sports organizer simply assumed that football belongs more to boys and other sports will 'naturally' attract more girls. While it is likely that there are girls who indeed prefer other sports above football, this is not because of a 'natural' preference for softer sports but part of the dominant discourse and organization of football as a masculine sport. Furthermore, the 'naturalized' connection of masculinity with strength, power, rough play and football, and femininity with softer sports through the language use of sports professionals, also overlooks the possibility of boys' preferences for other sports than football (Renold 1997; Swain 2000).

Importantly, an implicit gendered ordering is already present in the jargon and terminology that is used in football. During the matches, masculine terms are used, such as 'the last man' when referring to the position of one of the players, also when they are girls. Sometimes, I heard sports organizers, coaches or referees talk about 'the boys', when they referred to the football players, also in the case of mixed trainings or competitions. As I already showed above, a 'football' training or competition is often perceived as a boys' football training or competition, emphasized precisely by the absence of a gender marker. Boys, with their male bodies, are constructed as neutral and not as having sexed or gendered bodies (Puwar 2004; Wekker and Lutz 2001). As such, using the term 'football' without a gendered marker means boys' football. Girls' football is only recognized by the addition of the gender denominator. So, the organization of girls' hours in football does not only spatially and temporarily construct football as masculine but also discursively, through the naming of the trainings and competitions.

The construction of girls' bodies as bodies that are explicitly marked by gender is also related to the sexualization of girls' bodies in football. Girls mentioned that they were sometimes called 'whore' or 'slut', because boys think that girls just play football to impress boys. When I asked Jamila what the boys of the Schilderswijk Street League thought of playing against a girls' team, she said:

> They like it, to get attention from girls. And, right away, they think that they can win.

As became clear in the stories from Nora, Jamila and Ibrahim, some boys or adults interpret girls' play as sexualized performances to hit on the boys. Although girls and boys playing football together can certainly include an aspect of flirting, this is not something I have observed frequently. The girls I talked with all mention that they are not interested in flirting with boys in football; they really, primarily, want to practise their football skills. Actual dating and flirting takes place in domains other than football, such as the homework classes at the youth centre, where girls' access does not threaten boys' hegemony as much as in the masculinized football spaces. However, girls' participation in the masculinized domain of football is sometimes interpreted by other players as sexualized, because they do not take girls' participation as real football players seriously.

Other words that girls heard were 'butch' or '*manwijf*', a derogatory Dutch term literally translated as 'manwoman'. With these words, girls' football performances are not interpreted as sexualized, but their femininity is questioned with regards to a dominant perception of hegemonic femininity that is seen as not compatible with playing football. Puwar (2004) observed a similar dynamic in her research, in which the femininity of female leaders in organizations was questioned. Girls who play football are either 'stigmatized as lacking in full heterosexual femininity' or stigmatized based on sexual identity or reputation, in the case of sexualizing them (Clark and Paechter 2007, 270; see also Green and Singleton 2007, 116–17). Girls are subject to sexual labelling, since their football performances are perceived as threatening the heteronormative gender order (Clark and Paechter 2007, 270). Both sexualizing girls and questioning their femininity are ways of reconfirming hegemonic heteronormative masculinity in football (Renold 1997; 2003; Swain 2000, 96): when girls 'invade' the public sports playgrounds, hegemonic masculinity becomes threatened and needs to be rearticulated (Clark and Paechter 2007, 264). The gendered and sexualized discourses that were used in football by staff, trainers, football players and observers serve to reinforce the idea that football is inherently a masculine practice, in a time when that masculinity and male privilege is increasingly challenged by the increase of girls' playing football.

Yet, there were some different voices and experiences, especially from the younger girls and boys. There were boys who mentioned that, for them, 'it is normal that girls also play football'. The boys who play football at FGU, and who are thus used to play with girls, also do not think of football as primarily a boys' sport. When talking about FGU, Hafsa confirmed this:

> The boys who come here, they just *know* that girls can also play football.

These boys contest the idea that football is inherently a boys' sport. Girls themselves also contribute to changing discourses on gender and football, like Arzu (eleven years old). I met her at a 6 vs 6 Cruyff Court competition in the Schilderswijk and asked her whether she likes playing in the competition:

> Yes, I like it a lot, I would also like to join a football club. In the past, I thought that football was only for boys, but then we played football a lot at school and now I think, now I *know*, that football is also for girls!

Through playing football herself, she was able to change her own ideas on femininity and football, and frame football also as a girls' sport. It seems that these younger boys and girls may have a more flexible approach to gender, masculinity, femininity and football than the sports organizers and older people whom I discussed above. They, however, lack older or adult female role models in sports who also manage to embody those alternative conceptions of femininity and football, something I will come back to in the last section of this chapter.

Racialized and religious intersections

Central to Puwar's framework of 'space invaders' are not only gendered bodies but also racialized bodies who invade public spaces. The construction of public space is not only based on a gendered logic but intersects with racialized norms and structures of power and difference (Silverstein 2005; Stolcke 1993). Yet, contrary to the public spaces in Puwar's research, the public football playgrounds in the Schilderswijk are not spaces that are predominantly occupied by white bodies. In line with the ethnic composition of the Schilderswijk, most boys and girls in the public playgrounds have non-white backgrounds. Usually, public playgrounds reflect the ethnic composition of the area (Cevaal and Romijn 2011, 12), with a slight overrepresentation of the dominant ethnic group (Karsten 2003, 465). It is not surprising, then, that gender was most prominent in the stories of the girls, since they often shared racial/ethnic and religious backgrounds with the boys in the public playgrounds, whereas gender was a clear difference. Yet, the racialization of space, in intersection with religious difference and religious embodiments, is still an important aspect of the construction of norms and belonging in playgrounds. Also here, the construction of public spaces is not primarily depending on the *actual* numbers of racialized bodies in public spaces but shaped through dominant ideas, norms and discourses about who does and does not 'naturally' belong to places (Holston and Appadurai 1999; Massey 1994), and about what is considered appropriate behaviour in public spaces (Jaffe and A. de Koning 2015, 63; Puwar 2004).

Public spaces in multicultural neighbourhoods are given meaning through dominant ideas on racialized and religious 'others', Islam and young 'Moroccan' residents, as I have discussed in the previous chapters (M. de Koning 2008; A. de Koning 2013; 2016). As Muslim and Moroccan-Dutch women are often stereotypically portrayed as oppressed, passive and inactive, playing football is seen as 'alien' to racialized Muslim girls by white sports professionals and broader society (Ratna 2011; Samie 2013). Therefore, the girls in my research act not only as space invaders as girls but also as Muslim and Moroccan-Dutch girls in public spaces that are normatively constructed as white and secular (Bracke 2013; Moors and Salih 2009; Sunier 2009). In some of the playgrounds in the Schilderswijk in which Sportteam organizes sports trainings for ten-to-twelve-year-olds on weekdays after school, wearing a headscarf is discouraged. Peter, the coordinator of these playgrounds, discourages girls to play sports with a headscarf, because he thinks the headscarf does not belong in football and sports fields:

> I just don't want it. Already for ten years, we've been doing it like this, during gym classes at school it's also not allowed, and this is just an extension of the gym classes.

The implicit message is that football space is supposed to be an areligious or secular space and that Islamic religious markers are undesirable. Now and then, girls step up to discuss this issue with Peter, and, recently, he has allowed an older girl to wear her headscarf during kickboxing classes, because she is now in secondary school.[6] Although girls challenge his rules, in this case, the power to regulate Muslim girls' bodies in public sports spaces is still in the hands of a white man. How Peter's arguments are related to a broader discussion of Islam and culturalized citizenship in the Netherlands will be further discussed in Chapter 7.

A second way of constructing public football spaces as implicitly 'secular' through the spatial and temporal organization of football becomes visible by looking at the days and times football competitions and trainings take place. The 6 vs 6 Cruyff Court competition and other football activities usually take place on Wednesday afternoons, when most public, secular and Christian schools in the Netherlands finish early. Islamic schools, however, finish early on Fridays, because of the Islamic Friday prayers. During my observations of the 6 vs 6 Cruyff Court competitions in Amsterdam East, I became aware of this difference. Right next to the public playground in which the competition took place, an Islamic primary school was situated. This school finished at 3.00 pm, when the competition was already in full swing. Many of the children from this school came to the playground to watch the football matches, but none of them could participate because they were still in class when the competition started. When I asked some of the girls and boys from this school about football, they told me that they would have definitely liked to participate in the competition if it had been possible.

In the Schilderswijk in The Hague, there are two Islamic primary schools that finish early on Fridays and not on Wednesdays. The football activities organized by Sportteam in the Schilderswijk start at noon or 1.30 pm on Wednesdays, and at 3.00 pm on other weekdays. On Saturdays and Sundays, there are also sports activities in the playgrounds, but only in a few of them. Nevertheless, there are still plenty of activities children from the Islamic schools can participate in, and most of the schools in the neighbourhood do finish early on Wednesdays; so for practical reasons, it makes sense to start early on the Wednesdays. In Amsterdam, however, it was unfortunate to observe that the children from the school right next to the playground were not able to participate in the street football competition. This case points to a way of organizing football that is implicitly structured by the dominant Christian public calendar in the Netherlands, which makes it easy to overlook schools with other calendars, such as Islamic schools.

Football spaces are not shaped by a clear divide between religious or secular, but more through implicit or explicit ideas about which bodies are seen as the norm, in which spaces and when (Fadil 2011; Massey 1994; Puwar 2004). In one of the first quotes I presented in this chapter, Jasmine referred specifically to girls 'also with a headscarf' playing football in public playgrounds. Muslim girls who wear headscarves are even more noticeable as space invaders in public football spaces, because they are not perceived as the gendered and secularized norm in such spaces. Girls do not always like being explicitly noticed or singled out in 'male' football spaces due to their headscarves. When I attended the Schilderswijk Street League competition, there was a small film crew of two white men from the TV channel of ADO Den Haag, who were walking around in search of a spot to film the football matches from. Nadia (fifteen years old), one of the players on the only girls' team, asked me a bit upset:

Nadia: Are they going to film? Because I don't want to be filmed.
Kathrine: I don't know, I don't know them. But I can tell that man that you don't want to be filmed? Or do you want to tell him yourself?
Nadia: I rather not go myself, I think that's a bit unpleasant.
Kathrine: Okay, I'll tell him.
Nadia: Yes. Because then I'm again the only one with a headscarf you know, I don't like that.

In this space, in which Nadia was the only one wearing a headscarf, she feared being singled out by the film makers because of her headscarf. As the only girls' team in this 'boys'' competition, the girls already felt 'out of place', and being the only girl with a headscarf strengthened this feeling for Nadia, specifically when being visible on film for a wider, mostly white and non-Muslim, audience. She did not want to be singled out because of her headscarf in a space in which the gendered embodiment of religious adherence through a headscarf is not perceived as the norm. Therefore, Nadia did not want to be filmed and preferred me to communicate this to the film crew; otherwise, she still felt as if she would be attracting too much attention.

The racialization and secular norm of public football spaces is not limited to girls but also shapes Moroccan-Dutch and Muslim boys' position in public football spaces.[7] Although, in this research, I have predominantly studied the perspectives of girls, sometimes I do focus on boys to highlight their role and position in the (gendered) construction of football spaces. When I talked with Peter about public playgrounds in the Schilderswijk,[8] he expressed his experiences with those spaces:

Peter: Okay, it is really great that there is a square where you can make laps with your scooter, and a football field that everybody can use, really great. But then, for a trainer, let's say from Sportteam, it is quite a struggle to be there. All those big ... in The Hague, it are often Moroccan guys, or at least boys from the neighbourhood. And this trainer just has to know that, if they enter the playground with a bag full of balls to organize a sports hour, and they get a big mouth from the boys, that they can deal with it in their way. And yes, although people know me in the Schilderswijk, I cannot do it this way! I cannot show up with a bag of balls and then say, 'Yeah leave, I have to train here.'

Kathrine: And this is because you have a Dutch background?[9]

Peter: Because I am not from the neighbourhood. And every trainer belongs to a certain playground, a certain area. Yes, I did once walk here to this playground to ask something but yes you have to ... well ... watch out is a word that is too strong, but, like, it's not natural. Hamza, he's from the community centre, he's just a Moroccan of two metres high and if he says something should go this way, then it really happens that way. And I have to *ask* it, haha.

For Peter, the dominance of Moroccan-Dutch boys in public playgrounds means that they can potentially create trouble and might not listen to him. From his experience, public playgrounds in the Schilderswijk are constructed through a 'Moroccan' masculine norm, where he, as someone who is not from the neighbourhood and who has a white Dutch background, is considered 'out of place'. Although I can certainly understand that it is difficult for a sports trainer 'out of place' to claim ownership over a playground in order to organize a sports' hour, I cannot forego to see his experiences as part of a broader discourse in the Netherlands about 'Moroccan' boys in urban public spaces as a nuisance and a threat (A. de Koning 2013; 2016; Martineau 2006; Watson and Ratna 2011, 75).

Ibrahim also mentioned the boys in public playgrounds as a potential threat, when I talked with him about Sportteam's aim to attract more girls and their new strategy to have two staff members, including female staff members, in the playgrounds:

> Yes, but then those boys will harass her, although we do have female sports trainers now. Then you also need two other trainers, because what can I do? I cannot protect her if boys harass her, because I'm busy.

Here, Ibrahim frames not only girls but also female Sportteam staff members as potential victims of harassment in public playgrounds and boys as potential harassers. He did not mention 'Moroccan' boys specifically as a threat in this context but framed the boys in public playgrounds in the Schilderswijk as boys who grow up in unstable contexts in relation to family problems, poverty and unemployment, framing them as classed and gendered 'problematic' subjects in public playgrounds. How he takes on the protection of girls and women in playgrounds from these boys – by regulating the access of girls and women – is also a way to reinstall masculine dominance in public spaces (see also Prouse 2015).

Racialized (and classed) ethnic-minority boys are differently 'read' by adult sports professionals than white boys when they occupy public playgrounds. Although the perceived problem of 'hang-around youths' in urban spaces in the Netherlands is not limited to racialized boys, as conflicts also arise between white youths and adults, the issue of 'problematic' youths often slips into one of ethnic difference (Martineau 2006, 227). One reason for that is that the relation of ethnic homogeneity and space is differently perceived. When white boys are in the majority in public leisure spaces, that usually is not considered problematic, because the space is already seen as 'theirs' and white majorities are not seen as 'ethnically concentrated' (Watson and Ratna 2011, 76). However, when racialized ethnic-minority boys form the majority in public spaces, it is perceived as 'ethnic concentration' – even if they are diverse in ethnic backgrounds – and it is considered problematic (A. de Koning 2015a, 1218; El-Tayeb 2011; Rana 2014, 35–6; Vermeulen and Verweel 2009, 1215). 'There is a "normalization" of access to leisure and public space for dominant groups,' Watson and Ratna (2011, 76) argue, that is not there for racialized minority groups. Racialized boys' position in public spaces is thus not so much limited because they are a minority or because they are not allowed to physically occupy the space, but because, in discursive and cultural ways, their spatial dominance is framed as problematic, dangerous and as a threat.

Furthermore, sports projects are also an opportunity to stimulate boys' (and girls') behaviour that does fit normative ideas on appropriate behaviour in public sports spaces. Kayleigh, for example, mentioned how she teaches her pupils in the playgrounds 'to be on time, practise discipline, to give a call when they do not participate, and to help each other and not only think about yourself'. This topic of disciplining in sports will be further investigated in Chapters 6 and 7, but, here, it is useful to refer to Puwar (2004, 15), who also emphasizes the 'assimilative pressure to conform to the behavioural norm' on racialized subjects in (white and/or upper-middle-class) public spaces: 'Adherence to the norms and values of this hegemonic culture is almost a condition of entry', while the norms itself are not in question (Puwar 2004, 117).

Role models and/as space invaders

When I asked girls how they came into contact with playing football, most of them mentioned that they started to play with their fathers, brothers, cousins, uncles or neighbours. They have imitated much of the street football tricks from these fellow male football players. When I asked the girls whether they watch football on television, most of them said they occasionally watch national or international men's football (again, often with their fathers and brothers) and only rarely women's football. It is not that girls do not like women's football but that women's football receives much less media attention (Cevaal 2017; Elling, Peeters and Stentler 2017), and the players are therefore less known and less attractive as role models than male football players (Tilman and van Sterkenburg 2017, 253). The street football competitions in the Schilderswijk and The Hague also only pay attention to the professional men's team from the city, ADO Den Haag. For example, the Schilderswijk Street League does not play on the days on which ADO Den Haag's 'first team' plays its home matches, the organizer explained to me, so that the participants in the league can visit the match. Here, the 'first team' means the first men's team from the club; the first women's team is not taken into account. As such, both on the local level, in the media, and in the professional football players they encounter, the football girls in the Schilderswijk often have male role models.[10]

Sports organizations in the neighbourhood only marginally take into account girls' need or wishes for (male or female) role models; on this matter, their main focus is on the boys. Only boys participate in the trips that are organized for youths from the neighbourhood to visit professional football matches. It is not that girls are not allowed to attend these trips, but they are often simply forgotten. When I went to a girls' football hour in one of the community centres,

I saw many boys gathering at the entrance to pay a visit to ADO Den Haag. They looked very excited about their trip, and I wished I could join them to observe the whole event. However, the girls were left behind in the community centre with two interns who would give football training. Only one of the interns knew about the boys' trip; the rest of the girls were not aware of it and could therefore not demand to attend, had they wished so.

In another, rather extreme, case, Hafsa's girls' football team had won a national street football competition, and, as a prize, they received tickets for a professional women's football match in The Hague. But, she told me, a staff member of the community centre under which name they played gave these tickets to the boys' team who had not won anything in the competition. On top of that, he took the cup from them and placed it in the trophy cabinet of the community centre, a place the girls hardly ever visit, because they only receive their trainings at FGU and not at the community centre. It seems that the tickets served as a consolation prize for the boys to compensate for the fact that they lost in the competition, while the girls had won. In other words, the girls' team lost both the tickets for the women's match and the cup they had won, two important elements for the recognition of girls' football and the possibility of having female role models. Thus, on both local and (inter)national levels, girls' football role models are mostly men, and many sports organizers do not consider the importance of football role models for girls. Research on sports and role models shows otherwise: female role models in sports are important for girls, especially in sports that are dominated by men, such as football (Adriaanse and Crosswhite 2008; Vescio, Wilde and Crosswhite 2005). Female football role models can show girls that they can have success, despite the experiences of gender-related barriers in football (Lockwood 2006).

Hafsa told me that she never wants to play for the community centre anymore; she only wants to play for FGU, which is almost the only place where girls can find female role models in football. Women's leadership is explicitly promoted within FGU and girls can also become coaches and trainers. In most other football organizations in the Schilderswijk, the trainers, coaches, referees and organizers are male, occupying important spaces of leadership and power in football. Whereas many girls see themselves as (street) footballers, they often do not figure themselves as leaders in football. For example, when the girls' team in the Schilderswijk Street League was preparing for their match in the cloakroom, a younger boy, a brother of one of the girls, acted as self-appointed coach and instructed the girls on their positions and strategy. For him, it was more 'natural' to take up this position, since leadership in sports is implicitly and explicitly connected with hegemonic masculinity and is therefore not a position that girls easily claim for themselves (Claringbould and Knoppers 2013; Elling and Knoppers 2005).

Sportteam, however, is aware of the lack of female role models and leaders in their sports activities and tries to appoint more female Sportteam staff members. The coordinator of Sportteam, Frank, told me that it is a difficult matter, especially to attract female coaches with a Moroccan-Dutch or Turkish-Dutch background. One of the problems is that women are usually educated in social work and health and not in sports coaching, and a sports education is one of Sportteam's formal requirements. Frank explained:

> Chaimae, for example, does not have a sports education, so we really have to brush up that knowledge, we have to teach her how you create a good sports training. That is where she lags behind, like she's very good at playing football, and she has a lot of experience with that, but, still, that's different.

Because of this formal requirement of a sports education, and because many girls from the Schilderswijk choose to study social work or social health,[11] it proves to be very difficult to hire female sports coaches. Aliya, one of the FGU volunteers, also volunteered for Sportteam and later applied for a paid position at the organization. A week after her application, I asked her what the outcome was. Aliya responded disappointedly:

> Unfortunately, I didn't get the job. Because I do not know enough about sports. But I was good enough to do volunteer work for them for three years.

In this way, Sportteam holds on to norms and rules that do not fit with the daily reality of the Schilderswijk. In the talk I had with Frank, I noticed that Sportteam hardly considers the added value of having sports coaches with a social work and health education, although coaches have daily contact in public playgrounds with socially vulnerable youth, where such an education can be of high value. As such, also through the lack of female coaches and role models in football and public playgrounds in the Schilderswijk, the sport is constructed as dominantly a masculine sport.

When I talked with Nora about a meet-and-greet she attended with the professional women's football team from ADO Den Haag,[12] she talked about the lack of Moroccan-Dutch and Turkish-Dutch role models:

Kathrine: How did you like it, to see and to meet those girls or women?
Nora: Yeah, that was really nice, because you saw, like, a brown girl there, but, for example, you didn't see a Moroccan girl or so, no Turkish girls, really only Dutch or Surinamese girls like that.

Kathrine:	Yeah, you noticed that?
Nora:	Yeah, that was really remarkable because I thought, there are enough Moroccan girls who are as good as they are, why are they not there? Like that.
Kathrine:	Yes, and do you know why that is? I don't know actually …
Nora:	No, I really don't know. But if I get the chance to play on a professional team then I really would just do it.

Through the way in which Nora framed her experience of meeting the professional women's team, it becomes clear that seeing brown girls as part of the team was something that she valued, but she did wonder why there are no Moroccan-Dutch or Turkish-Dutch women playing at this professional level. Having role models from similar ethnic communities or with similar religious backgrounds is important for girls in football spaces that continue to be shaped by constructing Moroccan-Dutch Muslim girls 'out' of the norm. Also with regards to leadership positions in football, there are hardly any Moroccan-Dutch or Muslim female role models, as most trainers, coaches, referees, organizers and camera operators from Sportteam and other football competitions are Moroccan-Dutch or white men (see also Elling and Claringbould 2005; Claringbould and Knoppers 2013).

Nisa confirmed the importance of Moroccan-Dutch Muslim female role models in public playgrounds. When I asked her what had to happen to attract more girls to public sports playgrounds, she said:

> You should put a female role model there. For example, if mostly Moroccan girls are living in that area, as an example eh, then you have to put a Moroccan girl, with a headscarf, who looks like them, in that playground. So that she can show, like, girls, nothing is wrong, you can come. You know, this playground is ours, not only theirs. Like a role model.

Actually, Nisa herself acts like a 'space invader role model' for younger girls, when she plays football in public playgrounds with her friends. She claims the public space as 'ours' and not only 'theirs', and, with that, she shows other, younger girls that girls can play football and claim public playgrounds as well. She not only refers to girls as 'ours' but also frames an 'ours' that explicitly encompasses girls with Moroccan-Dutch and Muslim backgrounds. In this way, she avoids the risk that girls' football is seen as something only white or non-Muslim girls or women participate in, as is often the case with professional football role models. Girls from the Schilderswijk who act as space invaders, such as Nisa and Hanan, challenge not only the gendered and masculine norms of football spaces but also the racialized and secularized spaces of football in the Netherlands, in which whiteness and masculinity still function as the discursive norm. Hanan told me that when she started to organize girls' football in the Schilderswijk, it was an advantage that she was a Moroccan-Dutch woman herself:

> After the first weeks, we noticed already that more and more girls came, also from other neighbourhoods, yes, who also wanted to participate because, yeah, you were seen as a role model. Like, if she can do it as a Moroccan girl, why can't we?

In the previous section, I showed how Hafsa and her friends turned gendered expectations about girls as bad football players into their football strategy, thereby kicking back at and critiquing those expectations. In a similar way, Nora and her football team turned racialized expectations about Muslim girls and football into a winning strategy:

> People underestimate us. A lot. Two years ago, we played the National Street Football finals. The final was against a team from Heerenveen, and this was really a group with only Dutch girls.[13] And, of course, they thought: 'We will win, they are just Moroccan girls with headscarves, they cannot play football.' But in the end, yeah, we've beaten them to the max. But they really didn't expect that, because they thought we couldn't play, and they really underestimated us, so they played very nonchalant.

Kathrine: How did you notice this during the match?
Nora: They ridiculed us, laughed, such things. If we play against another team, then you see them laughing at us from the stands. Not that we care, because in the end we are the ones who run off with the cup!

Clearly, the best way to be a space invader and challenge racialized and gendered norms and expectations in public sports spaces is to win the match and leave the football court as winners. De Martini Ugolotti (2015) has shown how, in capoeira and parkour, the embodied use of public space is a way of reappropriating public spaces and of challenging dominant ideas of who belongs in public space, and, in my research, the use of public space by football girls is also important. However, in the case of football, there is an extra aspect inherent to the game, and that is the opportunity to literally *defeat* opponents and thereby to 'defeat' the dominant gendered and racialized constructions of sports spaces in the game itself (see also

Bale and Cronin 2003, 1, 5). Winning the match and being skilled in football are then the performative acts of kicking back at gendered and racialized norms and hierarchies in football spaces by reappropriating them.

To conclude, the spatial, embodied and discursive exclusion of girls in public sports playgrounds is not something unique for the Schilderswijk, or for Moroccan-Dutch or Muslim residents only. Lara, a social worker from Duindorp, a white working-class neighbourhood in The Hague, observed similar dynamics of public sports spaces as masculine, a lack of female role models, and a gendered discourse in football. In the other places of my fieldwork as well, I saw similar processes. This exclusion is a characteristic of male dominance in football and the marginal position of women's football in the Netherlands, on professional levels, in local and youth clubs, and in leadership positions in football (see also Prange and Oosterbaan 2017). Moroccan-Dutch and Muslim girls are not absent in public playgrounds but rather *pushed to the margins* through dominant masculine and racialized power relations. Or, in the words of Puwar (2004, 24): 'Here we see how it is too simple a story to say that women are simply excluded. ... Instead, through a set of hierarchies of inclusion they become included differently.' Furthermore, girls are not simply victims of these gendered and racialized hierarchies in street football spaces. They kick back at those hierarchies and actively and creatively reclaim football spaces as space invaders and as role models.

6

The street football competition: Girls only?

This chapter focuses on playing football in the Football Girls United (FGU) competition, a competition set up by Moroccan-Dutch women and girls from the Schilderswijk themselves. It discusses the experiences and motivations of girls to play football in this girls' football competition, in comparison with playing street football in public playgrounds. Contrary to what is popularly believed, the chapter shows that girls' motivations for playing in a girls' football competition are diverse and not limited to religious motivations, but primarily related to the spatial and dichotomous gendered and (hetero)sexualized organization of mainstream sports (Blazer 2015; Butler 1998; Jeanes 2011). Furthermore, the chapter reveals that the football practices of FGU are less strictly gender segregated than the name might suggest, as some boys are also involved in the FGU competition. Through engaging and disciplining boys and their football practices, FGU constructs football space and the meanings of masculinity, femininity and (hetero)sexuality in football space differently.

This chapter argues that gender segregation in sports is a practice that differs over time and place, and not a fixed attribute of Muslim girls' sport practices. This is an important addition to and critique on existing literature on Muslim women and sports (e.g. Benn, Pfister and Jawad 2011; Kay 2006), in which Muslim girls' football is approached only as a strictly gender-segregated practice, supposedly primarily informed by religious convictions. These studies reproduce popular and public representations of Muslim girls as inherently 'other' to white secular Western societies, while the ethnographic material in this book shows that Muslim girls share much of the broader concerns of gender and sexual norms and male dominance in football culture and in public playgrounds.

This chapter starts with a discussion of girls' motivations for playing in the specific girls' football competition of FGU, which include four aspects: social justice, friendship, embodied and physical contact, and football level. I argue that these motivations are related to, and a reaction to, the dominance of boys in 'regular' football in public playgrounds. In the second part, I discuss the role of boys and the constructions of gender and sexuality in the girls' football of FGU. I argue that FGU resists dominant constructions of gender and heteronormativity in football by organizing girls' football and promoting a gender education project that stimulates alternative and more inclusive constructions of masculinity, femininity and heterosexuality in football. Yet, in these performances of alternative masculinities and femininities, heterosexuality is still being reproduced as the norm in the sporting context of FGU.

Girls, power and gender segregation

The girls who play football at the FGU competition are very enthusiastic about the competition and the teams. They experience FGU as a nice and pleasant space to play football together, contrary to girls' experiences of playing football in public playgrounds where they often do not feel welcome, as showed in the previous chapter. The most important reason for girls' positive experiences with FGU is that it is a girls' competition; the whole organization of the competition and trainings is focused on girls, and they are thus never the only girl or the only girls' team. This does not mean that girls by definition only want to play football with girls; my observations and interviews show that most girls incidentally or structurally also play football with boys, both in public playgrounds and in FGU. There are, however, different preferences: some girls prefer to play with girls, for example, because they think that boys play too hard, while other girls do not care if they play with girls or boys. For Nisha (thirteen years old), one of the FGU football players, skill is more important than gender:

> FGU is my favourite place to play football, other places such as school are not my favourite, because, there, people think they can play football, but then, in reality, they really cannot. Here, they can.

I only spoke to three girls in my research who only want to play football in a space where there are no boys around, and their perspectives will be discussed in the section 'Only girls today'. Usually, the preference of girls depends on the context. When I asked a group of twelve-year-old girls who play football at a community centre in the Schilderswijk whether they prefer mixed football or girls' only football, Maya responded:

> Sometimes with boys and sometimes only girls.

Sahar, another player, added:

> Only with boys from our school class, because that's what we're used to, and we know them. We feel better with that. With other boys, you don't know how they react when you touch them by accident for example, like if they get angry or not.

Most girls thus do not think it is a problem to play with boys, but they prefer to play with boys they know, from the neighbourhood or from school. In FGU, the boys who participate and volunteer are boys they know and are familiar with. That is precisely the reason why girls do not think it is a problem that boys participate and help: they are known, and they are a minority.

The fact that boys are the minority in FGU is the most important and crucial difference with the presence of boys in public football playgrounds. Playing football in public playgrounds usually means that as a girl, you play 'with the boys'. In FGU, that is exactly the opposite: boys play amongst and 'with the girls'. Nora, football player and volunteer at FGU, described this in a striking way:

> I don't mind if there are boys playing with us, it's not like that, because amongst the volunteers are also boys. But there is more attention for boys' football and if we, if girls play with the boys, then we don't get the ball, or we are not picked. If the boys play with the girls, then it's different. Last year, we organized competitions with boys and girls mixed, that just went very well. But as soon as we participate in a boys' competition, then we're again the only girls who play. That's just different than a boys' group here between the girls.

It is noteworthy that Nora talked about boys' football and boys' competitions. Formally, these general competitions, such as the Danone Nations Cup or the Schilderswijk Street League, are not boys' competitions: they are for everybody. Yet, as I showed in the previous chapter, often only boys or a majority of boys participate in these football competitions, and many girls therefore see this as boys' football. Sometimes, the girls use the term 'boys' football' to refer to a competition that is specifically for boys, such as the 'masculine' counterpart of FGU: Futsal School Competition. In this boys' football competition, like in FGU, teams from schools and community centres play against each other in a football competition indoors. Notably, there is no gender marker in the name Futsal School Competition: only the general name for indoor football is used, 'futsal'. This implies again that 'general' football, or football without a gender marker, actually means boys' football. Girls' football, then, means a football space that is different than the regular football spaces; it is the counterpart or the exception that confirms regular football space as masculine.

Girls' football at FGU, therefore, is more an alternative for the gendered organization of public sports spaces than a space that is literally meant only for girls. The starting point is not that only girls are allowed in the FGU football spaces but that girls form the central players and can claim ownership of the football space. FGU, thus, is not a strictly gender-segregated space but a reaction to and intervention in the gendered construction of the football spaces at most clubs and public playgrounds (where boys dominate and claim ownership), and, thus, an alternative way of gendering football space (Massey 1994; Watson and Ratna 2011). As such, the girls in FGU do not think it is a problem that boys are involved in the girls' football competition. Nadia told me that she thinks it is extra nice to play in a girls' football competition, because of the people and the atmosphere:

> I really can do my own thing there. I always go home with a happy face. In other competitions there's never something specific for girls.

When boys joined FGU as volunteers, that did not make a difference according to Nadia: 'It just always stayed the same.' What matters to her, and the other players at FGU, is that, despite the involvement of boys, FGU is still a girls' competition, where girls are the majority and the point of departure. 'Majority' is not necessarily a majority in quantitative terms but more importantly a qualitative majority in terms of power and ownership of football spaces. Even when boys participate, or incidentally form the quantitative majority, the main focus of FGU stays on the girls and they feel they have more ownership in FGU than in public playgrounds. This is expressed in the name of the competition, Football Girls United, which explicitly includes the name 'girls'. The gendered power relations are also expressed through the organization of FGU competitions, in which girls make their own teams and decide themselves whether they want to allow boys or not on their teams. What is more, all girls are welcome in FGU, but certainly not all boys. Therefore, Nadia feels comfortable in the FGU competition; she decides with whom, when and where she's playing, contrary to public playgrounds, where boys are in charge.

For the football girls, the alternative gendering of football spaces, power and ownership at FGU provides a crucial difference compared with 'regular' football. This becomes clear in their motivations for and experiences of playing in FGU, from which I identified four different dynamics of gender and power. A first dynamic of the importance of a specific girls' football competition is a form of social justice for the girls. Many girls, and some boys, in my research mentioned that 'there is so much organized for boys; here, at FGU, finally something is now organized for girls'. Since 'regular' football trainings and competitions are often seen as boys' football, it feels right to also have a girls' football competition of their own, next to all the boys' competitions. Although the girls in my research generally think that boys and girls are equal, they experience that, in practice, this is not always the case, like Samira (eleven years old), who participated in a girls' football training:

Kathrine: What do you think about the football only being for girls? Or do you also play with boys?
Samira: Actually, it does not matter because nowadays boys and girls are the same. But it was also really nice, because it was safer, you could make friends and tell secrets.
Kathrine: And do you think it is important that there are separate sports for girls?
Samira: Actually, it should not be necessary, but it is also really nice. Because some girls wear a headscarf, so then it's nice, and there's also football only for boys: boys' football.

In Samira's comments, there is an implicit message that it is a bit out of date that girls would need their own football spaces. Yet, she justifies the existence of a separate girls' football training by mentioning that there is also boys' football. Most girls in my research think that, since there are already so many sports and leisure activities for boys (although, officially this is supposed to be general football for everybody), it is a form of social justice and equality that they get to have their own football competition as well.

Social justice can refer to equal access to facilities and resources (Elhage 2017), and to challenging intersectional structures of oppression such as racism and sexism in sports (Bilge 2014; Dhawan and Castro Varela 2016; Long and Spracklen 2011). Yet, social justice is not only about being 'equal' to boys or having equal opportunities but also about power and being in charge of football spaces: 'Social justice is about a fair distribution of material goods but also goes beyond material goods to things like respect, opportunity, power and honour' (Young, in Foley, Taylor and Maxwell 2011, 175). An idea of social justice is important for girls to be able to claim ownership and power in football spaces, like they do at FGU.

A second dynamic of gender and power in girls' experiences of their own football competition also became clear in the talk I had with Samira. She mentioned that it is nice to play with girls, so that she can make friends and share secrets. Here, playing football is related to making friends also outside of the football context, something that is more complicated when girls play in 'boys' football'. Friendships outside school and sports contexts are often structured along gender lines, especially in puberty (Thorne 1993, 47). Because of the limited leisure spaces for girls in the Schilderswijk, they have less opportunities to solidify their friendships in public spaces, away from their parents' supervision, than boys (Franke, Overmaat and Reijndorp 2014). When girls have their own football competition, it is easier for them to develop friendships than when they are the only or amongst the few girls in 'regular' football competitions. How these gendered friendships and relations are also shaped within heteronormative contexts in society and sports will be elaborated on later in this chapter.

A third dynamic in girls' experiences of girls' football is related to the embodied play itself and the construction of gendered bodies and heteronormativity in sports. Girls sometimes feel uncomfortable playing football amongst boys, as Hafsa told me when we talked about FGU's girls' football competition:

Kathrine: What do you think about the fact that this competition is for girls?

Hafsa: Ehm, I think it is actually very good that it's only for girls, since there are very few places where girls can play football. There aren't any football competitions for girls, also there aren't really any football clubs for girls. Everywhere it's really only boys. You can sign up for a boys' competition, but then you're in a group of four girls. Still then you're playing amongst the boys. You just start to feel uncomfortable then and so on. Here, it's girls amongst themselves, that's just much easier, yes. You can learn from each other.

In this quote, it is not entirely clear what causes Hafsa's uncomfortable feeling when she plays in a boys' competition. Later in the conversation, when I asked her how she thought about the boys who participate in FGU, she told me that, especially with the younger girls, it was no problem. With the older girls, such as of her age, it is, according to her, better when not many boys are present, or there are only boys whom they are familiar with. More girls expressed a feeling of discomfort when playing with (many) boys or with boys they do not know, and some related this to physical contact in the game. Football, especially the street football variant, is a sport with a relative degree of physical contact between the players – a reason why football was seen as unfit for women for a long time (Derks 2017). When girls are at an age during puberty in which their body is changing and developing, this physical contact can make girls feel uncomfortable, insecure and ashamed (Beauvoir 2011, 320; Evans 2006; Thorne 1993, 142); this is what Hafsa referred to when she talked about the 'older girls'. Samira mentioned that playing amongst girls can be nicer for girls who wear a headscarf. For some girls, wearing a headscarf marks the transition from girlhood to womanhood, and her comment about the headscarf should therefore not only be related to Islam but also to changing bodies in puberty and adolescence.

Especially during puberty, the dichotomous gender construction becomes more rigid and explicitly embodied through the separation between men's and women's bodies in domains such as sports, and becomes instilled with a heterosexual meaning (Martin 1996; Mora 2012; Swain 2003; Thorne 1993, 135). The (athletic) body is central in adolescents' construction of distinct gender identities; it is common that boys perform hegemonic masculinity through growing muscles and playing sports (Mora 2012; Swain 2003), whereas girls who play football often avoid growing muscles, since that is not considered 'feminine' enough (Jeanes 2011).[1] Heterosexuality functions as the main normative force in the development of children's gender and sexual identities, which are produced within a heteronormative framework (Butler 1998; Ortner and Whitehead 1981; Renold 2003; 2005;). Thorne (1993, 155), inspired by Adrienne Rich (1980), stated about the phase of adolescence: 'Transition to adolescence can be understood as a period of entry into the institution of heterosexuality.' It is in this context of 'entrance' in heterosexuality, and the embodied performance of hegemonic masculinities and femininities, that physical contact in sports can acquire a heterosexual connotation. This, then, can make adolescent players such as Hafsa, Samira and Sahar feel uncomfortable, especially when they play with boys they are not familiar with and whose reactions to physical contact they are as such not yet aware of (similarly, for boys it can be more comfortable to play with boys only, too).

The separation of girls' and boys' bodies into two strictly distinctive categories is not a 'natural' phenomenon in itself, but socially constructed based on gendered norms and practices in society (Butler 1990; 1993; Ortner and Whitehead 1981; Rosaldo 1980), for example, through the control and regulation of hormones in elite sports (Butler 1998; Caudwell 2003). The norm of gender segregation in football materializes sexed and gendered bodies in a heteronormative framework (Anderson 2008). As such, the girls' wishes to have their own football competition need to be placed within this context of gender segregation and heteronormativity in sports, and the development of gendered identities and sexed bodies in adolescence. Playing together with boys in football spaces that are always already sexualized and gendered constructs girls and boys as potential sexual partners rather than mere football buddies. Boys and girls who play football together always run the 'risk' that a sexual relation is assumed or attached to physical contact in the game. Thorne (1993, 71–2) observed in her research that trainers and teachers also try to avoid physical contact in leisure and sports between girls and boys in puberty because of heterosexual meanings. In the previous chapter, these heterosexual connections with playing football became clear in the sexualized discourses that girls experienced in playing football in public playgrounds: they were sometimes accused of 'playing for the boys'. The point mentioned earlier in this chapter, that it is easier for girls to develop friendships in girls' football competitions, also takes shape in a heteronormative context in which friendship is often conceptualized as same-gender friendship, and friendship between girls and boys is seen as more complicated (Renold 2005). Playing in a girls' competition with no boys or with only a few familiar boys might thus feel more comfortable for adolescent girls. Nisa, who organizes girls' football at a community centre, also noticed this: 'When girls play amongst girls, then they're different, they dare to play more.'

The girls' football competition that is organized by FGU is not a competition based on the traditional dichotomous separation of boys and girls in sports. Rather, it is a space where boys and girls play football together. In this alternative football space, the volunteers and football players deal with gender norms in heteronormative contexts in a different way, for example, through promoting (non-sexual) friendships between boys and girls. Because of this possibility, girls and boys are less quickly placed in a context of assumptions around sexual relations and can therefore play more easily and comfortably with each other. Contrary to what Van den Heuvel (2017) argues for elite women's football (where women's football also literally means football only for women, defined by regulation), the girls' football of FGU does have the potential to destabilize gender norms, precisely because it does not hold on to a fixed and rigid spatial binary of gender segregation. Rather than a gender-segregated space, girls' football at FGU is a space where (alternative) gender relations are central, through the organization of a girls' competition that encompasses boys. In the section on the role of boys in FGU, I will elaborate more on this point.

Next to gendered bodies, social justice and friendships in football, there is a fourth dynamic of gender and power in girls' experiences of and motivations for girls' football: the football level of boys and girls. Many boys and girls told me that they experience that boys are generally better at playing football than girls. When the difference in football level is too big, it can be less amusing for girls to play amongst boys, and any possible insecurities regarding their (changing) bodies can become amplified with insecurities about their football level and skills (Evans 2006). Sonia (twelve years old) told me that, in the future, she might want to play at an official football club, but only on a girls' team:

> Because yes, it's girls and then you know a bit what their level is. Maybe boys are better, and then you're on a team with boys and then you think 'Yes, they are better, what am I doing here then?'

Noha mentioned that she likes playing on a girls' team, but 'only with girls who are really good, otherwise that's useless', so she usually plays with boys. Level is thus important in determining with whom football players want to play, although many trainers, players and parents already assume that girls are less good at playing football. Noha, for example, saw the need to mention that she wants to play football with girls, but 'only if they're really good'. Evans (2006), in her research, found that girls prefer to play amongst girls, because they feel ashamed and insecure about their football skills compared with boys. In other words, level is an important factor in girls' preference for playing amongst girls or mixed, although level is inextricably attached to dichotomous embodied and gendered differences and separations in football.

Through sports performances in a binary gender system, gendered athletic bodies become naturalized, as if they exist as such in biology, although they are actually produced performatively: 'The contour that marks the athletic body is a contour produced over time, established again and again, the spatialized result of a certain repetition' (Butler 1998, 2). It is the result of the spatial separation and construction of (athletic) bodies in two dichotomous categories: men and women. Through repetitive performances of spatial segregation, football training and body stylization, girls' and boys' football performances, level and skills become inscribed onto their bodies. Because boys have more access to football spaces, and often receive better training than girls (see the previous chapter), there is a self-fulfilling logic in which boys become better football players than girls.[2] Differences in football level between girls and boys are maintained through this binary segregation, because, in Dutch football clubs, girls who are really good at football are often placed on the boys' teams (Siebelink 2016b), so the girls' teams cannot develop and will always stay at a level below the boys' teams.[3]

Girls wishing to play football amongst girls because of level thus need to be placed in this context; level is not a 'natural' difference of boys' and girls' bodies, but a consequence of the dichotomous spatial organization of sports. Their wish for their own football competition is, at the same time, also a performative reproduction of the gendered difference in football level and of gendered bodies in football, although with a difference, because some boys' bodies are also included in FGU.

In this first part of the chapter, I have shown how girls' experiences of and motivations for playing in a girls' football competition has four interrelated dynamics of gender, power and the gendered organization of football: social justice, friendship, sexed and gendered bodies, and football level. Girls' motivations for having their own football competition are not necessarily based on the wish to play in a strictly gender-segregated girls-only football competition, as is often assumed in research on gender and sports when it concerns Muslim women. The girls' wishes are rather a response to the dominant ways of constructing football space in gender-binary and hierarchical ways, with boys and men in dominant positions of power and girls being constructed as 'out of place' (Puwar 2004). The girls' practices and wishes in football are thus not primarily motivated by religious motivations or piety (except for the 'only girls today' case later in this chapter), as is often assumed in research on Muslim women and sports, but by the gendered and spatial organization of football.

FGU offers an alternative football space where girls, rather than boys, are the central players and where girls are in charge of organizing football in terms of friendship, level and embodied play, even if boys are present. The term 'girls' in Football Girls United is thus not a literal description, but a performative act (Butler 1993) to create a football space with alternative gendered power relations: a space where girls are in charge. The performative naming of 'girls' in Football Girls United is not only discursive but also creates a specific physical space of football that is different from 'regular' football spaces, such as the public playgrounds in the neighbourhood. The act of naming the competition a 'girls' competition' could be seen as a form of 'talking back' to the dominance of boys and men in football, thereby not managing to fully 'escape' the discursive gender constructions of football, as it is still based on the idea that a gender marker is needed to denote a 'different' football space. Within this spatial and discursive performative act of FGU, it remains the question what is specifically the role of boys in the football competition.

Boys, discipline and gender education

The first time I visited FGU, in March 2014, Hanan introduced the organization of the trainings and competitions to me and made clear the reason of boys' participation in the girls' competition:

> The competitions and trainings are only for girls, but boys can watch, just not too much. Some girls don't feel comfortable with that. First, we were very strict, like really only for girls. But it's also important that they learn how to deal with boys, they see them in their daily life as well. So now we're a little bit more flexible when it comes to that.

A month later, the boys and girls of FGU were playing football in one of the public playgrounds in the Schilderswijk, and I again talked about this issue with Hanan. She told me that, in 2008, when they started, she really wanted the competition strictly separated for girls:

> At that time, we thought that that was good. But now we want for boys and girls from the neighbourhood to get to know each other. You know, otherwise they only see each other in those shisha cafés, there is one around the corner.

One of the football players who sat next to us nodded affirmatively, and Hanan continued:

> Where in this neighbourhood do you see boys and girls interact with each other and learn how to interact with each other? Nowhere. Here, we teach girls how to deal with boys, and here we teach boys how they should deal with girls.

The participation of boys in FGU is thus not just a side issue but central in the gender and education goals of FGU. Hanan wants to not only provide girls with a safe space to play football amongst girls but also create a safe space where girls can interact with boys in leisure times and spaces.[4] As the initiator and coordinator of FGU, Hanan is, most of the time, the one to implement and focus on these gender relations amongst boys and girls in FGU. This is not an official policy but more an organic process based on the wishes and needs of the girls and in dialogue with them, much like the competition itself. In this case, it was an explicit wish of the girls in FGU to also involve boys in the competition, Hanan told me.

The goal of FGU is, as Hanan frames it, to create a space for girls and boys from the Schilderswijk to meet and engage with each other in a friendly way. This contrasts with other leisure spaces in the neighbourhood such as shisha cafés; as I sensed from her comment above, these are not known as positive spaces for boys and girls to meet each other. Hanging around in public squares or in shisha cafés with boys calls on unwanted sexual associations (see also Franke, Overmaat and Reijndorp 2014, 41). Hafsa told me that not only her parents think it is positive that she plays football at FGU, but also she herself that it is better to play football than to hang around outside:

> We're inside here, it's safe here; outside, you have many girls who hit on the boys, for example, by lying between the boys in shisha lounges. That's not for me, I rather play football. But that's my opinion, I don't know what others think about that. Others may think: 'Oh, she's playing football.'

An important difference is that, in FGU's girls' football, boys arrive in a space that is dominated and defined by girls, and where boys are present in order to create different and non-sexual relations between each other. In shisha cafés and the streets, this is the other way around: these are leisure spaces that are constructed and reproduced as masculine, mainly occupied by boys, and known for a sexualized atmosphere.

The preparation for the yearly finale of the FGU competition is a good example to look at the boys' role in creating new gender relations in football. The yearly finale is a festive closing of the football season with music, food, an award ceremony and spectators such as parents, residents and sponsors. A few weeks in advance, a group of about ten volunteers and football players gather after a football training to brainstorm about the set-up of the day. Jamal (thirteen years old), who had been a volunteer for a little less than a year at the time, told the group that he is a rapper and that he would like to sing a song at the finale, for example, the song *Helemaal naar de Klote* (translated: Totally Fucked Up) from the Dutch band The Partysquad. Hanan responded:

> It should be a good text, a text with respect. I want the parents to see that we do good things here. So, you can come up with a text yourself about girls who can play football very well and who deserve respect. But you can make that up on the melody of the *Helemaal naar de Klote* song.

The young boy became very enthusiastic and quickly made up the first sentence of his song: 'Girls are the best, come try and test!' ('*Meiden zijn de beste, kom het maar testen!*'). In this way, this boy was steered and educated to remake a rap about booze and barmaids, which can be interpreted as sexist, into a self-made rap about girls who are the best at playing football and who deserve recognition and respect. This is clearly a reaction to and an alternative for the dominant gendered power relations in public football playgrounds, where girls are seen as bad football players and where they are sexualized.

Although FGU is not a school, it does have some commonalities with schooling. In schools, there are regulations about who can occupy certain spaces when, there are written and unwritten rules about desirable behaviour, and there are implicit gender norms imposed on the pupils (Evans 2006; Morris 2005). Regulation and control of children's bodies is increasingly becoming the practice in the daily lives of children also in public leisure spaces (Christensen and Mikkelsen 2013; Harris 2004). Leisure and 'free' play in public spaces are becoming more and more institutionalized by adults, even though children's leisure used to be precisely identified by the absence of adults and institutions' control and regulation (Harris 2004). FGU is a space in which boys (and girls) are also disciplined and educated in appropriate gender relations and behaviours. It is a privileged site (namely, sport) for disciplining bodies in desirable ways, related to behavioural norms based on gender and heteronormativity (Dortants and Knoppers 2013; Foucault 1977; Martin 1998; Morris 2005). To create alternative gender and sexual relations in FGU, a separated space from 'regular' football is needed (see also Foucault 1977), in which there can be a level of control on which boys enter, and on which boys can be educated and steered according to the equal gender relations that Hanan promotes. It is necessary for Hanan to create a separated space to be able to implement disciplinary power that is based on alternative and more equal ideals of gender relations in football. Furthermore, Hanan expects that the boys take on an active role in organizing the girls' football competition and are not just there to hang around and watch the girls play. By taking on an active role as volunteer or trainer, they can be educated or trained in approaching girls with respect.

The gender relations that Hanan promotes also encompass different gendered spatial practices, as she frequently takes boys off the field who move the ball through the whole field without passing it to girls, or who play aggressively or egoistically. In some matches, boys are allowed to participate on the field, in others they are expected to remain at the sidelines or only defend the goal. Hanan disciplines the boys through limiting their spatial and embodied practices. She often calls from the sidelines that they should play together and cooperate. In this way, boys learn that they cannot claim football space as only theirs but that they have to share it with girls, or even give priority to the girls. Hanan aims to change dominant gender relations in football through gendered spatial practices on the field, as these spaces are not only gendered themselves, but, through space and spatial practices in football, gender relations are constructed and reconfigured (Jaffe and A. de Koning 2015; Massey 1994; Rosaldo 1980).

Many boys in FGU are cousins, brothers or neighbours of the football girls. Usually, the girls introduce the boys to FGU, so they have a voice in which boys participate in the girls' football, and the boys are known and familiar to (at least some of) the girls. Although Hanan has mentioned to me that boys are not allowed to just watch the girls' play, and can only come along if they actively participate as volunteers, referees or coaches, I did speak with a few boys who were spectators at first and only later became volunteers. Khalid, for example, who is in his early twenties:

> I've been coming here for five years already, but now a little bit less because I'm busy. I first came here to watch the girls, then I was like that, a young boy. Then, that was what you did, like, to impress. Then Hanan asked me if I wanted to help out and now I've been doing that already for five years.

Mansour (fourteen years old) became involved with FGU in this way, too. He sometimes came to FGU to watch the matches, and then Hanan asked him if he wanted to help with a small task, and later he helped more often. He is very positive about the girls' competition and he told me that the boys who volunteer also make sure that no unknown boys come to FGU. However, he emphasized, there are only boy volunteers as long as the girls agree.

During my talk with Mansour, we were sitting in the hallway of the sports complex, and a few boys came in. Mansour sent them away, but I could not follow the conversation because it proceeded in Moroccan Arabic.[5] After the boys went away, he said: 'They are not allowed in here.' It could be possible that, in that moment, he sent the boys away to enforce his previous statement to me, that the boy volunteers are also there to control other boys. Yet, at other moments, the volunteers of FGU also made sure to keep unknown or undesirable boys outside, for example, at the finale of the competition in May 2014: when I left the sports complex at the end of the day, there were volunteers in the hallway who quickly closed the door and who controlled who could enter. In other words, the role and regulation of boys in FGU is not always related to the specific tasks or roles boys pick up, but more importantly to only allowing 'good' boys entry to the girls' football spaces of FGU. Hafsa explained this to me in the following way:

Kathrine: There are quite a few boys on the staff and as volunteers in FGU, is that on purpose, that there are both boys and girls in FGU? Or is it just that everyone who wants to volunteer can just come?

Hafsa: No, because Hanan does look at whether they, whether they are really committed. Not that they just come for the girls, but that they are really there to volunteer and to learn girls how to play football. Not to score their phone numbers or something like that. But you also feel that, with the boys in FGU, they're just, they are here voluntarily, they come to teach football, and then they just quietly go home after. It's not like 'hey, hang around with me' or something.

Hanan said the following about the boys who volunteer in FGU:

> We can really benefit from good boys, like Ilias. But we just have to make sure that no strange boys come in.

'Good' boys are thus described as boys who come to FGU because they are committed to girls' football, have respect for girls and make sure that girls can play football in a context that is not overly sexualized. Mansour, Khalid and the other male volunteers describe their involvement in FGU as if they are training their own sisters or cousins in football. As became clear from the talk with Mansour, boys also take up roles as 'protectors' of girls, who, in that way, also become constructed as 'vulnerable' and in need of this protection. This reproduces the patriarchal idea that men need to protect women. 'Bad' boys are described as unknown or 'strange' boys who just come to the girls' football to watch the girls play, to hit on the girls or to look for a girlfriend, and they are unwanted in the FGU football spaces. When unknown boys come to FGU, Hanan first talks to them to get an idea of their motivations to join and to teach them about respect for the football girls.

When I visited FGU again in March 2018, Hanan was educating new boys who wanted to participate in the football at FGU, too. When I entered the sports hall, she had no time to extensively greet or introduce me, but she said, in a casual way, that she was still teaching 'Moroccan class' and that she would join me quickly after that. Here, she casually related her gender education project to the specific Moroccan-Dutch community to which most of the girls and boys in FGU belong, and where specific concerns regarding gender, sexuality, physical contact and public spaces can be experienced. As Green and Singleton (2007) also point out, discourses in local (ethnic or religious) communities about girls' and women's respectability and reputation, related to patriarchal ideas of honour and modesty, are an important concern in the decision of girls for appropriate sports and leisure activities. In my research, some girls, too, showed concerns regarding 'appropriate' leisure spaces, in which most girls agree that shisha cafés in the neighbourhood are not places they want or can visit, whereas FGU is a safe and welcome space for girls. The focus on respect in FGU risks to reinstall dominant norms and relations of gender and sexuality, in which girls, in turn, need to be respectable and protected.

Much attention in this book is paid to challenging gendered and racialized stereotypes of Muslim girls that are based on dominant ideas of Islam as backward and essentially oppressing women. The risk of this focus is to overlook the specific issues regarding gender and sexuality that Moroccan-Dutch girls and women struggle with. Two recent examples that Nadia Ezzeroili (2018) discussed in her opinion piece in Dutch newspaper *Volkskrant* are the phenomenon of exposure WhatsApp groups and the framing of Muslim women who are out late at night as *kechs* (whores). Although I have not observed this, some girls in my research also mentioned that boys called them whores because they played football in public playgrounds. The risk to overlook these issues is related to my own situatedness in the research as a white non-Muslim researcher from outside the Schilderswijk: specific experiences regarding Moroccan-Dutch communities are possibly much less emphasized by Hanan and the other girls to me and to other white Dutch people outside the neighbourhood, because they do not want to reinforce negative representations of Moroccan-Dutch and Muslim citizens. The experiences of girls as 'out of place' in public football playgrounds is not specific to or exclusionary of Moroccan-Dutch or Muslim women, or only the case in the Schilderswijk – this was something I found across the Netherlands in multiple places. Yet, the gendered, sexual, bodily, and spatial struggles and norms girls and women in public spaces in and outside football have to deal with, especially concerning respectability, have different histories and impacts on women with different ethnic, religious and socio-economic backgrounds (see also Dhawan and Castro Varela 2016).

Hanan's gender educational 'intervention' can thus be seen as working in multiple directions: within the public spaces of Schilderswijk and amongst youths with Moroccan-Dutch and Muslim backgrounds; within the dominant gendered spatial organization of football that creates girls as 'second-class' players; and outside the Schilderswijk, in relation to representations of Moroccan-Dutch and Muslim youths in broader Dutch society. She talks and kicks back at multiple audiences to create more equal football and leisure spaces. The work of Hanan and the other volunteers in FGU shows that specific gender and sexual struggles in both Moroccan-Dutch communities and in football are not inherent or fixed but are subject to change, creating possibilities for more equal opportunities, and this is precisely why they include boys in FGU. This 'positive' message is one that Hanan is keen on sharing with others, in allowing me as researcher in her football competition, but, for example, also through representations in social media, where she shared a picture of some of the boy volunteers with the caption: 'Moroccans are doing something good for their neighbourhood!'

The gender and sexuality norms the girls have to deal with, and the exercise of those norms in 'respectable' leisure spaces, are not only imposed on them by boys, parents or adults. There is also the exercise of self-discipline and the internalizing and 'naturalization' of norms (Foucault 1989, 251; 1977; Harris 2004, 115). This is, for example, visible in how girls themselves frame shisha cafés as inappropriate leisure spaces, like Hafsa did. Yet, the internalizing of norms is always performed with a difference; discipline is never one-directional but subject to performative resistance and change. Subjects, including children, do not just 'undergo' discipline but use discipline, resist and challenge discipline, and rework discipline, not in the least case through performative practices in sports (Butler 1993; 1998; Caudwell 2003; Dortants and Knoppers 2013; Dyck 2008; Markula and Pringle 2006). Gendered norms are always 'ideals which no gendered body fully or exhaustively embodies. … Indeed, such ideals are also transformed in subtle and significant ways in and through their public and dramatic performances' (Butler 1998, 4). This aspect of performative change is the focus of the next part, in which I look at how gendered norms in sports are reworked into alternative constructions of femininity and masculinity by the girls and boys in FGU through playing football. From the specific focus on the role of boys in FGU, I move to a broader discussion of the spatial organizations and intersectional constructions of gender and (hetero)sexuality in FGU's practice, and I illustrate this with two case studies: one on 'only girls today' and one on a boys-girls tournament, or the battle of the sexes.

Masculinity, femininity and heteronormativity

Hegemonic femininity, with ideals of being passive, decent, polite, physical attractive and slim, is difficult to combine with hegemonic ideals in football, where ideals that are perceived as masculine, such as power, competition and physical activity, are central (Azzarito 2010; Evans 2006; Friedman 2013; I. M. Young 2005; Morris 2005). Various scholars argue that, especially in women's sports, and, more specifically, in women's football, alternative performances of gender and femininity are, however, possible because of its radical altering of dominant gender norms in athletic performance (Butler 1998; Caudwell 2003; Pringle 2014). The 'spectacular public restaging' of women's sports can 'broaden the scope of acceptable gender performance' and pose performative resistance to hegemonic femininity (Butler 1998, 4).[6] According to Azzarito (2010), new hegemonic femininities have emerged in relation to sports and sports media, which produce an ideal of fit, healthy, sexy, strong, and sportive female bodies. Notwithstanding, these athletic femininities are still produced and only acceptable within a framework of heterosexual feminine performance (Evans 2006, 557; van den Heuvel 2017).[7]

However, an intersectional approach is needed here: race/ethnicity and religion co-determine to which specific bodies an ideal of athletic femininity as strong, sportive and slim is accessible. Azzarito (2010) argues that Muslim girls are constructed outside of this ideal, because they are often perceived as oppressed and inactive, supposedly because of their headscarf and covered clothing.[8] They are rather portrayed as unhealthy and 'at risk' (see also Abu-Lughod 2013; El-Tayeb 2011), as 'other' compared with the healthy, sportive, sexy and strong dominant performances of white femininity in the sports media that Azzarito has analysed. For boys, too, race/ethnicity, religion and class are central in disciplining bodies as desirable subjects in school or sports. Sports are normally a domain in which values, movements and actions that are seen as 'masculine', such as power, competition and dominance, are the norm (Shogan, in Pringle 2014, 401). Yet, for racialized and Muslim boys, especially in 'disadvantaged' working-class neighbourhoods, this 'masculine' behaviour is, in many public and educational contexts, not seen as the norm but as a problem (El-Tayeb 2011; Ferguson 2001; Jaffe-Walter 2016; Martin 1998; Morris 2005; Thorne 1993). Jaffe-Walter (2016, 144) argues, based on Danish research by Laura Gilliam: 'Rather than viewing the individual infractions of Muslim students through the lens of normative male adolescent behaviour, teachers see them through the lens of criminality and cultural deviance.' Racialized boys are systematically seen as a threat, as causers of problems, as deviant from the norm (El-Tayeb 2011, 7, see also previous chapters), and therefore more often subject to disciplinary forces than white or ethnic-majority boys (Ferguson 2001; Jaffe-Walter 2016; Morris 2005).[9]

The carefully formulated comments of Peter in the previous chapter about 'Moroccan' boys in public playgrounds can be seen as part of this dominant framing of 'Moroccan' boys as problematic. Another Dutch example in the context of sports is the statement made by football commentator Johan Derksen,[10] who said that there are too many 'Moroccan' boys at football clubs and that this is causing problems. They are, in his words, often good at kicking a ball but not disciplined enough to become real, professional football players. The constructions of masculinity and femininity in football are thus embedded in racialized power relations and hierarchies, in which Muslim or ethnic-minority boys and girls are perceived as essentially different from white 'secular' football players (El-Tayeb 2011; Silverstein 2005).

Sport is, in addition to school, an important domain for the disciplining and embodiment of national ideologies, citizenship and for the supposed integration of racial/ethnic or religious minorities (Besnier and Brownell 2012; Jaffe-Walter 2016, 33; Rana 2014; Silverstein 2000, 33). Gender and heterosexual norms are crucial in disciplining racialized and religious 'other' bodies, such as the norm in sports to take a shower together, naked, with same-sex sports players after the training. Boys and girls who are not comfortable in doing so, or who are already assumed to not want to take part in those norms because of their religious or ethnic background,[11] are constructed as not yet fully disciplined and integrated into Dutch national ideologies of gender, sexuality and sports.

In FGU, ideals and norms of gender and sexuality in relation to football, race/ethnicity and religion are differently produced. Dominant spatial gender norms of playing football are being transformed into renewed and more inclusive performances of femininity and masculinity, also in relation to religion and race/ethnicity. FGU promotes an inclusive interpretation of femininity that is not in conflict with playing football or wearing a headscarf. There is space in FGU for forms of femininity that are not necessarily based on hegemonic athletic femininities of slim, sportive and 'sexy' attractive bodies. Girls who wear headscarves or covered clothing are recognized and accepted as real football players, too. At the same time, other norms are installed within FGU, based on desirable behaviour of boys and girls: smoking and hanging around in shisha lounges are, for example, seen as less desirable activities for girls. There is also an alternative conception of masculinity in FGU, based on having respect for and recognizing girls as 'real' and good football players. Rather than reproducing hegemonic masculinity (Anderson 2008; Renold 1997; Swain 2000), boys are taught that it is normal for girls to play football, that girls also perform competition and athletic activity, and are thus 'in place' in football spaces and competitions. Furthermore, boys are educated to limit their claims on football spaces in FGU, as these are mainly reserved for the girls – contrary to football in public playgrounds – and they are not supposed to make comments about girls' bodies or to ask for their telephone numbers.

In FGU, Moroccan-Dutch Muslim boys are not perceived as a problem, and as threatening the supposed Dutch national values of gender and sexual emancipation (El-Tayeb 2011; Masquelier and Soares 2016; Mepschen, Duyvendak and Tonkens 2010; Wekker 2016), but as part of the solution for creating more equal opportunities for girls in football spaces in the Schilderswijk and beyond. Crucial here is that not only girls' performative football play poses challenges to dominant spatial constructions of gender and sexuality in football, but also boys' performative play, through playing and volunteering in the girls' football spaces of FGU. The role of boys as crucial actors in challenging hierarchical and exclusive gender relations in different (public) spaces is a topic that has increasingly gained attention in feminist activism over the past years,[12] and fits within a broader growing attention in feminist research on the various hegemonic and non-hegemonic performativities of masculinity (Anderson 2008; Archer 2003; Mora 2012; Renold 1997; 2005; Swain 2000; 2003). This does not implicate that patriarchal or heteronormative power relations are lifted (Renold 1997), but they are performatively reworked in different contexts and in relation to constructions of femininity and sexuality, as is also the case in and through sports.

FGU creates a separated and controlled girls' football space with norms that provide resistance to gender and sexuality norms in 'regular' football spaces. Masculinity is constructed as having respect for girls, and femininity is constructed as encompassing both football and Muslim embodiments and identities, in that both boys and girls performatively practise alternative gendered bodies and norms through playing football. Yet, norms in 'regular' football space are, at the same time, being reproduced in FGU, for example, the patriarchal idea that boys need to protect girls and the risk of reproducing patriarchal conceptions of girls' 'respectability', but also the norm of heterosexual orientation. A dichotomous difference between boys and girls is still present and reproduced, for example, through the difference in access: all girls are welcome, but only certain, 'good' boys are allowed in, and they have to first be educated by Hanan on the topics of respect, gender and sexuality. One of the aims of FGU is to challenge the sexualization of girls in football; yet, by placing this dynamic as part of regulating the relations between boys and girls, it assumes heterosexual orientation. In the following case studies, the norms and assumptions of gender and heterosexuality in FGU in relation to the different spatial ways of organizing girls' football in FGU are discussed. The case studies show that gender segregation in the girls' football competition is never stable but subject to changing needs, wishes and contexts.

'Only girls today'

Although football at FGU almost never means a 'real' gender-segregated space, it does in exceptional moments. On a Sunday afternoon in January 2015, Hanan asked the boys and girls who came for the girls' football to sit down on the benches in the sports hall, and said: 'I would like to ask all men and boys to leave. You can come back at half past four. I only want girls today.' The boys walked away and went to sit together in the hallway of the sports complex. I asked one of the volunteers why the boys had to leave, and Nora responded:

Nora:	A few girls don't like it when boys join.
Kathrine:	Why not?
Nora:	They wear a headscarf, a niqab,[13] and then they can play football without a headscarf here.

Shortly after, the three girls, Hilal, Lisa and Farida, about whom Nora was talking, came out of the locker room in sports clothes. I had not seen them before at FGU or at different football activities in the Schilderswijk. In the meantime, some volunteers were sticking trash bags over the windows of the sports hall, so that no one could look inside. Mansour came in the doorway to ask something, but Hanan responded angrily: 'No boys here now, no, really not!' Hilal walked to the other side of the hall and kept her hands before her face, saying: 'I don't know if there's a boy here.' Later, I again saw her watching the door carefully when it opened, to see who was entering. Hanan emphasized that no one was allowed to put pictures of the sports training on social media, something they normally do. Hanan did take a picture of Lisa, Hilal and Farida for social media, but in such a way that their faces were not visible. The girls also filmed each other, but they made sure their faces were not included.

When I had a short talk with Lisa, she told me that she thinks it is a pity that there were not that many girls of her age (twenty-one) present that afternoon:

Lisa:	For years, I didn't play sports, that's really clear to me now, your physical fitness vanishes really quickly! While, in the past, I used to be very sportive. And when I went to secondary school, I quit playing sports.
Kathrine:	Do you want to come here more often?
Lisa:	Do they do this every week here? Yes, then I would like to be with more girls of my age. I do miss football. Hanan is my neighbour, that's why she took us here this time.

When I asked the girls whether it is important that football is only for girls, Farida responded: 'For me that's important, yes.' I did not have time to ask them much more, because they had to return to the field, and I did not want to take their spare football time away by asking too many questions. I asked Hanan whether the boys mind that they had to leave: 'Oh no, they don't mind, they respect that. And still, they watch if no strange boys come in. They feel very responsible.' When the boys came back around 5.00 pm, they confirmed this. Mansour said: 'No, it's normal that they also get time to play football here, right?'

FGU thus also wants to create space and time for girls who do not want to play with boys because of their religious beliefs. Most of the times, boys are allowed in the football spaces of FGU, yet this time it was necessary to create a separated space within the space of FGU, one really only for girls. Although not physically present in the sports hall itself, the boys did play a role in making sure that no other boys were entering the sports complex. The organization of a real girls-only football training in FGU nevertheless remains an exception, as this was the only girls-only afternoon during my fieldwork period. Hanan told me that when they organize a mother–daughter sports day, they usually also play without boys and men, because mothers are not used to playing football, so it can be more comfortable for them when they only play with their daughters and other women.

The battle of the sexes

On a Wednesday afternoon in April 2014, the FGU volunteers organized a girls–boys tournament on their own initiative. This was the first time that FGU organized such a tournament for both boys' and girls' teams. When I arrived, the sports hall was full of boys and girls between eleven and fifteen years old. The matches had not started yet and the preparations were in full swing: the registration of the players, the forming of the teams and the set-up of the schedule. On the left side of the stands, the boys' teams were sitting and, on the right side, the girls'. Although the girls' teams and boys' teams sat separately, the volunteers of FGU sat mixed between the boys and the girls. They were there to make sure that the boys and girls stayed on their own half, and they guided and coached the teams during the tournament. Some of the boy volunteers of FGU sat between the girls, and Nina, also one of the volunteers, sat on the left side between the boys. Some other volunteers of FGU laughed about that, because Nina was the only girl from FGU to sit between the boys.

One of the volunteers said: 'She's looking for a boyfriend. But those boys are much younger than her, ha-ha!'

Then, the first match began, and the girls' teams played against the boys' teams. After every goal, a famous Moroccan song was played through the sound speakers. The boys' and girls' teams moved up quite equally in the rankings of the day. But, when Nisha and Ines's team had lost several matches, they asked two boys to be standby for their team, and to become substitute players when they were losing. Other girls told me that they sometimes use that same tactic, having boys as substitute players for when you really need them, in school football competitions. In the end, one of the boys played on Nisha and Ines' team, but they lost the match nevertheless. When the day was almost finished, and the finals were being played, Hanan told me that if the day proceeds well and if everyone likes it, she might organize boys–girls tournaments more often, but possibly only with the younger football players, as the boys between thirteen and fifteen years old are 'too noisy and they don't listen'.

This tournament made clear that the girls of FGU like to play with – or against – boys; this competition was their own initiative. It is, however, still the case that the boys and girls are separated and treated as distinct groups. Part of the fun was precisely to play as girls against the boys, as a kind of battle of the sexes. Such a battle follows from the dominant sexed and gendered binary segregation in sports. In challenging gender norms in sports, it is exciting and motivating for girls to challenge the biggest gender norm in sports: the hierarchical gender separation with boys at the top of the ranking. Nevertheless, if boys are needed for your own girls' team to win, they are more than welcome to join, as Nisha and Ines negotiated. Although this might reinstall the dominant idea that boys are better football players than girls, the difference with street football being played in public playgrounds, a I discussed in Chapter 5, is that, here in FGU, the girls are in charge of the when, how and why of letting boys join. The spatial and sportive performances of gender in football show that the performativity of gender is never a linear process, but one of messy negotiations of gender, bodies, play and winning. In some moments, gender norms and stereotypes are being challenged and resisted, in other moments – when winning is more important – they might be reinstalled. The kind of spatial segregation of boys and girls in FGU is one that is different and messier than the usual ways of gender segregation in sports. At the same time, this spatial segregation reinstalls and reproduces a dominant heterosexual orientation, as possible sexual relations between boys and girls continue to be negotiated, for example, when the volunteers were making fun of Nina, who sat between the boys.

My observations in FGU, where the girls most of the time also play with boys, run against the prominent focus on girls-only sports in debates and research on Muslim women. In these debates, it is assumed that gender segregation is crucial for Muslim girls' sports participation because of their religious beliefs, but this is too simplistic and overlooks the ways in which gender and sexuality norms in sports also shape Muslim girls' experiences and motives and are in turn shaped by them (see also Samie 2013). Girls' football at FGU cannot escape gender dichotomies of girls and boys in football either, but their spatial football practices are much more layered and nuanced than a simple rigid and fixed segregation. Moreover, while Muslim girls continue to be constructed as ultimate 'other' in Dutch society, they actually share much of the broader concerns of gender norms and male dominance in football and public playgrounds with their fellow female football players from all backgrounds. The next chapter will discuss the specific axes of religious difference and culturalized citizenship that they, as Muslim girls, also have to deal with.

7

Playing religion, gender and citizenship

Football Girls United's (FGU) competition in the Schilderswijk plays against the backdrop of polarized debates about Muslim immigration to Europe and about the integration of ethnic and Muslim minorities in urban multicultural neighbourhoods. In dominant discourses in media and politics, the starting point is that Moroccan-Dutch and Muslim citizens still need to be 'integrated' into Dutch society, even when they are born and raised in the Netherlands. This narrative of the lack of integration is also apparent in the context of girls' football. When I started my research in October 2013, Aisha, who had organized girls' football in Amsterdam for ten years, already told me that her football team was criticized because it consisted only of Moroccan-Dutch girls. It would supposedly not stimulate Moroccan-Dutch girls' integration in the Netherlands if they had their 'own' football team, she told me. In the Schilderswijk, similar concerns are being voiced by sports professionals and policy makers from the municipality. They relate the self-organized girls' football competition of FGU to a lack of cultural integration, citizenship and emancipation in Dutch society, and they question the boys' and girls' proper integration and gender and sexual emancipation in relation to their Islamic backgrounds. Football players in the Schilderswijk thus also become central subjects in debates on Dutch national identity and cultural citizenship in relation to Islam, gender and sports; and this is the topic of the current chapter.

The chapter places the experiences of the football girls within the wider constructions of culturalized citizenship in the Netherlands. It critically discusses the emphasis on Islam, gender and emancipation in debates about citizenship (Bracke 2012; Mepschen, Duyvendak and Tonkens 2010) and in neighbourhood sport projects (Rana 2014). In this culturalized citizenship, which is a set of cultural norms and practices defining what it means to be a 'good' or 'real' Dutch citizen (A. de Koning 2016, 116; Duyvendak, Hurenkamp and Tonkens 2010), Muslim girls are expected to 'integrate' and 'emancipate' in Dutch society through sports, while they are at the same time always also constructed as the Islamic 'other' because of their embodied religious difference. Gender and sexuality are prominent markers of the cultural norms of Dutch citizenship, using women's and sexual emancipation as indicator for the division between 'real' and second-class citizens – often Muslim or other religious or ethnic-minority citizens (Bracke 2012; Holston and Appadurai 1999; Mepschen, Duyvendak and Tonkens 2010; Wekker 2016).

I argue that gender, Islam and girls' football are caught in a paradox of culturalized citizenship in the Netherlands, in which full citizenship for Muslim girls is ultimately seen as incompatible. In this paradox, gender segregation in football forms a crucial axis through which differences between white Dutch citizens and Islamic 'others' are discursively brought into existence. I contrast this dominant discourse with the experience of the football girls themselves: according to them, their Islamic backgrounds are not always most important on the football field. In their football practices, they do not necessarily embody an identity based on religion or Islam but rather embody a football identity through winning. I therefore argue that playing football (and winning) forms an important performative and embodied practice through which culturalized constructions of Dutch citizenship can be challenged. The girls who play football at FGU incorporate differences of gender, Islam and race/ethnicity in their football strategies to win, which I analyse as kicking back and as the playing of citizenship (Lazar 2014; Nyhagen and Halsaa 2016).

Citizenship and 'integration' in neighbourhood football

The neighbourhood sport organizations in the Schilderswijk do not simply offer football or sports activities but also place their sports activities within a broader discourse of social participation, integration and citizenship, albeit not always very explicitly. For example, the Cruyff Court 6 vs 6 competition is related to enhancing social cohesion in urban neighbourhoods. The aim of the Cruyff Courts in general, and the 6 vs 6 competition in particular, is to get to know and involve oneself with youths from different backgrounds and to learn how to deal with each other in playing sports and in daily life. Cooperation, responsibility, respect, integration, social participation and creativity are central aspects of the competition, highlighted in the '14 rules of Johan Cruyff'.[1] Whereas most neighbourhood sports programmes and sports-for-development projects are used as a way of integrating marginalized people or people from ethnic-minority backgrounds (Besnier and Brownell 2012, 453; Jaffe-Walter 2016, 64; Silverstein 2000; 2002; Spaaij 2009; Vermeulen and Verweel 2009), at the Cruyff Court 6 vs 6 competitions, integration is seen as more of a mutual process, involving all youths who live in the neighbourhoods where the Cruyff Courts are placed. Since the Cruyff Courts are often found in urban spaces, but not only in 'disadvantaged' urban neighbourhoods such as the Schilderswijk, they actually involve a wide range of 'majority' and 'minority' youths in their sports activities for integration, participation, respect and social cohesion.

The other neighbourhood sports activities in the Schilderswijk are more specifically focused on the (supposed need of) integration, citizenship and respect of urban ethnic- and religious-minority youths. The Schilderswijk Street League and the activities of Sportteam intent to increase youths' and their parents' participation in the neighbourhood. In a business meeting about the Schilderswijk Street League, Jeroen from ADO The Hague, who set up the competition together with Sportteam, explained the goals of the Schilderswijk Street League:

> The goals of the Street League are: parents' participation, so that they can become the coaches of the teams; preventing nuisance; combatting obesity; transmitting norms and values, such as being on time, et cetera. The children can also get points for sportive behaviour, not only when they win a match. For instance, by showing respect, properly wearing their team uniforms, and we organize theme meetings for which they will get points if they participate. For example, about what's going on in the neighbourhood, which problems there are, such as radicalization and bullying, discrimination. For contributions to their neighbourhood, they can also get points, like baking pancakes for the neighbourhood, helping elderly with doing grocery shopping, cleaning up playgrounds. It's even better when children themselves think of a neighbourhood contribution, what best fits their neighbourhood. Furthermore, we engage with a project in which children learn to make short films about the neighbourhood, so that not only the football players but the whole neighbourhood becomes involved. So, in the end, not the best football player wins, but the most engaged team.

In this neighbourhood sports project, it is assumed that young residents need stimulation by way of earning points to engage with participation and citizenship activities, and that they still need to be educated into properly embodying norms and values such as punctuality and discipline.

Although such sports programmes are also used to combat obesity amongst children, much emphasis is put on the 'participation' aspect, as the quote above shows. Such neighbourhood citizenship projects usually only take place in 'disadvantaged' neighbourhoods and not in affluent or dominantly white neighbourhoods; in these latter places, it is assumed that citizenship education is either not necessary or that residents already engage in citizenship activities. The framing of such neighbourhood sport projects overlooks the fact that many girls and boys in the Schilderswijk already participate in sports and football, albeit in their own organized competition. Furthermore, what is interesting is that the Schilderswijk Street League project is not only targeted at children but also extended to their parents and the whole neighbourhood. The idea is that the 'disadvantaged' neighbourhood as a whole needs to be stimulated to engage with citizenship and integration activities, as the whole neighbourhood supposedly not yet fully fits within Dutch norms and citizenship.

Furthermore, the goal of neighbourhood sports projects and competitions is often to 'guide' youths to participation in official sports clubs: playing street football is seen as a first step towards membership of an official club (Hoekman et al. 2011a). In Dutch youth sports culture, participation in an official sports club rather than only playing football in public playgrounds is seen as 'real', 'proper' or 'full' sports participation. For example, Marieke from the municipality of The Hague, said the following about the municipality's sports policy:

> So, we think it is important that girls play more sports, but also that they do that in a sports club. And why do we think that is important, well, because playing sports in clubs leads to a more sustainable sports participation.

Thus, in sports policies, 'unorganized' forms of sports participation by minoritized groups are valued less than other 'official' forms of sports participation. The implicit cultural norm of sports participation in the Netherlands is that only playing sports in the controlled environment of an official football club is considered the ultimate embodiment of 'full' citizenship. This does not always fit within the experiences and wishes of youths in urban multicultural and working-class neighbourhoods: these sports clubs are further away and expensive, and some Muslim or Moroccan-Dutch children do not want to play there because they are afraid of experiencing racism and/or sexism. Furthermore, some girls in my research said that they prefer to play football in an urban football court rather than on a field, as matches in street football are more flexible and faster, and there is more space for technical tricks.

The focus on 'proper' integration, citizenship and social participation in neighbourhood and youth sports projects is not new. In the Time for Sport policy (2005) of the Ministry of Health, Welfare and Sport, youths were a specific target group, and sports were seen as a way to 'organize groups to play sports instead of loitering or hanging around' (VWS 2005, 6, translation mine). The ministry launched a large project in cooperation with the Ministry of Integration and Housing, called 'Participation Allochthonous Youth through Sport' (*Meedoen allochtone jeugd door sport*), which ran from 2006 to 2010.[2] Starting from the assumption that Moroccan-Dutch and Turkish-Dutch youths 'lag behind' in sports participation,[3] this project focused on encouraging ethnic-minority youths to participate more in sports through neighbourhood sports projects. From the aims of the project, the explicit connection with citizenship became clear:

> To create encounters between allochthonous and authochthonous youths and the involvement of their parents; to address the lagging participation of allochthonous youths in sports (integration in sports); to advance full citizenship and participation of allochthonous youths in society and countering social isolation (integration through sports); and to address and prevent nuisance and problematic behaviour (education through sports). With this, the failure in Dutch society can be prevented and reintegration accomplished. (VWS 2006, 2, translation mine)

These goals show that 'allochthonous' youth, meaning non-Western migrant youth, though many of them are born and raised in the Netherlands, are not yet seen as full citizens in terms of cultural citizenship but rather as potential *failures*. The Participation project provides specific attention to the transmission of norms and values, respect and tolerance, social skills and cooperation, resilience and emancipation, the learning of discipline and self-control, and the regulation of aggression (VWS 2006, 3), which can be seen as crucial aspects of Dutch cultural citizenship, according to this project. Van Sterkenburg (2011, 24), discussing the Participation project, argues, in line with Wekker (2002) and Lorde (2007, 116): 'Sport is used here to bring the cultural norms and values of allochtonen closer to those of autochtonen while rendering the group of (white) autochtonen normative.'

Religious and ethnic minorities are portrayed as if they can only become full citizens through sports, discipline, integration and empowerment. Although women's bodies are central in debates about integration, emancipation and citizenship, the focus on gender and sexuality in 'integration' discourses clearly also plays out on (immigrant or Muslim) men's bodies (Silverstein 2000, 27). Anthropologist Paul Silverstein showed how, in France, ideologies of nationalism and citizenship are projected on male Muslim bodies through governmental youth sports projects and corporate sports advertisements. During the Algerian Civil War in the 1990s, Muslim boys in *banlieues* in France, mainly with Algerian backgrounds, were depicted as potential terrorists and supporters of radical Islam, in a context in which Muslim religious difference was discursively constructed as 'inassimilable to French secular standards' (Silverstein 2000, 31; see also Fernando 2016; Selby 2011). Seeing sports as the privileged site of disciplining citizens into norms and ideologies of national citizenship, the French nation state organized neighbourhood sports projects in *banlieues* as an alternative for or even against Islamic community organizations. Through sports, the state sought to construct and discipline youths into secularized and individualized citizens to whom Islam would only be a private matter and who would therefore be compatible with secular French citizenship and national belonging. 'Practitioners of such an Islam would play soccer [football] by day, pray to Allah at night, and vote in municipal elections every two years,' Silverstein (2000, 32) summarizes expressively.

Although Silverstein's article is based on the French context in the 1990s, there are striking resemblances with contemporary Europe, where young Muslim boys from 'disadvantaged' neighbourhoods are similarly represented as potential terrorists in the context of a renewed fear of radical Islam after 9/11 (Archer 2009; El-Tayeb 2011; Masquelier and Soares 2016) and, more recently, the rise of IS. Muslim girls and women are also increasingly represented within a framework of Muslim radicalism and Jihad, yet they are more often framed in terms of being victims rather than aggressive perpetrators (Abu-Lughod 2013; El-Tayeb 2011). Neighbourhood sports programmes often have specific projects for Muslim (and Hindu) girls – suggesting that the 'standard' sports projects are implicitly targeted at boys (see also Chapter 5). In these programmes, Muslim girls are represented as the most inactive and oppressed, and in need of help and assistance with emancipation and participation in sports and society (e.g. in the programmes by VWS 2006; KNVB 2009; 2014). Whereas ethnic-minority or Muslim boys are often perceived as too visible and a threat in public spaces, and thus in need of disciplining and regulation, ethnic- and religious-minority girls are perceived as not visible enough in public spaces and thus in need of emancipation (Harris 2004; Rana 2014).

In this line of thinking, the visibility of Muslim girls in public spaces is presented as an indicator of their level of emancipation in Dutch society. Yet, as I will point out later, Muslim girls' actual visibility in public spaces is, in practice, more ambiguous. Neighbourhood sports projects, such as the Participation project, thus often aim at emancipation in the case of Muslim women and girls, and at regulation of supposed aggression and criminal behaviour in the case of Muslim boys (Rana 2014, 33). Rana (2014) argues that this (often implicit) differentiation based on race/ethnicity, religion and gender in neighbourhood sports programmes, while aiming at integration and social cohesion, actually reinforces racial/ethnic and gender inequality and differences in sports.

Although the Participation project has officially ended, the focus of much current neighbourhood sports programmes is still on social participation and citizenship in a broader context of social participation in the Dutch welfare state (Tonkens 2014) and in migration and integration policies (Asscher 2013; 2015).[4] The Participation project has set the tone for subsequent sports projects in 'disadvantaged' neighbourhoods, such as Sportimpuls,[5] where integration, becoming a 'good' and 'healthy' citizen, and social cohesion are also central (Rana 2014). These neighbourhood sports programmes also fit into the broader increasing regulation of youths' free and leisure time in urban neighbourhoods: organized sports are, contrary to 'just' hanging around in the streets, seen as a 'meaningful realization of leisure time' (VWS 2005, 5, translation mine; see also Harris 2004).

In 2008, Hanan started organizing the FGU girls' football competition with subsidy from the Participation project. She received the subsidy – for renting the sports hall and the coordination of the competition – to encourage the sports participation of Muslim and Hindu girls in The Hague. When, in 2010, the Participation project ended, the municipality took over the financial contributions, but the subsidies dried up in the following years. Since 2015, FGU has not received any substantial subsidies, so the competition was forced to scale down. According to Hanan, this was because FGU was apparently not successful enough, since they did not attract as many players as the boys' competition did. As in the whole range of women's football, here boys' football served as the norm to which the 'success' of girls' football was held as well. In the next part, I will show how these discourses of culturalized citizenship play out on the girls' football in the Schilderswijk, focusing in particular on the issue of gender segregation from the perspectives of sports and neighbourhood professionals.

A paradox of Islam, gender and girls' football

During my research in the Schilderswijk, I interviewed several policy makers from the municipality of The Hague who are responsible for the Schilderswijk neighbourhood, youths or sports in the city. I asked them what they thought about youths' sports participation and about the girls' football competition FGU in the Schilderswijk. Mariet, one of the policy makers, replied:

> I think it's one of the most backward things you can imagine. Look, backward till a certain age though, because, during puberty, different feelings arise. Like I was raised at a time when there were still girls' schools and I was in such a girls' school, and then there was a rival boys' school we had lots of exchanges with. Like lots of exchanges that even resulted in marriages. And actually, I have to say, I thought it was nice and comfortable to be only with girls. Because boys, yeah, they are quite different, they find other stuff important. Because the last year was a mixed school and then, suddenly, we had those footballing *Henkies* that I thought well … But yeah, I don't stimulate it here. Because the reason here is not puberty; it are completely different motivations.

Kathrine: Like what kind of motivations?

Mariet: Traditional religious motivations. So, I don't support that, I think there are much more normal attitudes if you play mixed football with boys and girls. Because now you see it's always a bit tensed. Boys don't know how to deal with girls and girls don't know how to deal with boys.

In this quote, it becomes clear that although Mariet acknowledges from her own experiences that it can be comfortable to be exclusively with girls – especially during puberty – she does not want to ascribe this experience to the footballing girls in the Schilderswijk. She assumes that because these girls have a Moroccan-Dutch or Muslim background, their reasons to play football with girls only have to do with tradition and religion, and not with puberty, as she experienced herself.

Other organizers of youth sports in the Schilderswijk, too, mentioned in the interviews that they recognize the desire to play sports with people of their own gender. For example, Peter played on a volleyball team with only men and experienced it was very different and less 'natural' when two women joined their team: 'With men, it was just more convenient because the net can also be put high,' he said. Or Hanan, who told me that, when she was younger, she preferred to play on a girls-only football team. In the conversations about this topic, the Dutch words '*gewoon*' (just, ordinary, naturally) and '*lekker*' (in this context meaning nice and comfortable) were often expressed. It appears that, for many adults, both white and non-white Dutch, it feels more 'natural' and comfortable to play sports with people of the same gender.

For white Dutch people, however, gender segregation in sports is seldom discussed as problematic, as it is seen as a normal consequence of puberty, or as part of 'natural' physical differences between men and women. This is not surprising, as the organization of sports is built on the premise of sexed and gender-segregated bodies, based on the idea of 'natural' physical differences between sexed bodies (Anderson 2008; Butler 1993; Caudwell 2003; Siebelink 2016b).[6] Furthermore, gender segregation serves to materialize men's teams and masculinity as the norm (Anderson 2008; Caudwell 2003). This is illustrated by the fact that Mariet only criticizes the girls' competition for gender segregation and not the boys' competition. So while gender segregation for white Dutch people is normalized, when exercised by Muslim or Moroccan-Dutch girls, gender segregation in sports is considered, at least by Mariet, an anomaly based on fundamental religious motivations and a lack of integration in Dutch society and culture. Indeed, Rebecca Alpert (2015, 30) also poses the question of 'why religions are criticized for gender segregation when it is a universally accepted dimension of sports culture'.

The different meanings that are given to gender-segregated sports practices are an example of 'how sexual regulation operates through the regulation of racial boundaries' (Butler 1993, 20) and vice versa, including the construction of racialized religious difference of mainly Muslim citizens (Wekker 2016). Gender differentiation and segregation of white Dutch people is seen as superior and more advanced, in which a dual gender system is based on supposed 'natural' bodily differences. On the other hand, gender differentiation and segregation of racialized and Muslim girls is interpreted as backward and based on traditional cultural or religious convictions. To compare, white girls' football teams are never problematized regarding gender segregation. Muslim girls' spatial football practices become a paradoxical part of cultural and sexual constructions of citizenship in which Muslim sports players are constructed as unintegrated and unemancipated in Dutch society. According to Dutch cultural discourses on integration and citizenship, religious and ethnic 'others' first need to become 'modern', 'gender equal' and liberated from their 'backward' religion before they can segregate again. The emphasis that is put on playing 'mixed' football is only a prerequisite for educating and disciplining ethnic and Muslim 'others' into dominant Dutch norms and values, but is not in itself part of these norms and values for white Dutch people.

Mariet, however, was the only person I spoke with who had such strong opinions about separated girls' football in the Schilderswijk as backward and undesirable. Others, such as Marieke from the municipality and Peter from

Sportteam, support and facilitate girls-only sports hours, yet do so in a way that also reinforces racial/ethnic and religious difference through gender and sexuality and vice versa. Marieke deals with gender segregation in sports in the following way:

Kathrine: How do you, the municipality, think about football being separate for girls and boys in the Schilderswijk?

Marieke: Yeah, that's difficult for us. Eh, mainly because … look, I'm from the sports section and here we believe it's important that you can exercise sports well, so it's important to connect to the level and wishes of the target group that wants to play sports. So, that means that, if we organize a competition, we have to think carefully about the entry levels, and then the difference between boys and girls is very important, that's just the case in sports. Therefore, we have … there are just physical differences and other things based on which teams are divided. So, that's what is important for us, that you can exercise a sport properly, and then you have to make a difference.

Only from a political point of view, ehm, around the discussion of diversity and Islamic backgrounds, that has become a charged topic. So, for example, we have had a whole issue around segregated swimming and if, with the segregated swimming, arguments are involved from belief, faith, then, politically, it becomes a sensitive topic. And then we have the VVD in the city council and they would say that they don't want that. And the CDA, they are also quite, eh, strict in that.[7] So, up until now, we offer, from within the municipality, no segregated swimming. For this reason. So, it's a difficult topic for the municipality.

Kathrine: And how do you deal with this topic in other sports? For example, with the girls' football competition?

Marieke: Well, we always make the link just with sports and not with faith. And with what works for these children. How they want it. So, in that way, we of course try to avoid the faith issue a bit. Because of course it plays a role and it also has to do with why precisely playing segregated is that important, that they, from their own beliefs and cultural background, feel safe in there.

Like Mariet, Marieke also makes a distinction between an 'accepted' gender segregation in sports, here motivated by sports level and 'natural' physical differences between boys and girls, and a problematized gender segregation in sports based on Islamic faith. Unlike Mariet, Marieke is not 'against' separate girls' football in the Schilderswijk and actually aims to facilitate it, motivated by the municipality's policy of making sports accessible for everybody. She, however, still thinks that Islamic reasons are at the core of Muslim girls' motivations for playing football separately (see also Samie 2018, 46), yet covers this up by politically focusing on the accepted motivations for gender-segregated sporting: the supposed 'naturally' different bodies of girls and boys and the difference in sports level that are a result of that.[8] In this way, she facilitates girls' football by reinforcing sexed and gender differences and stereotypes in football: girls cannot compete with boys in football because of 'natural' differences and therefore need their own competition. This is even more ironic because FGU's gender education, as explained in the previous chapter, aims to do exactly the opposite: teaching boys and girls that girls can be as good at football as boys are, and creating a space where boys and girls can play football together on equal terms.

Peter from Sportteam facilitates a segregated girls' football hour in his playground too, besides the 'regular' football hours during which mostly boys play. According to Peter, most girls are 'too nice' to play with boys, and then 'it just doesn't work'. Only if girls really want to and if they are good enough, they can play on the 'regular' boys' team. Peter's motivation for a separate girls' team follows the same line of argumentation as Marieke's: based on football performance level and differences between boys' and girls' bodies, it is better to have girls play football separately. Yet, facilitating girls-only football is also a way to implement Peter's informal headscarf policy. He discourages and does not allow girls to wear a headscarf during the sports hours he organizes in the playground. This is rather an informal policy, as Peter explained to me that he cannot forbid them from wearing a headscarf 'because that would go against freedom of religion'. Rather, he told me, he will have a conversation with the girls to discourage it.[9] When I asked him why exactly he does not want girls to wear a headscarf during the sports hours, he explained that it is not a matter of safety – they all have special sports headscarves – but more a way of drawing a line:

> Actually, yeah, I just don't want it, because where is the line then? What is now a headscarf could become a *burqa* tomorrow.

So, facilitating girls-only sports without boys or men being present – besides football, girls-only dance classes are also organized in Peter's indoor playground – makes girls more willing to take off their headscarf while playing sports, and this is exactly what Peter aims for.

In the following quote from the interview, Peter's ideas on girls-only sports are further articulated, when I asked him about separated sports hours for girls:

> I do think it's good if there are certain sports where girls can just take off their headscarves, with blinded windows for all I care, with the door closed and with a female teacher, but! Then it must be a teacher who's pedagogically sound, who, for all I care, also only takes off her headscarf herself in that moment, while she wears one the rest of the week. But she should look at the world around her with an open mind. So, nuancing what is happening, like now in Paris [the Charlie Hebdo shooting],[10] and being able to communicate openly about that with the girls. So, also being pedagogically and didactically experienced. And not just saying like, 'now, take off your headscarf, we're going to dance, and eh, I think this and that is the truth'. And then putting on the headscarf again and going outside. Ehm, it should be a real teacher, it must have added value.

As becomes clear, at Sportteam, segregated football or sports is accepted and facilitated, yet for Peter there is always the risk of radicalization. He relates a separate girls' hour and girls' headscarves in his playground, where mostly girls with Muslim and ethnic-minority backgrounds play, to radical Islam and terrorism. A separated girls' team, then, is accepted as long as it has an 'added value', which, for Peter, means teaching appropriate norms and values to the girls. There is an explicit connection between sports, education and citizenship here. Sports is used to 'draw a line' between which bodies are desired and which are not – such as covered bodies – in dominant Dutch, presumed secular, norms and values of sexual emancipation and freedom. Sport is used here to cultivate a secular embodied citizen – one who looks at the world in an 'open' and 'nuanced' way. I find this strikingly corresponding with how Wekker (2016, 166) critically describes white Dutch self-representations as 'deeply tolerant, ethically elevated and justified, colour-blind, and antiracist'. By emphasizing these values, it is assumed that white Dutch norms and values are ethically elevated, and Muslim girls do not yet have an open mind and tend more towards Islamic fundamentalism ('this and that is the truth'), radicalization ('it could become a *burqa* tomorrow')[11] or even terrorism ('Paris'), especially if they play sports in gender-segregated spaces. Although gender-segregated football hours support the no-headscarf policy, it is, for Peter, also intimately connected with 'radical Islamic' ideas. As I mentioned before, when it concerns white Dutch people, gender-segregated sporting is rather seen as a 'natural' consequence of physical differences between gendered bodies than associated with radical ideologies. In the al-Qaida case in this chapter, I will further discuss the discursive connections that are made between gender, the embodied practice of sports and radical Islam in public spaces.

Mariet, Marieke and Peter explain Muslim girls' gender-segregated sporting practices from a purely Islamic perspective, as if their gendered and spatial sports practices only stem from a traditional religious and ethnic background. In this way, they do not recognize or acknowledge that Muslim girls are also situated in gendered and sexual power dynamics in the domain of (Dutch) sports itself (see also Samie 2013), particularly street football in public playgrounds, where girls are marginalized and cannot easily claim those spaces. As I have discussed in the previous chapter, this gender dynamic in public sports spaces is the most important reason for girls to organize themselves and to play football in a girls' competition, where they can be in charge of the football space and the game. By focusing only on religious motivations for gender segregation in sports, or on supposed 'natural' physical differences, the social construction of football and public sports spaces as normatively and dominantly masculine are overlooked.

Mariet, Marieke and Peter assume that public sports spaces are neutral spaces, where everybody can and should participate equally (Jaffe and A. de Koning 2015, 55) – that is, until 'natural' physical differences do not allow for this anymore. If Muslim girls play in their own segregated football spaces, they assume this is simply because of their religious or ethnic-minority background. Furthermore, these assumptions overlook the fact that the girls' football of FGU is not so much a strictly gender-segregated space, given the central role of boys in the competition, but more a discursive naming of a football space to challenge dominant gendered power structures in football. Interestingly, only a girls' football competition is perceived and 'read' as gender segregation in this paradox of gender, Islam and girls' football. A boys' competition is supposedly not marked by gender and not interpreted as gender segregation but as the 'standard' or 'neutral' version of the sport.

This problematization of girls' football in the Schilderswijk is also related to a problematization of racial/ethnic and religious segregation in many neighbourhood (sports) policies. Muslim women who play football together are framed as ethnic and religious minorities who 'withdraw in their own communities' and thus refuse to participate in wider Dutch society.[12] These 'own communities' are assumed to be homogeneous, even if they consist of girls with diverse ethnic or religious backgrounds. Ironically, ethnic homogeneity in white (sports) settings is hardly questioned, while sports clubs with mostly 'ethnic minorities' are often more ethnically diverse than white clubs (Rana

2014, 35–6; Vermeulen and Verweel 2009, 1210). These ethnically diverse sports clubs are nevertheless seen as homogeneous, because of a racialized discourse in the Netherlands in which all non-white Dutch citizens are framed as 'others', and as obstructing proper integration and citizenship. In integration and sports policies, ethnic homogeneity is framed as if it is a deliberate choice of Muslim or ethnic-minority citizens to live and sport in ethnically and religiously segregated spaces, while, in fact, spatial and ethnic segregation in neighbourhoods, schools and sports clubs most of the time can be explained from class or socio-economic factors, or by white people's self-segregation (see Chapter 4).

In her research on a women's basketball team in the UK, Samie suggests that the ethnic make-up of sports spaces and clubs is often a reflection of the ethnic composition of a neighbourhood and that 'the Asian-only demographic of the team was not a deliberate endeavour, but an outcome of the high demand for sports and leisure opportunities from women in the local area' (2013, 262). It is likely that this is also the case in the Schilderswijk, where there is a high demand amongst boys and girls to play football, resulting in enough teams and competitions to play football in the neighbourhood itself without having to go outside the neighbourhood and mix with football players from other places. This is in sharp contrast with the dominant representation of Muslim girls in sports policy texts as 'inactive' and as 'lagging behind' in playing sports. Gendered and racialized spatial segregation in sports are thus central aspects of the construction of Muslim girls as unemancipated and unintegrated in Dutch sexual norms and citizenship, but, they are also connected to a religion/secular dichotomy in Dutch culturalized citizenship that is crucial in differentiating between white Dutch citizens and Islamic 'others'.

Religion is normatively framed as a private matter: it should be practiced in churches or homes and not in public spaces, which are normatively constructed as 'secular' (Bracke 2013). Especially public sports spaces are assumed and expected to be secular, despite the existence of sports clubs with Christian denominations in the Netherlands.[13] Similarly, public schools in the Netherlands are framed as being 'secular', although many of them take the Christian tradition as guideline for cultural participation. For example, Peter told me that, at the public primary school he is affiliated with as a sports teacher, all children are expected to participate in the Christmas celebrations, and he talks about the importance of attending the celebrations at his sports lessons. Christianity is, contrary to Islam, seen as 'harmless' to and coexisting with the secular norm of public space, as it is perceived as being part of the national identity and heritage, whereas Islam, as 'othered' religion, is not (van den Hemel 2014; Oosterbaan 2014).

The presence of Muslim girls' bodies in the public spaces of schools and sports is seen as contradictory to the perceived secular 'nature' of Dutch public space (Butler 2008; Jaffe-Walter 2016, 40).[14] The no-headscarf policy of Peter is one example of the 'secular' norm of public sports space: the public sports playground should be free from Islamic religious signs such as the headscarf, and sports is used to teach and discipline girls into the Dutch cultural and 'Christian secular' norm – they are not supposed to be wearing a headscarf but are expected to participate in Christmas. This secular norm that is installed in the public playgrounds produces a gendered division, as it directs Muslim girls to play football inside (where they can take of their headscarves), invisible from the audience, whereas the presence of (Muslim) boys in the public playgrounds is considered unproblematic for keeping the space 'secular'.

Within this normative secular/religious construction of public spaces, it is assumed that if Muslim girls play football with a headscarf, the football space automatically becomes a priori an Islamic space – the football space becomes religionized, which, in turn, conflicts with the secular norm. Yet, the girls in my research themselves experience and frame football space above all as a football, and not as a religious, space, as I will show in the next section. In the views of the policy makers and sports professionals in my research, playing football in a separated girls' space or playing football with a sports headscarf is perceived as a threat to the secular norm of public spaces, rather than as a normal aspect of sports culture and practices. The sports professionals and policy makers I interviewed reduced Muslim women's practices and experiences solely to 'being Muslim', and do not acknowledge that their practices are also informed, or even primarily informed, by the gendered, sexualized and racialized norms in football culture in the Netherlands.

The reduction of Muslim girls' football practices solely to their Muslim background points to a paradox of Muslim girls' football participation that is inherent in Dutch culturalized constructions of citizenship. In sports and neighbourhood policies, Muslim girls are constructed as in need of integration and emancipation, because of their racialized and religious 'difference' within dominant white Dutch society and because of their supposed gender and sexual oppression. Sports, especially football, are often used as the privileged domain to 'integrate' or 'discipline' Muslim youths into the desired forms of cultural and sexual citizenship. It is worth repeating here that the FGU competition also precisely aims at girls' emancipation in the Schilderswijk and in public football spaces. As I have shown in the previous chapter, they create a separated girls' football competition as a counterspace to the male-dominated street football spaces where girls are often excluded. The paradox is that, when girls with Moroccan-Dutch and Muslim backgrounds play football in a girls' football competition, it is not interpreted as integration or as a normal aspect of sports culture but as essentially linked to their alleged traditional religious backgrounds and therefore contrary to integration. In this situation, it is impossible for these girls to be regarded as full citizens, because their sportive performances will always 'fail' within dominant constructions of cultural and sexual citizenship, where they are and stay essentially positioned as 'different' and 'other' from white Dutch sporting culture and society.

Even more, the construction of Muslim girls as essentially 'other' within Dutch society becomes articulated precisely when Muslim women or girls become more visible in public spaces, such as when playing football, as anthropologist Sunier (2009, 475) argues:

> The more closely Muslim women are involved in European societies, the more their religious background seems to become a problematic issue. As long as the veiled lady cleans our buildings, looks after our children, or cooks our food, in other words keeps a certain occupational and social distance to the rest of society, there is no need to get disturbed and to raise the religious question. But when they enter 'our' life worlds, something else is at stake.

Muslim women become perceived as a 'problem' when they become more visible as social actors, in presumed secular public spaces (Göle 2006), while, at the same time, they are 'expected', according to integration and emancipation policies, to increase their participation in public (sports) spaces. This is the paradox in Dutch integration and citizenship discourses: Muslim women need to become integrated and emancipated, but it is simultaneously and precisely their successful integration and emancipation in public spaces that subsequently frames them as problematic (Henkel 2009b, 476). Dutch cultural and sexual constructions of citizenship are thus always unreachable goals, yet crucial to construct essentialized differences between white Dutch citizens and racialized and religious 'others'. In the next two case studies, I will further illustrate how the girls in my research are constantly negatively defined by their 'Islamic otherness' in football spaces in the Schilderswijk.

The al-Qaida case

In an interview with Noor (twenty-one years old) and Aliya, both volunteers at FGU, we talked about wearing a headscarf while playing sports, and Noor told me the following story:

> One day, it was so funny, it was a comment about us, I laughed about it a lot. We were playing football and most of us were wearing a headscarf, we were with five girls. Then a Dutch guy passes by on his bicycle, and, when he sees us, he says: 'Is this a training camp for al-Qaida or something?' Bahahaha. And I had to laugh about what he said. And I thought, how can you make this up, how could you possibly be thinking about al-Qaida?!

Islamic clothing, here, is associated with a radicalized body and bodily practice ('training for al-Qaida') on the football field. I asked Noor and Aliya how they felt about this situation, and both mentioned their laughter about such comments, and they expressed a certain resigned attitude towards the issue. They mentioned that they do not really care about such comments and framed it as ignorance on behalf of the people who say such things:

Noor: Yeah, what can I say about it, it's a comment they make, and we just don't pay attention to it. I don't care because they don't know what a headscarf means, so then I don't talk to these people. If you know what a headscarf means, you don't talk about al-Qaida, because then you know what it really means.

Aliya: Yes, I actually don't mind when they say something to me about a headscarf. I really don't mind; if I were to receive such a comment, I think I would also laugh! It's just a joke. Perhaps I would say 'Hey, join us! Then you can also wear a headscarf!'

Noor: Indeed! Bahahaha.

Just like in Peter's playground, in this case there is also an immediate association of Muslim girls who wear headscarves and play football with terrorism and Islamic radicalism (see also Nyhagen and Halsaa 2016). When girls wear a headscarf, they are more directly recognizable as Muslims than boys are, invoking a reaction based on Muslim girls' embodied religious difference (Smiet 2014, 17–18). In addition, for (Muslim) boys, exercising and playing football in public playgrounds is seen as 'natural' and therefore not suspicious. For Muslim girls, playing football is not related to 'just' playing football but is seen as an outstanding 'Islamic' presence in supposed 'secular' and 'masculine' public spaces of football. The connection with radical Islam or Jihad is then apparently obvious, even if it is a joke. This case is a clear illustration of the paradox of gender, Islam and girls' football in Dutch cultural and sexual citizenship discourses: the Muslim girls in this case participate in Dutch society and embody Dutch norms of emancipation and integration by playing the national Dutch sport football in public playgrounds, but since they always already embody visible 'Islamic otherness', their football activities in public spaces are primarily read as related to Islam and seen as problematic and a threat rather than as emancipation (Göle 2006; Henkel 2009a; Sunier 2009).

While Noor and Aliya laughed about the situation, I was shocked at hearing their experiences of playing football being related to radical Islam. According to Noor and Aliya, other girls might also laugh about the joke, as they did, but some girls might become aggressive and think the guy is a racist. For Noor, her reaction to such comments also depends on the situation: most of the time, she is too busy playing football to notice or react at all. It shows that girls employ different strategies, talking back, silence and kicking back, to deal with such 'microaggressive' experiences (Jaffe-Walter 2016, 134).

The laundry case

While most of the time there are also boys involved in the FGU activities, once or twice a year, they organize a real girls-only football training, also discussed in the previous chapter. After Hanan asks the boys to leave, I am sitting with the girls on the benches; we are dividing the teams before playing. While Hanan is explaining what we will do today, three white middle-aged men with hockey sticks and sports bags walk past us to the exit of the sports hall. The last one of them stops, looks around, and says: 'So, can I leave my laundry here?' Hanan immediately responds to the man, but I cannot hear what she says, as the girls around me get very agitated and shout: 'He's a racist!' Some girls stand up from the benches and raise their hands. I get really angry as well because of his comment, so I cannot recall exactly what happened afterwards. I remember that Hanan stays calm and says to me and the girls: 'Well, we shouldn't pay attention to those kinds of people,' before continuing her explanation of the training and start playing football.

A couple of days later, I met Hanan at a community centre for an interview, and she said:

I've organized girls' football in several community centres and neighbourhoods. And still that's not always accepted. Or like that man from Sunday!? Yes, you got very angry, me too, and, if the girls hadn't been there, I would've hit him, but now I couldn't because the girls were there. So, I said to him: 'Oh, because we wear a headscarf you ask this? That's racist.' And then he reacted like 'well, well, well'. But you know, next Sunday, I will go a little bit earlier to the sports hall and then I'll confront him with what he said. Then I'll ask him: 'Sir, what did you mean by that?'

Reflecting on my own emotions during this encounter with the man, I felt personally humiliated and shouted 'He's a sexist!' in the uproar. When I heard the other girls shout 'racist', I was surprised for a second, because, as a white privileged woman in the Netherlands, at that moment I could only personally experience his comment in a sexist way. As Hanan pointed out, for her and the girls it was through being visibly Muslim through the headscarf that they understand this comment first and foremost as racist, an example of the racialization of Muslim women's bodies. This laundry question has thus strong racial, gendered and class meanings and refers not only to gendered labour but moreover to racialized and classed gendered labour.[15] Here, the paradox of gender, Islam and girls' football also becomes clear: in the football space of FGU, where Hanan and the volunteers teach boys and girls gender equality and respect, and aim for girls' emancipation in sports and society, the girls experience harsh racism, sexism and classism. Because of their gendered and racialized religious difference, the girls were not seen as 'normal' football players and as participants in Dutch society; in this case, they are rather being reduced to the stereotyped and feminized lower-class 'foreigners'' job of laundry washers for upper-class white male hockey players.[16] Such a comment relegates the 'integrated' and 'emancipated' football girls back to the private space of the home, where they are expected to act as cleaning ladies (Sunier 2009, 475).

Interestingly, in this case, the girls used the term 'racism' to express and describe the laundry question; I was the only one mentioning sexism. In other talks or interviews too, girls expressed both racist and sexist experiences under the term 'racism', for example, in a short interview I had with a girls' football team at the Cruyff Court 6 vs 6 competition in the Schilderswijk:

Kathrine: Sometimes, people say that football is more for boys, what do you think about that?
Amira: That's totally not true.
Hind: That's really racist.

Kathrine: Why is that racist?
Hind: Because they discriminate between boys and girls, that's racist.

The girls recognize that the sexism at work in the laundry comment and in football in general is racialized and classed sexism and, therefore, they refer to this as racism. It is in the first place their visible difference of brown skin and a headscarf that sets them apart from the white norm secular that persists in Dutch society, and therefore for these girls, experiences of sexism are also always racialized. When Muslim girls play football in their own girls' competition, this is not seen as a normal part of the gendered organization of sports but interpreted as an essentialist Islamic practice by sports professionals and in Dutch discourses on integration, emancipation and culturalized citizenship. Public football spaces subsequently become framed as religionized or 'Islamized'. Yet, in the girls' own identifications and football practices, Islam is not always at the forefront, as the next section will show.

Playing religion, ethnicity and citizenship

From the girls in my research, I seldom heard Islamic explanations or motivations for playing in a girls' football competition. Most research participants never expressed any interest in having their own segregated sporting space according to Islamic ideologies or because of their Muslim backgrounds, except for the three girls in the 'only girls today' case in the previous chapter. Most girls rather want to have their own football space as an alternative to the male-dominated public football playgrounds and to resist dominant gender norms in football. Samie (2013) argued as well that the sports participation of the British Pakistani Muslim women in her research was not so much shaped by Islamic or religious factors but by discourses and norms of female bodies exhibiting heterosexual appeal by being fit and sexy ('hetero-sexy'). Furthermore, FGU does not consider itself as a Muslim football competition, although most of the girls in FGU have Moroccan-Dutch and Muslim backgrounds. Yet, the football players often mentioned that FGU is not a football community for Moroccan-Dutch or Muslims only but for all girls in the Schilderswijk and adjacent neighbourhoods. Nora explained to me:

> We're not like: 'This place is only for headscarves or Moroccans or Muslims', because we also have Christian girls, or Catholics, or different backgrounds with a different skin colour.

Contrary to Nora's claim, I did not encounter Christian or Catholic girls during my fieldwork at FGU, but I suspect that she referred to a few of the white Dutch girls who participated irregularly in FGU and whom she assumed had Christian religious backgrounds. I did not explicitly ask all football players about their religious beliefs, identities or practices (which was a deliberate choice, see Chapter 2). Yet, in our talks about playing football and its relation to gender and ethnic and religious backgrounds and identities, most of the girls and boys mentioned that they identify as Muslim. What that meant for them in daily life, however, was diverse. In the talks they had amongst each other on the football field, some girls and boys mentioned religious engagements, such as going to Sunday mosque classes, taking Arabic and Quran classes, finding halal candies and trying to pray regularly. Others did not mention their involvement in such religious activities and saw Islam merely as a cultural-religious guide for norms and values in daily life.

When I asked the FGU football players in what ways their religious backgrounds or beliefs mattered on the football field, many responded with the word '*gewoon*' in Dutch, meaning something like 'just, normally', implying that playing football and Islam are not in conflict, like Nisa's response shows as well:

> I'm just a girl who likes to play football and who believes in Islam.

Some players immediately said: 'Faith does not matter, it does not make a difference.' It became clear to me that many football players, especially the younger girls, were not very interested in talking about their faith or religion with me. After all, they were there to play football, not because of any religious matters. Some might have wanted to avoid talking with me about Islam, because of the stigmatization of Muslims in the Netherlands; others might not have been interested in religion because of their young age. In this context, insisting to talk about Islam seemed strange and problematic to me, as I did not want to suggest that I was reinforcing stereotypes about Muslim girls in sports. It was thus mainly during conversations in which my research participants opened up themselves to talk about religion that I pursued to ask about religious matters.

A few players made clear, sometimes implicit, how they incorporated religious beliefs in their activities on and off the field. Hanan, coordinator of FGU, was one of them. After a football training, we were driving to a restaurant for an interview when she saw a woman with a *niqab* (face veil) walking in the street. Agitated, she told me:

> Look, that woman in *niqab*, I'm against that. Islam requires you to be open and welcoming. To be open to society and your neighbours. And, therefore, we welcomed you in our competition. A *niqab* is not open, you shut yourself off.

In the quote, Hanan refers to the way she and the FGU volunteers were willing to participate in my research and were open to my research questions. I was not the only person from outside the Schilderswijk or the Moroccan-Dutch Muslim community to be welcomed in FGU; a few times a year, the volunteers organize a football competition with girls from other neighbourhoods in The Hague to get to know each other, including girls from predominantly white Dutch neighbourhoods. For Hanan, to be open and welcoming to people from outside the neighbourhood is linked to her Islamic faith, although this was probably also prompted by her wish to challenge negative stereotypes of the Schilderswijk and its Muslim residents.

Other football players perform their religious belief mostly by way of moral behaviour on the field. When I asked whether there are girls with different religious backgrounds at FGU, one of the boy volunteers, Mansour, said:

> This is not important at all. Yes, most are Muslim. But everyone is treated the same. For example, if I do something racist, that's not okay. Or last week, there was a girl who became ill. Then we took her to the side, and we cared for her. We have to take care of each other.

It happened more often in my research that, when I asked about religion or Islam in FGU, research participants would at first respond that religion does not matter, after which they started to talk about 'being nice for each other on the field'. For many of my research participants, including Mansour, Islam was not a main concern in FGU. Only when I explicitly continued to ask them about religion, they connected Islam to morality, values of care and (gender) equality on the field, all things FGU explicitly strives for.

There were, however, some signs of Islamic convictions in playing football, for example, in the wish of some girls to play football in sports clothes that also cover their legs. For them, playing football with bare legs would be a mismatch with wearing a headscarf, but it was also related to not wanting to play in 'boys' clothes'[17] and to a hesitance to show too much of their (sexualized) body in athletic revealing poses when boys are looking. Religion or Islam on the football field thus always intersects with the gender and sexual dynamics in sports culture and football, and Muslim girls' experiences should therefore not only be discussed and explained from a religious perspective.

In relation to the competition aspect in football, sometimes ethnic identifications were explicitly performed or mentioned on the football field rather than religious identifications. I talked with Mona and Sabia, two football players in their twenties from a women's football team in Amsterdam, about how one's ethnic background influences playing football. At first, they mentioned that ethnicity does not play a role, because everyone on the field is just a football player.

Mona: I want to enter the football field as a footballer and not as Moroccan or Dutch or whatever. And we also leave the field as a footballer.
Sabia: Except when we win.
Mona: Indeed, then we are Moroccan, ha-ha!

Although they were clearly joking, it is also a playful but serious engagement with dominant perceptions of Moroccan-Dutch Muslim women in the context of discrimination, racism and Islamophobia on and off the football field. Explicitly identifying as Moroccan when one wins can be interpreted as a form of kicking back towards dominant power structures and stereotypes in Dutch society. A football player from FGU also told me that, especially when a 'Moroccan' team plays against a 'Dutch' team, they insist on winning:

Then you just don't want to lose, *definitely* not from Dutch people.

Winning on the football field is a way to challenge dominant perceptions and stereotypes of Moroccan-Dutch Muslim girls in Dutch society. The girls performatively reclaim and play with ethnic identification markers and perform a dominant position on the field through winning. In this way, the girls in my research kick back at the 'othered' and marginalized position that is often attributed to them in dominant perceptions of Moroccan-Dutch Muslim girls as inactive, bad football players and as oppressed, whilst at the same time drawing on those dominant perceptions. Fatima El-Tayeb has conceptualized this reclaiming of ethnicity as 'queering ethnicity' in the case of hip hop in European public space and describes it as 'forms of resistance that destabilize the ascribed essentialist identities not only by rejecting them, but also through a strategic and creative (mis)use' (2011, xxxvi).

In Chapter 5, I showed how Hafsa and her friends use gendered expectations about girls as bad football players in their strategy. Similarly, some other girls told me that they employ gendered and racialized stereotypes about Moroccan-Dutch Muslim girls in their football strategy as well: they at first play very shyly and act as if they are afraid of the ball, so that the other team becomes sure that they will win. At some point, they switch to full force and impress the opponents by making one goal after another. They reclaim categories of ethnic and religious difference to resist stereotypes and prejudices *and* at the same time to win the match. Nora's story about the National Street Football Finals, which I discussed in Chapter 5, serves as a good illustration here as well. Nora told me about the expectations of white Dutch players that Moroccan-Dutch Muslim girls cannot play football and how their opponents laughed when she and her team members entered the football field with headscarves. However, Nora also mentioned that, in the end, she and her team members did not care that much about prejudices and stereotypes because they won the match. The way Nora and her teammates deal with stereotypes about them as Moroccan-Dutch Muslim girls is incorporated within the game of football itself, where winning is the ultimate goal. Just as winning is a strategy to resist and challenge dominant gender stereotypes in football playgrounds in relation to boys, winning is also a strategy to challenge stereotypes and prejudices about Moroccan-Dutch Muslim girls on the football field. Just as with the idea of talking back, Muslim girls kick back at multiple discourses and multiple audiences by playing football.

Contrary to the policy makers and sports professionals' assumptions, girls' football experiences indicate that many of them do not primarily see themselves as Muslims or as believers on the football field but simply as football players. Although her story shows otherwise, Nora actually believes that religious, racial or ethnic backgrounds should not matter on the football field, but that simply playing football is the most important:

Kathrine: How does it feel when people have such prejudices about you?
Nora: Yeah, I think there is no need for them, because, in the end, we are as good as them, or well ... Yeah, no one is better than the other. So. But I don't really care, we all have the same blood, right? We are all humans, so ... If you have a headscarf or if you are brown or black or whatever, if you can play football you just play, that's not because of your skin colour or your descent or your beliefs.

Sport scholar Ratna also found, in her research on women's football in the UK, that the women did not want to be described in ethnic terms but as 'players of women's football' (2011, 261). The girls in FGU do not necessarily 'invade' football spaces as Muslims, because that would still make them 'other' or 'different' from the perceived 'natural' (white, male) occupants. They invade the spaces as football players who happen to be Muslim and who claim that they equally belong to urban public spaces as white or secular Dutch girls and as boys do. Farah (twelve years old) told me in an interview about a recent experience in which she was not welcome in a public football playground because of her ethnic and religious background. At the end of her story, she said:

> Whose space is this in the Netherlands? It's surely as much my space as it is a blonde Dutch girl's space!

By playing football and claiming public football spaces, my research participants claim belonging to public spaces as football players and as Dutch citizens (see also van den Brandt 2019, 296, 306; van Es 2019, 154).

For the Muslim football players in my research, Islamic or religious practices and identities are not the most important on the football field, nor do they play football because of any religious motivations. They describe themselves primarily as football players and not as Muslims, and it is as football players that they claim access to Dutch public football spaces. I am not suggesting that the football players are not pious or religious in general or in other spaces, but, on the football field, religion or Islam is not their primary concern. Samie (2013) arrives at similar conclusions in her research on British-Muslim women in sports, who prioritize their gendered and sexual identities on the field rather than their religious identifications, as a response to both gender ideals in sports and to British stereotypes about Muslim girls. In other words, although girls primarily see themselves as football players, ethnic and religious identities are inescapable in relation to how other football players perceive them and in relation to dominant Dutch discourses of Muslim girls (see also van den Brandt 2019, 308; Bracke 2011). The girls in my research are very much aware of Dutch stereotypical representations of them as oppressed Muslim and Moroccan-Dutch girls, and, in response to these stereotypes, they do play with the categories of ethnicity and religion. For example, they playfully reclaim an identity as Moroccan when they win a match or incorporate stereotypes of Muslim girls in their strategy to win a match. They challenge dominant Dutch constructions of Muslims as 'other' by embodying the popular Dutch sport football and identifying primarily as football players. Foregrounding an identity as football player is a response and resistance to dominant Dutch discourses on Muslim girls, cultural citizenship, and racist and Islamophobic prejudices.

Until now, I have mainly discussed citizenship in relation to the culturalization of citizenship, as discourses about what it means to be a 'good' or 'real' Dutch citizen. In that, there is a paradox in which Muslim girls are always constructed by their religious difference and continue to be seen as racialized and religious 'others', even when they engage with football, a popular practice that is often taken as indicator for properly embodying Dutch citizenship. However, I have also shown how the girls in my research use football to challenge and resist dominant discourses on Muslim girls and cultural constructions of citizenship. Current conceptualizations of culturalized citizenship offer limited space to include these forms of resistance. Research on the culturalization of citizenship mainly focuses on the level of dominant discourses and representations of citizenship, and not on actual practices of citizenship and marginalized subjects' resistances (El-Tayeb 2011). Approaching citizenship mainly from the perspective of the dominant discourses and norms about citizenship overlooks how citizenship is also something that is always performed, practised and lived. Citizenship is produced not only through dominant discursive (sexual and cultural) norms but, importantly, also through public, political and embodied practices that negotiate and question precisely those norms (Jaffe and A. de Koning 2015; Lazar 2014; Nyhagen and Halsaa 2016).

Nyhagen and Halsaa conceptualize citizenship as a lived practice: 'An emphasis on citizenship as lived practice is based on the idea that citizenship is not so much a fixed attribute of a particular group but rather involves contested, fluid and dynamic processes of negotiation and struggle' (2016, 60). Actions of negotiation and resistance in turn contribute to changing dominant perceptions of citizenship: citizenship 'is a dynamic construct which shifts as much due to the actions of those excluded from citizenship as those with the greater power of full membership' (Lazar 2014, 72). Occupying urban public spaces through street demonstrations, neighbourhood-based social gatherings or creative forms of protest such as graffiti are contemporary forms of citizenship action (Lazar 2014, 76), and this could also include playing street football.

In the Schilderswijk, practices of citizenship extend beyond football, although FGU itself is also an important domain for practising inclusive citizenship for the girls. Previously, I already mentioned the youth centre in the Schilderswijk where discussions are organized on societal and local issues, such as discrimination, unemployment, radicalization, crime and the relationship between youths and the police in the neighbourhood. It is run by three men from the Schilderswijk, and they help young residents with all kinds of issues: school and homework, finding a job, gaining self-confidence and so on. FGU cooperates with the youth centre, and Hanan always takes a group of girls from FGU to the events of the youth centre to stimulate girls' and women's participation in the discussions and trainings. Her participation works in two ways: it gives girls opportunities to become engaged in activities that can help them in their studies and work, and it challenges the normally dominantly masculine spaces of the youth centre. The girls from FGU also take part in other volunteer activities in the Schilderswijk: they help in an elderly nursing home, collect money and food for homeless and poor people in the neighbourhood with Ramadan, and participate in diner events at which residents with different backgrounds can meet each other in the Schilderswijk. Once a year, the girls from FGU participate together in the Dutch 'Royal Games' (*Koningsspelen*).[18] Next to stimulating girls' participation in the male-dominated spaces of football, FGU also encourages girls' participation in other traditionally male-dominated spaces in the Schilderswijk, such as politics and public debates.

Even if dominant culturalized constructions of citizenship create Muslim girls as 'second-class' citizens, playing football is a way in which Muslim girls do perform and 'play' citizenship. Playing football is in itself a citizenship practice, but in the Schilderswijk, girls' football also opens doors to other forms of citizenship practice, through volunteering and engaging in political debates. Through performative actions and practices of citizenship, the football girls redefine and reconceptualize what it means to be a Dutch citizen. They do not uncritically take part in neighbourhood sports projects for the integration, disciplining and emancipation of Muslim girls and boys, but adopt football as a citizenship practice to create their own sports practices and recreate citizenship more inclusively (see also Silverstein 2002).

The citizenship practices of the girls and boys in the Schilderswijk take place in relation to national belonging, by emphasizing that they belong to Dutch public spaces as Dutch citizens, but also in relation to local belonging and local practices in the neighbourhood in which they live and play. Citizenship is not only produced at the national level, but also in the city, where local spaces and practices of citizenship are 'challenging, diverging from, and even replacing nations as the important space of citizenship' (Holston and Appadurai 1999, 3). In these local citizenship activities in and beyond football, the girls and boys claim that they are already part of Dutch society and that they do not need to become Dutch citizens through culturalist discourses of integration or emancipation (van den Brandt 2019, 296, 306; van Es 2019, 154). According to Jaffe-Walter, this is precisely what being an active citizen entails, and critically analysing society is the best citizenship practice: 'Critiquing the norms, values, and institutions that produce inequalities helps students to be more engaged in society' (2016, 171). The football girls in the Schilderswijk claim not only football spaces as theirs but, by playing football, also the discursive spaces of Dutch citizenship.

8

Girls who kick back

This ethnography of girls' street football in the Schilderswijk functions as a critical perspective on contemporary dynamics and intersections of gender, race/ethnicity, religion and citizenship in Dutch society. It is situated in the context of three related societal developments in the Netherlands. First, girls' football has seen an enormous growth over the past years, both in official clubs and in other, more 'unorganized' football spaces such as urban playgrounds (Romijn and Elling 2017, 24), despite the still dominant image of football as a masculine sport. Street football has become increasingly popular amongst Moroccan-Dutch girls in urban multicultural neighbourhoods such as the Schilderswijk. The girls' football competition that formed the ethnographic body of this book, Football Girls United (FGU), is a living example of the popularity of football amongst ethnic-minority and Muslim girls in urban neighbourhoods.

The increased presence of ethnic-minority and Muslim girls in public football spaces relates to the second point, which is about the political and public anxieties around the increasing visibility of migrants, Islam and Muslim bodies in European cities (A. de Koning 2016; Modest and A. de Koning 2016; Oosterbaan 2014). Muslim citizens have become constructed as the ultimate religious and racial/ethnic 'others' in hegemonic Dutch society, with gender and sexuality as central 'markers' of the division between white Dutchness and Muslim 'others' (Wekker 2016). In this narrative, the histories of Moroccan low-skilled labour migration to the Netherlands and the residence patterns of Moroccan migrants in historically lower-class neighbourhoods such as the Schilderswijk are actively forgotten and ignored.

Third, these national discourses on Dutch identity, gender and Muslim 'others' play out specifically in those urban working-class neighbourhoods that become constructed as 'disadvantaged'. Discourses about Muslim 'others' feed into the construction of urban Muslim and ethnic-minority youths in these neighbourhoods as 'problematic' (A. de Koning 2015a; 2016). In turn, neighbourhood sports programmes are implemented as part of the policies to improve 'disadvantaged' neighbourhoods and to integrate its ethnic-minority and Muslim youths into dominant Dutch society (Rana 2014), usually through the most popular national sport: football. The starting point of these policies is that Moroccan-Dutch and Muslim citizens still need to be 'integrated' in Dutch society, even if they are born and raised in the Netherlands. Muslim and ethnic-minority girls form a specific target group of neighbourhood sports programmes because of their assumed lack of participation in sports and lack of emancipation.

In a paradoxical way, this assumption leads back to the first point: sociological research that shows that ethnic-minority girls' participation in (street) football is actually vastly increasing; yet these numbers are often not included in official statistics, which are based on club membership only (Elling and Knoppers 2005; Romijn and Elling 2017). Muslim girls' increasing football participation, thus, provides challenges to persisting assumptions and perceptions of Muslim girls as 'inactive' and 'oppressed', to popular perceptions of the visibility of Islam in urban neighbourhoods as a threat and to football as a domain of masculine nationalistic performance and identity.

Girls do not readily accept how public spaces in the Netherlands and in their neighbourhood are gendered, racialized and religionized through dominant discourses of ethnic-minority and Muslim girls as 'other'. Rather, by playing football and 'invading' public playgrounds, they performatively recreate and kick back at racialized norms of gender, ethnicity and religion in public spaces and in football. The girls literally and discursively play with the categories of religious difference, gender, ethnicity and citizenship, and create more inclusive and more equal public football spaces in the Schilderswijk, to which Muslim and Moroccan-Dutch female football players also belong. Playing football, thus, refers not only to 'non-serious' acts of leisure or recreation but also to the critical engagement and performative acts of gender, race/ethnicity, religion, space and citizenship. By playing football, girls and boys in the Schilderswijk also kick back at those social and epistemological categories of difference in a playful yet critical manner. The remainder of this chapter will present the different discourses and audiences that the football girls are in dialogue, in play or in competition with. Furthermore, it looks forward to much needed topics of future research in the fields of gender, sport, religion, race and 'Muslim youth'.

Kicking back at (representations of) the Schilderswijk

Chapter 4 has shown how political and popular representations of the Schilderswijk install a myth of the problem neighbourhood, which is a narrative that only pays attention to the social problems in the neighbourhood, supposedly related to ethnic minorities, gender oppression and Muslim youths, and not to residents' actual experiences of living in the neighbourhood. This book therefore aimed to create more nuanced perspectives on the Schilderswijk. In doing so, the ethnographic material revealed that young residents' own experiences and perspectives of their neighbourhood are generally positive, because of the proximity of other children, friends and neighbours. Playing football together not only contributes to their positive experiences but also provides a way to combat the negative representations of their neighbourhood in politics and media by inviting children and youth from other places to their football competitions in the Schilderswijk. Simply playing football together is already a way of kicking back at those representations of the neighbourhood, as it critiques the idea of the Schilderswijk as 'no-go' area.

The football girls in this research also specifically kick back at popular perceptions of Islam and Muslim bodies as a threat in urban neighbourhoods. The girls who participate in FGU see the competition as an important counter-message to the sensational messages in the media and in research about Islamic radicalism, youth riots, crime and backwardness in the neighbourhood. Part of that counter-message was explicitly cooperating with me as a researcher in the football competition, so that they could share the 'football story' of the Schilderswijk and not the story of 'disadvantage' and of 'problematic' Muslim youth. At the same time, the girls acknowledge that there are certain issues at stake regarding their exclusion in the public spaces in their neighbourhood, specifically in the sport and leisure spaces. FGU is a response not only to stereotypical representations of the Schilderswijk but also to the actual situation in the neighbourhood in which girls have no equal access to its public playgrounds. Creating more sport and leisure spaces for girls in the Schilderswijk, without excluding boys, is the core aim of FGU, and thereby they also kick back at the gendered organization of public space in marginalized urban neighbourhoods.

Kicking back at football culture

For girls in the masculine terrain of football, playing the game is also a way of performative resistance to the gendered norms and constructions of football space, in which girls act as 'space invaders' (Puwar 2004). Girls are not simply 'outsiders' in public football spaces but contribute to constructing public football spaces differently by their increasing 'invasions' of and claims on public football spaces. Football girls are both insiders, by exposing the hidden (masculine) norm through their embodied presence in the playgrounds, and outsiders, as they precisely do not embody that norm. So, girls kick back at the gendered organization of and the masculine dominance in football. By playing this game, they show that football is the domain not only of hegemonic masculine nationalistic performance and identity but also of performing alternative and new femininities and identities in sport.

FGU is not a football competition based on the traditional dichotomous spatial segregation of boys and girls, as is the norm in sports, but aims to create more inclusive football spaces with different spatial performances. Both girls and boys performatively create more inclusive gender norms in FGU, for example, a femininity ideal that encompasses both football and Muslim embodiments and identities. Thereby at the same time, they *reproduce* some gender and sexual norms, for example, related to the ideas that boys need to protect girls and that girls deserve respect and thus must embody respectability, and the fact that heterosexuality still functions as the norm in the sporting context of FGU. Although girls' football at FGU cannot fully escape gendered and heterosexualized dichotomies of boys and girls in football, their girls' football practices, which include boys, are much more layered and nuanced than a simple rigid and fixed gender segregation.

Muslim girls' motivations for playing in a *girls'* football competition are thus not so much shaped by religious motivations but more by the gendered dynamics of public football spaces, where girls do not embody the masculine norm. The ethnographic material of Chapters 5 and 6 has demonstrated that the dichotomous gendered and sexualized organization of sports and the related gender and sexual norms and hierarchies in football are dominant in shaping girls' football experiences, and not religious or Islamic factors. As Samie (2013) also argues, Muslim women's participation in sports is not necessarily shaped by Islamic or religious motivations and convictions but by discourses and norms of gendered and (hetero)sexualized bodies in broader ('secular') football culture.

By playing football, they thus critically kick back not only at football culture but also at dominant discourses on Muslim girls.

Kicking back at discourses on Muslim girls

In Dutch society, including the sport sector, there are persisting assumptions and perceptions of Muslim girls as 'inactive' and 'oppressed', and their religious background is often seen as the most prominent aspect in their lives, also on the football field. Yet, for the young football players in this research, religion and Islam are not at all their primary interests on the football field, but they rather want to win the match and identify as a football player. As part of their performances as football players, however, they do take up and 'play' with the categories of religious difference and Islam: they take up dominant perceptions of Muslim girls as 'oppressed' and 'inactive' and incorporate them in their football tactics to win, thereby kicking back not only at their opponents on the football field but also at these stereotypical discourses. Furthermore, Muslim girls' participation in *girls'* football is often not interpreted as a successful integration or as a normal aspect of sports culture, but as essentially linked to gender segregation and their alleged traditional religious backgrounds and therefore contrary to integration. They are framed as not fully citizens in Dutch society, but by playing football in Dutch public spaces, girls position themselves as *already* part of the Dutch nation. They kick back at those discourses of culturalized citizenship by the performative play of winning and by claiming Dutch public football spaces as football players.

Similarly, most research on Muslim women and sport has a simplistic focus on gender-segregated sporting and the headscarf, thereby studying religion as a barrier for 'full' participation in sports. Studies of Muslim women's agency, on the other hand, have a limited perspective on agency as primarily stemming from religious practices or piety, which does not correspond to the experiences of the football girls in this research. These studies focus on the agentic aspect of religion but do so by centralizing mainly perspectives and experiences of observing pious women in explicitly and predominantly religious settings. While I do not deny that, for women in these settings, piety can indeed be their primary and main source of religious identification and agency, this is not the case for all religious or Muslim women and girls. Agency for the footballing girls in my research is not necessarily performed through pious or religious embodiments, but through playing football. The focus of these studies on piety and explicit religious identifications does not correspond with the anthropological lived realities of the girls in this book who 'happen to be Muslim' and who play football together.

In the context of their football activities, the girls in this book did not necessarily aspire to lead very pious, observant lives or engage with explicit Islamic or religious (sports) organizations; they engaged with what often is considered the 'secular' practice of playing football. I put secular in quotation marks, because there is no such thing as a purely 'secular' practice: what is constructed as secular is always produced through what is constructed as religious and vice versa. This book has shown the importance of also studying perspectives and experiences of Muslim girls outside explicitly religious spaces such as mosques or religious women's groups, as Muslim women's lives are not confined to these spaces only. The empirical focus of this book on football practices made it possible to not approach their lives and experiences primarily from a religious perspective but from a perspective of their navigations in spaces that were not explicitly religious. In this way, I was able to focus on an aspect of Muslim girls' daily lives that is often forgotten: their embodied leisure practices in the public playgrounds in their neighbourhoods. The football players in this book, therefore, also kick back at the epistemological categories – 'Muslim', 'Islam', 'religion' – that researchers use to study them, but that do not always correspond with their daily lives and practices.

This book shows how differences of religion, race/ethnicity and gender are being taken up by a group that is often overlooked in feminist and anthropological research on Muslim youth and gender: the young women who 'happen to be Muslim' and for whom piety is not their main practice or interest but playing football is. It shows how categories of difference, such as race/ethnicity, religion and gender, are not fixed but reproduced, resisted and changed by the actions and performances of girls themselves in different spaces. The focus on girls' football also proved to be a 'fresh' approach during the ethnographic fieldwork, as it was partly a departure from the problematic 'Islam research industry' (Abbas 2010, 133) and the overemphasis on 'Muslim youth', because it first and foremost approached the research participants as football players and not as Muslims. This 'new' scholarly entrance in their lives provides also a new entrance in knowledge production on racialized Muslim youth in the Netherlands beyond a religious perspective.

Kicking forward

I propose that future research should focus more on these 'other', non-religious aspects of Muslim girls' lives, such as education, work, leisure and sports. Feminist and anthropological research on Muslim youth and gender should not only focus on pious women in religious spaces but also engage with sports as an embodied practice of women's agency. It is time to pay attention to these spheres of life and to move beyond the limited focus on religion and Islam in studies of Muslim women. Future studies of sports and leisure can enhance understandings of the ways in which agency in Muslim girls' lives is performed not only through religion or Islam but also through other domains that are not explicitly religious. In this way, the shared experiences of girls with diverse religious and ethnic backgrounds can be emphasized, rather than Muslim girls' 'religious difference' in European public spaces. Also, broadening the empirical focus opens up discussions on the relevance of the categories that are currently used in feminist and anthropological research. Is it really relevant to categorize 'Muslims' as 'Muslims' in every research setting? It risks reproducing the existence of 'Muslims' as a separate and 'othered' group in the Netherlands and Europe more broadly, while the girls in this research have made clear that they are also just football players who would like to win the game.

Future research could also explore some issues that were not explicitly part of this research but are nevertheless important in relation to girls' football and public spaces. How sexual desire, falling in love and sexual identities are part of girls' football is a topic on which more research could be done. This is especially interesting in relation to the historical development of women's football as a space for the performances of non-heteronormative sexualities, which is now rapidly changing in current heterosexualized representations of women's football and female football athletes. How the performance of normative and non-normative sexualities plays out in non-professional street football in multi-ethnic and multireligious neighbourhoods is an important topic of further investigation.

This also raises new questions about the relation between girls' street football and the professional national women's team, the *OranjeLeeuwinnen*, with which I started this book. How does the growing participation of Muslim and Moroccan-Dutch girls in street football translate into the Dutch professional women's football teams, in which, until now, no Muslim and Moroccan-Dutch women have played? The relationships between street football, club football and women's professional football globally, with attention to gender, race/ethnicity, religion and citizenship as categories of difference, and the access of girls with diverse backgrounds to professional football, is an important topic for further research.

In this book, I have argued that conceptualizations of Muslim women's agency should attend to the experiences of Muslim girls not only from a religious or Islamic point of view but also by taking into account spatial and embodied practices that are not explicitly religious. Muslim women's agency is not always necessarily performed through religious embodied practices or in religious spaces but can also be formed through sportive embodied practices, such as playing football, in public spaces. Then, indeed, the 'Muslim' in Muslim women's agency is a question, not a given. By playing football in public spaces, girls also performatively play with – and kick back at – the racialized categories of 'Muslim', gender, ethnicity, Islam, religion and citizenship. Hence, they urge us to rethink the categories of analysis that we use, and often take for granted, as feminist and intersectional scholars of religion, Islam, gender and sport.

This book has identified the specific embodied and creative elements in sport and play (such as tactics, winning, naming of teams) that girls use to resist and critique dominant discourses, and I have conceptualized these practices as 'kicking back'. Through playing street football, Muslim girls kick back at dominant discourses and assumptions about them, thereby necessarily also drawing on those discourses, yet in a creative, performative fashion. In this way, kicking back will also apply to contexts other than only sport. Kicking back does not rely on discursive responses or (political) speech – indeed not something that is easily available for children and youth with diverse backgrounds – but highlights youth's embodied and playful responses and agencies in urban public spaces.

Notes

Chapter 1
Introduction

1. https://atria.nl/nieuws-publicaties/overig/atria-berichten/gloria-wekker-welverdiend-winnaar-joke-smitprijs-2017/ (accessed 8 January 2022). The Joke Smit *oeuvre* prize was that year awarded to Gloria Wekker, anthropologist and Emeritus Professor of Gender and Ethnicity at Utrecht University. The prize was awarded to Professor Wekker because of her long-term fight to improve the position of Black women in the Netherlands. She is known for her work on gender, sexuality, ethnicity and race in Suriname and the Netherlands. Together with other feminist scholars, she has introduced intersectionality, in Dutch known as *kruispuntdenken*, to the Netherlands. According to the jury, Professor Wekker played a crucial role in academic and societal debates on the topics of gender and ethnicity, and contributed profoundly to educating and stimulating students, journalists, activists and other people on these topics.
2. As in other countries, the headscarf is important in this representation of the lack of 'integration' in Dutch society. The decade-long debate on women's Islamic dress in public spaces resulted in the parliament's approval of a ban on the face veil in public areas such as schools, hospitals, government buildings and public transport in 2016 by the House of Representatives (*Tweede Kamer*) and in 2018 by the Dutch Senate (*Eerste Kamer*). As of August 2019, the law came into effect. Officially, all face covering is prohibited in public spaces such as education and care facilities, public transport and government buildings (not only a face veil), except when necessary for sports, professional matters or events. A penalty can be imposed on a person wearing a face cover: https://www.rijksoverheid.nl/onderwerpen/gezichtsbedekkende-kleding-in-de-media-boerkaverbod/gezichtsbedekkende-kleding-gedeeltelijk-verbieden (accessed 9 January 2022).
3. Like all other names of organizations and persons in this book, Football Girls United is a pseudonym.
4. Examples of such programmes are the national *Time for Sport Note* (*Tijd voor Sport Nota*) of the Ministry of Health, Welfare and Sport, and the *Participation Migrant Youth through Sports* programme, a collaboration between the aforementioned ministry with the Ministry of Integration and Housing. Rana (2014, 37–9) and Van Sterkenburg (2011) have discussed these programmes in more detail, and

I come back to these programmes in Chapter 7. Important to note, although these programmes talk about 'migrant youth', they mostly aim at second-generation migrant youth, thus girls and boys who are born and raised in the Netherlands with parents born elsewhere.

5 As is the case in many other national contexts, such as Canada (Dyck 2012).
6 In this book, I will use gender markers for both men's and women's sports, thus talking about 'men's football' and 'women's football'; just the term 'football' is meant for both.
7 This is also the case in global sport-for-development projects that, for example, portray sporting Afghan girls as 'emancipated' and 'agentic' but thereby overlook ongoing global structural inequalities and reproduce a postfeminist discourse that assumes that gender equality has already been achieved in the Global North (Thorpe, Hayhurst and Chawansky 2018).
8 This gap between intersectionality research and research on religion, religious agency and gender is also present in broader feminist research, as has been noted, amongst others, by Singh (2015; see also van den Bogert 2018).
9 In the selection of this literature, I have focused on the European context. There is more literature on Muslim women and sports in Muslim-majority countries, for example, by Homa Hoodfar (2015).
10 I agree with Van Es (2018) that (too) much research on Muslim women focuses on young Muslim women, which makes invisible the life experiences of middle-aged and older Muslim women, and thereby mistakenly suggesting that Muslim women's emancipation is a new or recent phenomenon from the younger generation only. It is, however, seldom the case that women or girls under eighteen years old are taken into account, let alone girls in their early teenage years, so I suggest it is also important to include this age group.

Chapter 2
An ethnography of Muslim girls' street football

1 The results of this research, carried out by Utrecht University and Leiden University and funded by NWO (the Dutch Research Council), can be found in the Dutch book *Vrouwenvoetbal in Nederland* (Women's Football in the Netherlands), edited by Prange and Oosterbaan (2017).
2 This is an initiative of the Cruyff Foundation, a Dutch NGO that builds street football playgrounds in neighbourhoods and organizes, in collaboration with local partners, a yearly competition: the 6 vs 6 Cruyff Court Competitions. At the end of this chapter, I discuss the different (girls') football organizations and spaces that I have researched in more detail.

3 This is Arabic for 'Thank God' and an often-used expression amongst Muslims in the Netherlands and amongst people in Arabic-speaking countries.
4 In Dutch: '*Het blijft toch een Marokkaan, hè.*'
5 With formal sports clubs I mean sports clubs that have an official status as a sports club and are affiliated to a national sports federation. Usually, sporters pay a yearly membership fee and play in the local, regional and/or national competitions.
6 In Dutch: *buurtsportvereniging.*

Chapter 3
Histories of Moroccan-Dutch youth: Migration, politics and street football

1 In 2021, at the time of writing, there were 416,518 Dutch citizens with a Moroccan background (CBS 2021). These numbers, as calculated by the Dutch organization on statistics (CBS), only include the first and second generations. From the third generation onwards, Dutch citizens with Moroccan (or other ethnic) backgrounds are counted as having a 'Dutch background' in CBS's statistical reports on 'migration and integration' (CBS 2016). Although their definition of 'migrant background' only includes the first and second generations, the CBS also incidentally provides data on the 'third generation'.
2 *Gastarbeiders* in Dutch.
3 From the Moroccan migrants who arrived between 1965 and 1966, one-third stayed in the Netherlands, and of those arriving between 1972 and 1973, half (Bouras 2012, 51–2).
4 See the work of Guno Jones (2014, 323–4) for a more detailed discussion of Moluccan migration to the Netherlands.
5 NOS (2016), 'Samsom en Spekman Niet Vervolgd voor Marokkanenuitspraken', *NOS*, 14 April. Available online: https://nos.nl/artikel/2098694-samsom-en-spekman-niet-vervolgd-voor-marokkanenuitspraken.html (accessed 20 January 2021). In public debates in the Netherlands, crime statistics are often presented in relation to ethnic background/descent, emphasizing the relatively high representation of people with migration backgrounds in crime. But this is an incorrect and incomplete statement. Social-economic status is the most important factor relating to crime. Differences in ethnic groups are largely explained by demographic and socio-economic factors (Huijnk and Andriessen 2016).
6 Mark Rutte (2017), 'Aan alle Nederlanders'. Available online: https://vvd.nl/content/uploads/2017/01/briefvanmark.pdf (accessed 28 February 2022). Translation by Omar Achfay.

7 https://imagineic.nl/projecten/pannas-en-akkas/ (accessed 26 August 2021).
8 https://imagineic.nl/projecten/pannas-en-akkas/ (accessed 26 August 2021).
9 https://imagineic.openbeelden.nl/media/693622/Panna_s_en_Akka_s (accessed 26 August 2021).
10 https://imagineic.nl/projecten/pannas-en-akkas/ (accessed 26 August 2021).
11 https://imagineic.openbeelden.nl/media/693622/Panna_s_en_Akka_s (accessed 26 August 2021).

Chapter 4
Being young in a contested neighbourhood

1 In Dutch: *studiefinanciering*.
2 The online database from the city of The Hague uses the Dutch concepts '*allochtoon*' (people with a migration background, including the second generation) and '*autochtoon*' (native). For a critical discussion of these racialized concepts, please see Wekker (2016, 23).
3 For example, the Dutch newspaper *Trouw* published a special magazine named *Back in the Schilderswijk* (2015), after they had to retract an article about a supposed sharia triangle in the Schilderswijk, based on questionable and unverifiable sources: https://www.trouw.nl/home/terug-in-de-schilderswijk~a3d6017c/ (accessed 14 January 2018).
4 Maarten Zeegers (2016), *Ik was een van hen. Drie jaar undercover onder moslims* (I Was One of Them. Three Years Undercover amongst Muslims) is mostly about the neighbourhood Transvaal in The Hague, but it also discusses the neighbouring Schilderswijk; Hendrik Jan Korterink (2017), *Crimescene Schilderswijk: Misdaadbiografie van de beruchtste wijk van Nederland* (Crimescene Schilderswijk: Criminal Biography of the Most Notorious Neighbourhood in the Netherlands); Martin Schouten (2017), *Schilderswijk*; and Eric de Vroedt (2017, Dutch National Theatre), *The Nation*.
5 The series ran for two seasons with thirteen episodes in total: https://www.ad.nl/den-haag/scherpe-kritiek-op-rtl-serie-over-de-schilderswijk~abfd17c1/ (accessed 15 January 2018).
6 Historian Klein Kranenburg, who wrote extensively about the Schilderswijk, has a similar tendency to frame white inhabitants as the 'true' or 'authentic' inhabitants of the Schilderswijk. In his chapters about the Schilderswijk from the 1960s until the 1980s, he only presents narratives from white Dutch residents who lived in the Schilderswijk in this period, while, already in 1977, 15 per cent of the residents were Surinamese and Antillean, and 15 per cent came from Mediterranean countries (Geense 2004). In this way, he creates an image of the Schilderswijk as white and

portrays migrant residents and their children as people who did and do not really belong to the Schilderswijk and its social history. These groups almost only come into his story when talking about the problems white residents experience with migrants in the neighbourhood, while the experiences of the migrants themselves are ignored. In this way, Klein Kranenburg reproduces an image of the neighbourhood as authentically a white space and constructs non-white citizens 'out' of the history of the neighbourhood and the Netherlands, and 'in' contemporary discourses on urban 'disadvantaged' neighbourhoods and its social problems.

7 https://www.volkskrant.nl/politiek/wilders-in-de-haagse-schilderswijk-ik-waan-me-niet-in-nederland~a3444643/ (accessed 15 January 2018).
8 https://www.ad.nl/den-haag/asscher-tempert-onrust-over-schilderswijk~aa459f84/ (accessed 15 January 2018).
9 https://www.trouw.nl/home/trouw-trekt-tien-procent-artikelen-van-ramesar-in~a3d04121/ (accessed 15 January 2018).
10 https://www.nrc.nl/nieuws/2014/09/19/in-de-schilderswijk-zijn-ze-het-zat-1422849-a676475 (accessed 15 January 2018).
11 https://www.volkskrant.nl/nieuws-achtergrond/van-aartsen-verbiedt-alle-demonstraties-schilderswijk~b2e69df2/ (accessed 15 January 2018).
12 These interviews and talks were conducted before the protests in the summer of 2015 against police brutality, when, for five nights, there were riots and clashes between (young) residents and the police. In the research by Duijndam and Prins (2017, 125–33), young residents often did refer to those riots when talking about the Schilderswijk, which, according to them, emerged because of a lack of communication and response from the police after the killing of Mitch Henriquez. Yet, even the riots in 2015 (and the riots in 2020 and 2021 due to the Covid pandemic lockdowns) do not contradict the otherwise positive and peaceful experiences of young residents beyond those five exceptional days.

Chapter 5
Invading the public football playground

1 This is similar to the gendered use of space at football clubs, where the boys come first when it comes to the use of the football field and other facilities (Elling 2015, 20; Williams 2003), and where girls often have to use the lesser maintained fields and cloakrooms, which are sometimes further away or in a bad state.
2 The 6 vs 6 competitions from the Cruyff Foundation are an exception, as they explicitly stimulate girls' participation in the competition. They have two parallel competitions: one for boys and one for girls, and, officially, a local Cruyff Court is

only allowed to participate in the competition if they have at least one girls' team as well (although, in practice, as I found out, that is not always the case).

3 In Chapter 2, the different football initiatives in the Schilderswijk have been explained. The Schilderswijk Street League is a competition organized by ADO Den Haag, the professional football club of the city, in cooperation with Sportteam and community centres in the Schilderswijk. At the start of the competition, all participants went to the football club for the official launch and to sign a contract of participation.

4 A panna court is a small football court, especially designed for the form of street football that centres around (individual) skill, speed, technique and tricks (such as the panna trick, where you shoot a ball through the legs of your opponent).

5 In this chapter, it is my aim to show how gender norms shape and construct public sports spaces, and the different embodied practices and performances in those spaces. Yet, the relation between gender, bodies and space also works the other way around. Through the gender-segregated organization of football – and sports in general – different gendered uses of the body by boys and girls are reproduced. To speak with Butler, through the repetitive performances of the gendered and footballing body, differences between girls' bodies and boys' bodies in football are reproduced and become 'naturalized', as if they exist 'naturally' in this way. In the next chapter, I will discuss how gendered, sexed and sexualized bodies are produced through the spatial organization of sports.

6 This headscarf issue is only an issue when Peter himself is in charge of the 'official' sports trainings in the playgrounds after school; when FGU organizes football trainings in the same playgrounds in the evenings and on the weekends, Peter does not see it as a problem that girls play football with a headscarf.

7 An important topic in this regard is the relationship between youths, especially boys, and the police in the Schilderswijk. In the previous chapter, I briefly discussed this topic, but here it is beyond the scope of the chapter, as I focus mainly on public space in relation to sports organizations and football. For a recent research about the experiences of girls and boys from the Schilderswijk and their trust in the police, see Duijndam and Prins (2017).

8 Here, we talked about the majority of freely accessible public playgrounds in the Schilderswijk, and not the playground that he coordinates and where he is the 'boss'.

9 Here, I meant a white Dutch background. But because it is not common in the Netherlands to talk about whiteness as a racial/ethnic category, and because it can provoke heavy responses of denial, ignorance and anxiety (Wekker 2016), in many cases when I talked to white sports professionals, I tried to avoid those wordings, not to lose their willingness to talk with me. In hindsight, I doubt this choice, as I certainly recognize that this reinforces the construction of Dutchness with a strong white norm and the exclusion of non-white bodies as part of Dutchness.

10 In the literature on gender and sports, the concept of the role model is often defined in a broad way: a role model is someone who inspires an individual or a group of people, and who is perceived as exemplary or worthy of imitation (Adriaanse and Crosswhite 2008; J. A. Young et al. 2015). Family members (especially mothers) and peers are much more often described by adolescent girls as important sports role models than sports stars (J. A. Young et al. 2015; Vescio, Wilde and Crosswhite 2005).

11 Most likely because sports studies are also dominantly perceived as masculine.

12 They met the professional women's team when they won the street football competition and received the cup and the tickets, which were later given to the boys, as I have described.

13 Also here, with 'Dutch girls', she means white Dutch girls. See, for a discussion on racial language in football, Van den Bogert (2021).

Chapter 6
The street football competition: Girls only?

1 Here, I am mainly talking about non-professional female football athletes and not about professional football players. However, Van den Heuvel (2017, 163) has shown that some professional female football players also prevent their bodies from becoming more muscular because it does not fit the standards of hegemonic heterosexual femininity. However, female athletes' growing muscles can also be seen as resistance to gender and body norms (Butler 1998).

2 Anthroplogist Annie Blazer has included an illuminating footnote in her book, based on sociologist of sport Michael Messner's work, about the separation of girls' and boys' bodies in sports, one that is relevant to quote here:

> Michael Messner argues that the age at which boys and girls are separated athletically is when girls are, for the most part, taller and stronger than boys. He points out that separating boys and girls at that age prevents boys from experiencing outperformance by girls, which would challenge cultural assumptions that males are athletically superior to females. (Blazer 2015, 269, note 10)

3 Amongst football professionals in the Netherlands, the issue of girls' football and gender-segregated or mixed football is a hot topic, also within the Royal Netherlands Football Association (KNVB). In these discussions, different pros and cons are being discussed for both gender-segregated and mixed football, related to level, talent and skill development, physical difference, facilities, and girls' and parents' wishes and needs (Siebelink 2016a; 2016b). Currently, the KNVB presents the following options

in a report on girls' football: mixed football where girls play on a girls' team in the 'boys' competition' (possible only until the age of fifteen years, because of 'physical differences'), or mixed football where talented girls play on 'boys' teams' in the 'boys competition', which is possible until the age of nineteen (Siebelink 2016b, 8). Playing with a girls' team in a separate girls' competition is also possible, but this is not encouraged by the KNVB. In other words, although the KNVB encourages 'mixed' football rather than gender segregation, 'mixed' still means that girls play in the 'boys' competition'. As such, a discursive gender segregation of boys and girls is still at the core of thinking and talking about youth football in the Netherlands. This discursive gender segregation is related to ideas on 'natural' and physical differences between sexed bodies, differences in skill and development, and the dominant position of boys in football through framing the competition as a 'boys' competition'.

4 Of course, the school is also a space where boys and girls interact, and school spaces have never been mentioned as a problematic space of boys' and girls' interactions in my research (see also M. de Koning 2008). Yet, in this book, the focus is on public and leisure spaces outside the more strict and controlled spaces of school, education and learning. Besides FGU, most leisure spaces in the Schilderswijk are seen as problematic by girls and their parents, such as the shisha cafés and hanging around in public spaces late at night (see also Chapter 4).

5 It was highly exceptional that girls and boys talked with each other in Moroccan Arabic in FGU, except for the use of certain Moroccan Arabic terms or concepts for daily objects and practices related to food, marriage or famous Moroccan football players.

6 Whereas women's football was traditionally seen as a lesbian sport (Caudwell 1999), its popularity nowadays seems to exist on the premise of heterosexual attraction to the (elite women's) football players (Elling, Peeters and Stentler 2017; van den Heuvel 2017). The stereotype of women's football as a lesbian sport, and the emphasis that is consequently put on heterosexual appeal to resist that stereotype, is particularly strong in professional women's football. In my research, I have encountered neither the stereotype of women's football as a lesbian sport nor such strong emphasis on heterosexual appeal. Yet, it does show the larger context of how gender and heteronormativity are produced in women's football in the Netherlands and beyond.

7 This book does not discuss the individual sexual choices and desires of the girls and boys, as this was not part of the data collection (the research focused primarily on playing football) and it was not a topic the girls brought up themselves. Lesbian desire is an important topic in literature of (adult) women's football, but this did not come up in my research. The 'absence' of talking about sexual desire might also have to do with the relatively young age of many of my research participants and with the taboo of (talking about) sexual desire.

8 Although Azzarito speaks about Muslim girls, she acknowledges that this subject position is about intersecting dynamics of race/ethnicity, class and religion.
9 Research in US schools has pointed out that this is also increasingly the case for racialized Black girls (Crenshaw, Ocen and Nanda 2015).
10 In the television programme 'Voetbal Inside', 11 April 2016, RTL. Although the men in the football talk show programme are heavily criticized by feminists and anti-racists for their racist, sexist, and trans- and homophobic comments, the programme still appears to be popular amongst Dutch football fans.
11 In the same football talk show, Johan Derksen stated about Moroccan boys that they 'all take a shower while wearing their underwear'.
12 For example, the European project IMAGINE on the role of boys and men in gender equality and the prevention of sexual intimidation and sexual violence: http://www.emancipator.nl/imagine/ (accessed 9 November 2018).
13 Although, here, Nora talked about a *niqab*, I later saw that these girls did not wear a face veil but a *khimar*, which covers the whole body but leaves the face uncovered.

Chapter 7
Playing religion, gender and citizenship

1 https://www.cruyff-foundation.org/en/about/14-rules/ (accessed 15 January 2018).
2 Interestingly, as Rana (2014, 37) points out, soon after the start of the project, its name changed from 'allochthonous' to 'all' youths, indicating a shift away from policies for specific target groups and the use of alternative words for 'allochthonous', such as 'new Dutch'. Subsequently, the policy texts referred to 'neighbourhood residents' instead of 'allochthonous youths'. In other words, the focus on disadvantaged neighbourhoods in the sports project stayed, thus implicitly still referring to youths with migrant backgrounds, as 'neighbourhoods' came to stand in for 'multicultural' or 'allochthonous' youths. Rana states: 'Even if the words change: ... "*alle*" instead of "*allochtone*", the underlying discourse does not. Implementing sports programmes as part of neighbourhood regeneration efforts supposedly transcends ethnic profiling, but in everyday practice social categorizations are still implicitly reproduced' (Rana 2014, 45).
3 As I also explained earlier in this book, this supposed 'lack of participation' is likely the case because the numbers of sports participation are often based only on official club membership, whereas ethnic-minority and urban girls often play sports in public playgrounds without being a member of a club (Hoekman et al. 2011b; Romijn and Elling 2017, 24).

4 For example, the 'participation statement' from Minister Asscher of Social Affairs and Employment that migrants have to sign, with a strong focus on Dutch norms and values: https://participatieverklaring.com/en/ (accessed 20 January 2018).
5 https://www.zonmw.nl/nl/onderzoek-resultaten/jeugd/programmas/programma-detail/sportimpuls-jeugd-in-lage-inkomensbuurten/ (accessed 20 January 2018).
6 With a few exceptions in cheerleading (Anderson 2008) and the Dutch sport *korfball*, where mixed teams are the norm. However, both in cheerleading and *korfball*, the gendered and sexed spatial organization of the sport is still crucial, albeit in different ways: cheerleading is constructed as a discursively feminized space (Anderson 2008), and, in *korfball*, gender differentiation on the field is practised through the defence rules of the sport (men may only defend men and women may only defend women).
7 The VVD is the conservative liberal democratic party and the CDA the Christian democrat party. On a national level, these two parties formed the coalition Rutte-1 from 2010 to 2012 together. They received extra coalitional support from the PVV, the xenophobic and populist 'party for freedom' led by Geert Wilders, which meant 'a swing to the right of the entire political spectrum' (Wekker 2016, 110). It is not unlikely that this has also influenced the local government and policies in The Hague.
8 This also explains why gender-segregated swimming is more difficult to facilitate by the municipality: it is not about competition but about individual 'fitness' swimming, and the argument of gender segregation based on sports level and physical differences can therefore not be used.
9 Here, I am talking about the sports hours organized by Sportteam in this playground, on weekdays after school. Peter follows the same policy as the primary school that his playground is attached to, and of which he also uses the indoor sports hall. At the school, headscarves are not allowed during physical education classes. On Saturdays, when FGU uses Peter's playground, they can set their own rules. Wearing a headscarf, like in all of FGU's activities, is not a problem then.
10 He refers to the Charlie Hebdo shooting in Paris which took place on 7 January 2015.
11 I am aware that wearing a face veil (in popular language often called a *burqa*) and radicalism and terrorism are different things, and that wearing a face veil is more often a sign of adhering to Salafism than of radicalization. Salafism means adhering to orthodox or 'pure' Islam and is not necessarily related to jihadism. This is only the case for a small group of Salafis who adhere to the jihadist Salafi groups. The other two groups are the political and puritan Salafi's and they condemn violence (M. de Koning, Wagemakers and Becker 2014). Yet, in dominant Dutch discourses, these practices are conflated, and wearing a face veil is often associated with

radicalization and terrorism (M. de Koning, Wagemakers and Becker 2014) and seen as a threat to Dutch society and the Dutch nation state (Moors 2009).

12 In several policy documents, 'withdrawing in their own communities' is framed as one of the causes for a lack of integration in the Netherlands. For example, this is the case in the Integration Memorandum of 2007–11 from the Housing, Neighbourhoods and Integration section of the Ministry of Housing, Spatial Planning and the Environment (WWI/VROM). The name of the Memorandum is 'Make Sure You're Part of It!' (*Zorg dat je erbij hoort!*) and signals the fact that 'people withdraw in their own ethnic circle or their religious faith and live, so to speak, with their backs to society' (VROM/WWI 2007, 5, translation mine). Minister Asscher from Social Affairs and Employment also expressed his concern of migrants in 'parallel communities', who do not feel the need to meet or communicate with others (Asscher 2013, translation mine).

13 Which is a remnant of the former pillarization of Dutch society (Bracke 2013).

14 The norm of public space as secular and religion as private is more an idealized conception than a lived practice and has been challenged throughout Dutch history by different religious 'others': Catholics and Muslims (Tamimi Arab 2014, 11–12).

15 Domestic jobs such as caretaking and cleaning are often undertaken by migrant women in white Dutch households, and for a long time those were the only jobs available for migrant women (Marchetti 2016; Sunier 2009, 475). Although now the situation is more diverse, the image of domestic work is still very much constructed through a racialized, gendered and classed difference.

16 In the Netherlands, hockey is known to be an upper-class sport, and non-white people are often assumed to belong to the working class. The sports hall where this incident took place lies at the border of the Schilderswijk and the more affluent city centre, so it caters to sports people with diverse classed, racial/ethnic and religious backgrounds, who rent the sports hall.

17 In most of the community centres where girls play football, except for FGU, they only have boys' team uniforms available. As this is another sign of football still being seen as a masculine sport, girls like to have their own recognizable outfits, also as a recognition of football as a girls' sport.

18 The *Koningsspelen*, or the Royal Games, are sportive activities organized by the Johan Cruyff Foundation and the Richard Krajicek Foundation for primary school children around the national Dutch holiday King's Day, on which the birthday of King Willem Alexander is celebrated. During the Royal Games, adults and children dress in the colour orange (an orange *Djellaba* [Moroccan traditional dress] was worn by Peter), which is the national colour of the Netherlands, the royal family, and the national football team and all other national sports teams.

References

Abbas, Tahir. 2010. 'Muslim-on-Muslim Social Research: Knowledge, Power and Religio-Cultural Identities'. *Social Epistemology* 24 (2): 123–36. https://doi.org/10.1080/02691721003749919.

Abu-Lughod, Lila. 1990. 'Can There Be a Feminist Ethnography?' *Women & Performance: A Journal of Feminist Theory* 5 (1): 7–27. https://doi.org/10.1080/07407709008571138.

Abu-Lughod, Lila. 2002. 'Do Muslim Women Really Need Saving? Anthropological Reflections on Cultural Relativism and Its Others'. *American Anthropologist* 104 (3): 783–90. https://doi.org/10.1525/aa.2002.104.3.783.

Abu-Lughod, Lila. 2013. *Do Muslim Women Need Saving?* Cambridge, MA: Harvard University Press.

Adjepong, L. Anima, and Ben Carrington. 2014. 'Black Female Athletes as Space Invaders'. In *Routledge Handbook of Sport, Gender and Sexuality*, edited by Jennifer Hargreaves and Eric Anderson, 169–78. London: Routledge. https://doi.org/10.4324/9780203121375.

Adriaanse, Johanna A., and Janice J. Crosswhite. 2008. 'David or Mia? The Influence of Gender on Adolescent Girls' Choice of Sport Role Models'. *Women's Studies International Forum* 31 (5): 383–9. https://doi.org/10.1016/j.wsif.2008.08.008.

Ahmad, Aisha. 2011. 'British Football: Where Are the Muslim Female Footballers? Exploring the Connections between Gender, Ethnicity and Islam'. *Soccer & Society* 12 (3): 443–56. https://doi.org/10.1080/14660970.2011.568110.

Aitchison, Cara Carmichael, ed. 2004. *Sport and Gender Identities: Masculinities, Femininities and Sexualities*. London: Routledge.

Alpert, Rebecca T. 2015. *Religion and Sports: An Introduction and Case Studies*. New York: Columbia University Press.

Amir-Moazami, Schirin. 2010. 'Avoiding "Youthfulness"?: Young Muslims Negotiating Gender and Citizenship in France and Germany'. In *Being Young and Muslim: New Cultural Politics in the Global South and North*, edited by Linda Herrera and Asef Bayat, 189–206. Oxford: Oxford University Press.

Anderson, Eric. 2008. '"I Used to Think Women Were Weak": Orthodox Masculinity, Gender Segregation, and Sport'. *Sociological Forum* 23 (2): 257–80. https://doi.org/10.1111/j.1573-7861.2008.00058.x.

Archer, Louise. 2003. *Race, Masculinity and Schooling: Muslim Boys and Education*. Berkshire: Open University Press.

Archer, Louise. 2009. 'Race, "Face" and Masculinity: The Identities and Local Geographies of Muslim Boys'. In *Muslims in Britain. Race, Place and Identities*, edited by Peter Hopkins and Richard Gale, 74–91. Edinburgh: Edinburgh University Press.

Asad, Talal. 2003. *Formations of the Secular. Christianity, Islam, Modernity*. Stanford: Stanford University Press.

Asscher, Lodewijk F. 2013. 'Participatieverklaring'. Den Haag. Available online: https://www.tweedekamer.nl/kamerstukken/brieven_regering/detail?id=2013Z25324&did=2013D51653.

Asscher, Lodewijk F.. 2015. 'Participatieverklaring'. Den Haag. Available online: https://zoek.officielebekendmakingen.nl/kst-32824-115.html.

Azzarito, Laura. 2010. 'Future Girls, Transcendent Femininities and New Pedagogies: Toward Girls' Hybrid Bodies?' *Sport, Education and Society* 15 (3): 261–75. https://doi.org/10.1080/13573322.2010.493307.

Azzarito, Laura. 2018. 'Re-Focusing the Image of the "Superwoman" with "No Colour": "Writing Back to the Centre" from a Globalised View'. In *New Sporting Femininities: Embodied Politics in Postfeminist Times*, edited by Kim Toffoletti, Holly Thorpe and Jessica Francombe-Webb, 135–57. Cham: Palgrave Macmillan.

Bale, John, and Mike Cronin, eds. 2003. *Sport and Postcolonialism*. Oxford: Berg.

Beauvoir, Simone de. [1949] 2011. *The Second Sex*. New York: Vintage Books.

Benn, Tansin, and Gertrud Pfister. 2013. 'Meeting Needs of Muslim Girls in School Sport: Case Studies Exploring Cultural and Religious Diversity'. *European Journal of Sport Science* 13 (5): 567–74. https://doi.org/10.1080/17461391.2012.757808.

Benn, Tansin, Gertrud Pfister and Haifaa Jawad, eds. 2011. *Muslim Women and Sport*. London: Routledge.

Berg, Marguerite van den, and Willem Schinkel. 2009. '"Women from the Catacombs of the City": Gender Notions in Dutch Culturist Discourse'. *Innovation – The European Journal of Social Science Research* 22 (4): 393–410. https://doi.org/10.1080/13511610903108877.

Besnier, Niko, and Susan Brownell. 2012. 'Sport, Modernity, and the Body'. *Annual Review of Anthropology* 41: 443–59. https://doi.org/10.1146/annurev-anthro-092611-145934.

Besnier, Niko, Susan Brownell and Thomas Carter. 2018. *The Anthropology of Sport: Bodies, Borders, Biopolitics*. Oakland: University of California Press.

Bilge, Sirma. 2014. 'Whitening Intersectionality: Evanescence of Race in Intersectionality Scholarship'. In *Racism and Sociology*, edited by Wulf D. Hund and Alana Lentin, 175–206. Zürich: Lit Verlag.

Blazer, Annie. 2015. *Playing for God: Evangelical Women and the Unintended Consequences of Sports Ministry*. New York: New York University Press.

Boeije, Hennie. 2010. *Analysis in Qualitative Research*. London: Sage.

van den Bogert, Kathrine. 2018. 'Religious Superdiversity and Intersectionality on the Field'. *Tijdschrift Voor Genderstudies* 21 (1): 27–44. https://doi.org/10.5117/TVGN2018.1.BOGE.

van den Bogert, Kathrine. 2021. '"If Geert Wilders Has Freedom of Speech, We Have Freedom of Speech!": Girls' Soccer, Race, and Embodied Knowledge in/of the Netherlands'. *Transforming Anthropology* 29 (1): 58–72. https://doi.org/10.1111/traa.12201.

Bolin, Anne, and Jane Granskog. 2003. 'Reflexive Ethnography, Women, and Sporting Activities'. In *Athletic Intruders: Ethnographic Research on Women, Culture, and Exercise*, edited by Anne Bolin and Jane Granskog, 7–25. New York: State University of New York Press.

Bouras, Nadia. 2012. *Het Land van Herkomst: Perspectieven Op Verbondenheid Met Marokko, 1960-2010*. Hilversum: Uitgeverij Verloren.

Bracke, Sarah. 2008. 'Conjugating the Modern/Religious, Conceptualizing Female Religious Agency: Contours of a "Post-Secular" Conjuncture'. *Theory, Culture & Society* 25 (6): 51–67. https://doi.org/10.1177/0263276408095544.

Bracke, Sarah. 2011. 'Subjects of Debate: Secular and Sexual Exceptionalism, and Muslim Women in the Netherlands'. *Feminist Review* 98 (1): 28–46. https://doi.org/10.1057/fr.2011.5.

Bracke, Sarah. 2012. 'From "Saving Women" to "Saving Gays": Rescue Narratives and Their Dis/Continuities'. *European Journal of Women's Studies* 19 (2): 237–52. https://doi.org/10.1177/1350506811435032.

Bracke, Sarah. 2013. 'Transformations of the Secular and the "Muslim Question": Revisiting the Historical Coincidence of Depillarisation and the Institutionalisation of Islam in the Netherlands'. *Journal of Muslims in Europe* 2 (2): 208–26. https://doi.org/10.1163/22117954-12341264.

van den Brandt, Nella. 2019. '"The Muslim Question" and Muslim Women Talking Back'. *Journal of Muslims in Europe* 8 (31): 58–72. https://doi.org/10.1163/22117954-12341404.

Brah, Avtar, and Ann Phoenix. 2004. 'Ain't I a Woman? Revisiting Intersectionality'. *Journal of International Women's Studies* 5 (3): 286–312. https://vc.bridgew.edu/jiws/vol5/iss3/8.

Braidotti, Rosi. 2008. 'In Spite of the Times: The Postsecular Turn in Feminism'. *Theory, Culture & Society* 25 (6): 1–24. https://doi.org/10.1177/0263276408095542.

Brooks, Abigail, and Sharlene Nagy Hesse-Biber. 2007. 'An Invitation to Feminist Research'. In *Feminist Research Practice: A Primer*, edited by Sharlene Nagy Hesse-Biber and Patricia Lina Leavy, 1–26. Thousand Oaks: Sage.

Brubaker, Rogers. 2013. 'Categories of Analysis and Categories of Practice: A Note on the Study of Muslims in European Countries of Immigration'. *Ethnic and Racial Studies* 36 (1): 1–8. https://doi.org/10.1080/01419870.2012.729674.

Buch, Elana D., and Karen M. Staller. 2007. 'The Feminist Practice of Ethnography'. In *Feminist Research Practice: A Primer*, edited by Sharlene Nagy Hesse-Biber and Patricia Lina Leavy, 187–222. Thousand Oaks: Sage.

Bucholtz, Mary. 2003. 'Theories of Discourse as Theories of Gender: Discourse Analysis in Language and Gender Studies'. In *The Handbook of Language and Gender*, edited by Janet Holmes and Miriam Meyerhoff, 43–68. Malden: Blackwell.

Buma, Sybrand H. 2017. *'Verwarde Tijden!' Die Om Richting Vragen. HJ Schoo Lezing 2017*. Amsterdam: Elsevier.

Burrmann, Ulrike, and Michael Mutz. 2016. 'Sport Participation of Muslim Youths in Germany'. In *Sport in Islam and in Muslim Communities*, edited by Alberto Testa and Mahfoud Amara, 33–49. London: Routledge.

Butler, Judith. 1990. *Gender Trouble: Feminism and the Subversion of Identity*. New York: Routledge.

Butler, Judith. 1993. *Bodies That Matter: On the Discursive Limits of 'Sex'*. New York: Routledge.

Butler, Judith. 1998. 'Athletic Genders: Hyperbolic Instance and/or the Overcoming of Sexual Binarism'. *Stanford Humanities Review* 6 (2): 103–11.

Butler, Judith. 2008. 'Sexual Politics, Torture, and Sexular Time'. *British Journal of Sociology* 59 (1): 1–23. https://doi.org/10.1111/j.1468-4446.2007.00176.x.

'Buurtmonitor Den Haag'. 2017. Available online: https://denhaag.buurtmonitor.nl/home.

Çankaya, Sinan. 2015. 'De Ruimtelijke Regulering van Risicovolle Burgers Tijdens Proactief Politiewerk'. In *Diversiteit En Discriminatie: Onderzoek Naar Processen van in- En Uitsluiting*, edited by Marija Davidovic and Ashley Terlouw, 103–21. Amsterdam: Amsterdam University Press.

Carrington, Ben. 2008. '"What's the Footballer Doing Here?" Racialized Performativity, Reflexivity, and Identity'. *Cultural Studies <=> Critical Methodologies* 8 (4): 423–52. https://doi.org/10.1177/1532708608321574.

Carrington, Ben. 2010. *Race, Sport and Politics: The Sporting Black Diaspora*. London: Sage. https://doi.org/10.4135/9781446269244.

Caudwell, Jayne. 1999. 'Women's Football in the United Kingdom: Theorizing Gender and Unpacking the Butch Lesbian Image'. *Journal of Sport & Social Issues* 23 (4): 390–402. https://doi.org/10.1177/0193723599234003.

Caudwell, Jayne. 2003. 'Sporting Gender: Women's Footballing Bodies as Sites/Sights for the (Re) Articulation of Sex, Gender, and Desire'. *Sociology of Sport Journal* 20 (4): 371–86. https://doi.org/10.1123/ssj.20.4.371.

Caudwell, Jayne. 2011. 'Reviewing UK Football Cultures: Continuing with Gender Analyses'. *Soccer & Society* 12 (3): 323–9. https://doi.org/10.1080/14660970.2011.568097.

CBS. 2016. *Jaarrapport Integratie 2016*. Den Haag: Centraal Bureau voor de Statistiek.

CBS. 2021. 'Hoeveel Mensen Met Een Migratieachtergrond Wonen in Nederland?' Dossier Asiel, Migratie En Integratie. 2021. Available online: https://www.cbs.nl/nl-nl/dossier/dossier-asiel-migratie-en-integratie/hoeveel-mensen-met-een-migratieachtergrond-wonen-in-nederland-.

Cevaal, Astrid. 2017. 'In de Sportmedia Blijft Vrouwenvoetbal Bijzaak'. In *Vrouwenvoetbal in Nederland: Spiegel En Katalysator van Maatschappelijke Verandering*, edited by Martine Prange and Martijn Oosterbaan, 191–208. Utrecht: Klement.

Cevaal, Astrid, and David Romijn. 2011. *Pubers, Panna's & Playgrounds: Opvattingen van Jongeren over Het Sporten Op Moderne Playgrounds*. 's Hertogenbosch: W.J.H. Mulier Instituut.

Christensen, Pia, and Miguel Romero Mikkelsen. 2013. '"There Is Nothing Here for Us..!" How Girls Create Meaningful Places of Their Own through Movement'. *Children and Society* 27 (3): 197–207. https://doi.org/10.1111/j.1099-0860.2011.00413.x.

Claringbould, Inge, and Annelies Knoppers. 2013. 'Understanding the Lack of Gender Equity in Leadership Positions in (Sport) Organization'. In *Managing Social Issues: A Public Values Perspective*, edited by Peter Leisink, Paul Boselie, Maarten van Bottenburg and Dian Marie Hosking, 162–82. Cheltenham: Edwards Elgar.

Clark, Sheryl, and Carrie Paechter. 2007. '"Why Can't Girls Play Football?" Gender Dynamics and the Playground'. *Sport, Education & Society* 12 (3): 261–76. https://doi.org/10.1080/13573320701464085.

Collins, Patricia Hill. 2000. *Black Feminist Thought: Knowledge, Consciousness, and the Politics of Empowerment*. New York: Routledge.

Crenshaw, Kimberlé Williams, Priscilla Ocen and Jyoti Nanda. 2015. *Black Girls Matter: Pushed out, Overpoliced, and Underprotected*. New York: African American Policy Forum and Center for Intersectionality and Social Policy Studies. Available online: https://www.atlanticphilanthropies.org/wp-content/uploads/2015/09/BlackGirlsMatter_Report.pdf.

Crul, Maurice, Jens Schneider and Frans Lelie. 2013. *Super Diversity: A New Perspective on Integration*. Amsterdam: VU University Press.

Dagkas, Symeon, Tansin Benn and Kelly Knez. 2014. 'Religion, Culture and Sport in the Lives of Young Muslim Women: International Perspectives'. In *Routledge Handbook of Sport, Gender and Sexuality*, edited by Jennifer Hargreaves and Eric Anderson, 198–205. London: Routledge.

Davis, Dána-Ain, and Christa Craven. 2016. *Feminist Ethnography: Thinking through Methodologies, Challenges, and Possibilities*. Lanham: Rowman & Littlefield.

De Martini Ugolotti, Nicola. 2015. 'Climbing Walls, Making Bridges: Children of Immigrants' Identity Negotiations through Capoeira and Parkour in Turin'. *Leisure Studies* 34 (1): 19–33. https://doi.org/10.1080/02614367.2014.966746.

Deeb, Lara. 2015. 'Thinking Piety and the Everyday Together: A Response to Fadil and Fernando'. *HAU: Journal of Ethnographic Theory* 5 (2): 93–6. https://doi.org/10.14318/hau5.2.007.

Deeb, Lara, and Mona Harb. 2013. *Leisurely Islam: Negotiating Geography and Morality in Shi'ite South Beirut*. Princeton, NJ: Princeton University Press.

Derks, Marjet. 2017. 'Nette Vrouwen Zweten Niet: Sportvrouwen van Marginalisering Naar Profilering'. In *Vrouwenvoetbal in Nederland: Spiegel En Katalysator van Maatschappelijke Verandering*, edited by Martine Prange and Martijn Oosterbaan, 37–59. Utrecht: Klement.

Dhawan, Nikita, and Maria do Mar Castro Varela. 2016. '"What Difference Does Difference Make?": Diversity, Intersectionality, and Transnational Feminist Politics'. *Wagadu* 16 (16): 11–39.

Dortants, Marianne, and Annelies Knoppers. 2013. 'Regulation of Diversity through Discipline: Practices of Inclusion and Exclusion in Boxing'. *International Review for the Sociology of Sport* 48 (5): 535–49. https://doi.org/10.1177/1012690212445279.

Duijndam, Corina, and Baukje Prins. 2017. *Geboren En Getuige in de Schilderswijk: Verhalen van Jongeren in Een Haagse Wijk over Vertrouwen in de Politie*. Den Haag: De Haagse Hogeschool.

Duyvendak, Jan Willem. 2011. *The Politics of Home: Belonging and Nostalgia in Western Europe and the United States*. New York: Palgrave Macmillan.

Duyvendak, Jan Willem, Menno Hurenkamp and Evelien Tonkens. 2010. 'Culturalization of Citizenship in the Netherlands'. In *Managing Ethnic Diversity after 9/11*, edited by Ariane Chebel d'Appolonia and Simon Reich, 233–52. New Brunswick: Rutgers Universtiy Press.

Dyck, Noel. 2008. 'Anthropological Perspectives on Discipline: An Introduction to the Issues'. In *Exploring Regimes of Discipline: The Dynamics of Restraint*, edited by Noel Dyck, 1–22. New York: Berghahn Books.

Dyck, Noel. 2012. *Fields of Play: An Ethnography of Children's Sports*. Toronto: University of Toronto Press.

Echo. 2013. 'Straatvoetbal Is Een Lifestyle'. *Stadsblad De Echo*, 18 September. Available online: https://imagineic.nl/content/uploads/2020/01/Straatvoetbal-is-een-lifestyle-Echo-18-september-2013.pdf.

El-Tayeb, Fatima. 2011. *European Others: Queering Ethnicity in Postnational Europe*. Minneapolis: University of Minnesota Press.

El-Tayeb, Fatima. 2012. '"Gays Who Cannot Properly Be Gay": Queer Muslims in the Neoliberal European City'. *European Journal of Women's Studies* 19 (1): 79–95. https://doi.org/10.1177/1350506811426388.

Elhage, Hassnah Z. S. 2017. 'De Strijd Om Gelijkheid in Het Nederlandse Voetbal'. In *Vrouwenvoetbal in Nederland: Spiegel En Katalysator van Maatschappelijke Verandering*, edited by Martine Prange and Martijn Oosterbaan, 80–98. Utrecht: Klement.

Elling, Agnes. 2004. 'Bewegende Beelden: Sport, Sekse En Etniciteit'. *Tijdschrift Voor Genderstudies* 7 (1): 44–57.

Elling, Agnes. 2005. 'De Hollandse Dames Zwemclub, de Islamitische Waterlelies, En de Vraag van Wie Het Zwembad Is'. In *Cultuur En Migratie in Nederland. Veranderingen van Het Alledaagse 1950–2000*, edited by Isabel Hoving, Hester Dibbits and Marlou Schrover, 227–48. Den Haag: Sdu Uitgevers.

Elling, Agnes. 2015. 'Feminisering van Sportieve Ruimten'. *Agora* 31 (1): 20–2. https://doi.org/10.21825/agora.v31i1.1993.

Elling, Agnes, and Annelies Knoppers. 2005. 'Sport, Gender and Ethnicity: Practises of Symbolic Inclusion/Exclusion'. *Journal of Youth and Adolescence* 34 (3): 257–68. https://doi.org/10.1007/s10964-005-4311-6.

Elling, Agnes, and Inge Claringbould. 2005. 'Mechanisms of Inclusion and Exclusion in the Dutch Sports Landscape: Who Can and Wants to Belong?' *Sociology of Sport Journal* 22 (4): 498–515. https://doi.org/10.1123/ssj.22.4.498.

Elling, Agnes, and Rens Cremers. 2021. 'Sportgedrag En Ervaren Racisme Etnische Minderheden'. Utrecht: Mulier Instituut.

Elling, Agnes, Ivo van Hilvoorde and Remko van den Dool. 2014. 'Creating or Awakening National Pride through Sporting Success: A Longitudinal Study on Macro Effects in the Netherlands'. *International Review for the Sociology of Sport* 49 (2): 129–51. https://doi.org/10.1177/1012690212455961.

Elling, Agnes, Rens Peeters and Leonne Stentler. 2017. 'Tussen Nieuwe Heldinnen, Voetbalbabes En Lerende Amateurs'. In *Vrouwenvoetbal in Nederland: Spiegel En Katalysator van Maatschappelijke Verandering*, edited by Martine Prange and Martijn Oosterbaan, 209–36. Utrecht: Klement.

ERIC. 2013. 'Informed Consent'. *Ethical Guidance*. Lismore, Australia. Available online: http://childethics.com/wp-content/uploads/2013/10/ERIC-compendium-Ethical-Guidance-Informed-consent-section-only.pdf.

van Es, Margaretha A. 2016. *Stereotypes and Self-Representations of Women with a Muslim Background*. London: Palgrave Macmillan.

van Es, Margaretha A. 2018. 'Islam, Intersectionaliteit En Superdiversiteit. Ofwel: Wie Interesseert Zich Voor Moslima's van Boven de Veertig?' *Tijdschrift Voor Genderstudies* 20 (1): 69–74. https://doi.org/10.5117/TVGN2 018.1.MARG.

van Es, Margaretha A. 2019. 'The Promise of the Social Contract: Muslim Perspectives on the Culturalization of Citizenship and the Demand to Denounce Violent Extremism'. *Ethnic and Racial Studies* 42 (16): 141–58. https://doi.org/10.1080/01419870.2019.1600710.

Essed, Philomena, and Kwame Nimako. 2006. 'Designs and (Co)Incidents: Cultures of Scholarship and Public Policy on Immigrants/Minorities in the Netherlands'. *International Journal of Comparative Sociology* 47: 281–312. https://doi.org/10.1177/0020715206065784.

Evaldsson, Ann-Carita. 2003. 'Throwing like a Girl? Situating Gender Differences in Physicality across Game Contexts'. *Childhood: A Global Journal of Child Research* 10 (4): 475–97. https://doi.org/10.1177/0907568203104006.

Evans, Bethan. 2006. '"I'd Feel Ashamed": Girls' Bodies and Sports Participation'. *Gender, Place & Culture* 13 (5): 547–61. https://doi.org/10.1080/0966369060 0858952.

Ezzeroili, Nadia. 2018. 'Waarom Het Woord Kech Ons Altijd Treft Als Een Mokerslag (En Aanhaken Bij #MeToo Lastig Is)'. *Volkskrant*, 3 January 2018. Availble online: https://www.volkskrant.nl/opinie/waarom-het-woord-kech-ons-altijd-treft-als-een-mokerslag-en-aanhaken-bij-metoo-lastig-is~a4556745/.

Fadil, Nadia. 2011. 'Not-/Unveiling As an Ethical Practice'. *Feminist Review* 98 (1): 83–109. https://doi.org/10.1057/fr.2011.12.

Fadil, Nadia, and Mayanthi Fernando. 2015. 'Rediscovering the "Everyday" Muslim: Notes on an Anthropological Divide'. *HAU: Journal of Ethnographic Theory* 5 (2): 59–88. https://doi.org/10.14318/hau5.2.005.

Farooq, Samaya. 2011. '"Tough Talk", Muscular Islam and Football: Young British Pakistani Muslim Masculinities'. In *Race, Ethnicity and Football: Persisting Debates and Emergint Issues*, edited by Daniel Burdsey, 145–62. New York: Routledge.

Ferguson, Ann Arnett. 2001. *Bad Boys: Public Schools in the Making of Black Masculinity*. Ann Arbor: University of Michigan Press.

Fernando, Mayanthi L. 2014. *The Republic Unsettled: Muslim French and the Contradictions of Secularism*. Durham: Duke University Press.

Fernando, Mayanthi L. 2016. 'The Unpredictable Imagination of Muslim French: Citizenship, Public Religiosity, and Political Possibility in France'. In *Muslim Youth and the 9/11 Generation*, edited by Adeline Masquelier and Benjamin Soares, 123–50. Santa Fe: School for Advanced Research.

Foley, Carmel, Tracy Taylor and Hazel Maxwell. 2011. 'Gender and Cultural Diversity in Australian Sport'. In *Sport and Challenges to Racism*, edited by Jonathan Long and Karl Spracklen, 167–84. Basingstoke: Palgrave Macmillan.

Fonow, Mary Margaret, and Judith A. Cook. 2005. 'Feminist Methodology: New Applications in the Academy and Public Policy'. *Signs: Journal of Women in Culture and Society* 30 (4): 2211–36. https://doi.org/10.1086/428417.

Foucault, Michel. 1977. *Discipline and Punish. The Birth of the Prison*. New York: Vintage Books.

Foucault, Michel. 1989. *Discipline, Toezicht En Straf: De Geboorte van de Gevangenis*. Groningen: Historische Uitgeverij.

Franke, Simon, Lenneke Overmaat and Arnold Reijndorp. 2014. *Plekken van Betekenis in de Schilderswijk: Publiek Domein Als Strategie*. Haarlem: Trancity.

Friedman, Hilary Levey. 2013. *Playing to Win: Raising Children in a Competitive Culture*. Oakland: University of California Press.

Gagen, Elizabeth A. 2000. 'Playing the Part: Performing Gender in America's Playgrounds'. In *Children's Geographies: Playing, Living, Learning*, edited by Sarah L. Holloway and Gill Valentine, 213–29. London: Routledge.

Geense, Paul. 2004. 'De Ontwikkeling van Schilderswijk En Bouwlust'. In *Interetnische Contacten Op Portieken En in Voetbalclubs*, edited by Theo Veld, 9–24. Rotterdam: ISEO.

Göle, Nilüfer. 2006. 'Europe's Encounter with Islam: What Future?' *Constellations* 13 (2): 248–62. Available online: https://f.hypotheses.org/wp-content/blogs.dir/96/files/2012/11/2006-Europe-s-Encounter-with-Islam-What-Future.pdf.

Green, Eileen, and Carrie Singleton. 2007. '"Safe and Risky Spaces"': Gender, Ethnicity and Culture in the Leisure Lives of Young South Asian Women'. In *Geographies of Muslim Identities: Diaspora, Gender and Belonging*, edited by Cara Aitchison, Peter Hopkins and Mei-Po Kwan, 109–24. Aldershot: Ashgate.

Hall, Stuart. 1997. 'The Work of Representation'. In *Representation: Cultural Representations and Signifying Practices*, edited by Stuart Hall, 13–74. London: Sage.

Hall, Stuart. 2017. *The Fateful Triangle: Race, Ethnicity, Nation*. Edited by Kobena Mercer and Stuart Hall. London: Harvard University Press.

Haraway, Donna Jeanne. 1988. 'Situated Knowledges: The Science Question in Feminism and the Privilege of Partial Perspective'. *Feminist Studies* 14 (3): 575–99. https://doi.org/10.2307/3178066.

Hargreaves, Jennifer, and Patricia Vertinsky, eds. 2007. *Physical Culture, Power, and the Body*. London: Routledge.

Harris, Anita. 2004. *Future Girl: Young Women in the Twenty-First Century*. New York: Routledge.

van den Hemel, Ernst. 2014. '(Pro)Claiming Tradition: The "Judeo-Christian" Roots of Dutch Society and the Rise of Conservative Nationalism'. In *Transformations of Religion and the Public Sphere. Postsecular Publics*, edited by Rosi Braidotti, Bolette Blaagaard, Tobijn de Graauw and Eva Midden, 53–76. Basingstoke: Palgrave Macmillan.

Henkel, Heiko. 2009a. 'Are Muslim Women in Europe Threatening the Secular Public Sphere?' *Social Anthropology* 17 (4): 471–73. https://doi.org/10.1111/j.1469-8676.2009.00086_1.x.

Henkel, Heiko. 2009b. 'Response to Thijl Sunier'. *Social Anthropology* 17 (4): 476–7. https://doi.org/10.1111/j.1469-8676.2009.00086_3.x.

van den Heuvel, Nathanja. 2017. 'Gendersegregatie versus Emancipatie En de Toekomst van Het Nederlandse Topvoetbal'. In *Vrouwenvoetbal in Nederland: Spiegel En Katalysator van Maatschappelijke Verandering*, edited by Martine Prange and Martijn Oosterbaan, 171–88. Utrecht: Klement.

Hirschkind, Charles. 2011. 'Is There a Secular Body?' *Cultural Anthropology* 26 (4): 633–47. https://doi.org/10.1111/j.1548-1360.2011.01116.x.

Hoekman, Remco, Agnes Elling, Jan-Willem van der Roest and Fleur van Rens. 2011a. 'Meedoen Alle Jeugd Door Sport: Georganiseerde Sport Bewijst Zich'. In *Zonder Doel Kan Je Niet Scoren: Momenten Met Focus Op Sportparticipatie van Kansengroepen*, 17–25. Brussels: Demos vzw, kenniscentrum voor participatie en democratie.

Hoekman, Remco, Agnes Elling, Jan-Willem van der Roest and Fleur van Rens. 2011b. *Opbrengsten van Meedoen. Evaluatie Programma Meedoen Alle Jeugd Door Sport*. 's-Hertogenbosch: W.J.H. Mulier Instituut.

Hoff, Stella, Jean Marie Wildeboer Schut, Benedikt Goderis and Cok Vrooman. 2016. *Armoede in Kaart 2016*. Den Haag: Sociaal en Cultureel Planbureau. Available online: https://digitaal.scp.nl/armoedeinkaart2016/assets/pdf/armoede_in_kaart_2016-SCP.pdf.

Holston, James, and Arjun Appadurai. 1999. 'Cities and Citizenship'. In *Cities and Citizenship*, edited by James Holston, 1–18. Durham: Duke University Press.

Hoodfar, Homa, ed. 2015. *Women's Sport as Politics in Muslim Contexts*. London: Women Living under Muslim Laws.

hooks, bell. 1989. *Talking Back: Thinking Feminist, Thinking Black*. Boston: South End Press.

hooks, bell. 2015. *Talking Back: Thinking Feminist, Thinking Black*. New York: Routledge.

Houdijk, Gijs, and Mike Ekelschot. 2014. 'Sporten in de Schilderswijk'. In *De Maakbare Stad. Rondkijken in Den Haag. Haagse Sociale En Culturele Verkenningen 3*, edited by Vincent Smit, 33–8. Den Haag: Lectoraat Grootstedelijke Ontwikkeling, De Haagse Hogeschool.

Huijnk, Willem, and Iris Andriessen. 2016. *Integratie in Zicht?* Den Haag: Sociaal en Cultureel Planbureau.

Ifekwunigwe, Jayne O. 2017. '"And Still Serena Rises": Celebrating the Cross-Generational Continuities of Black Feminisms and Black Female Excellence in Sport'. In *The Palgrave Handbook of Feminism and Sport, Leisure and Physical Education*, edited by Louise Mansfield, Jayne Caudwell, Belinda Wheaton and Beccy Watson, 111–31. London: Palgrave Macmillan. https://doi.org/10.1057/978-1-137-53318-0_8.

Jaffe-Walter, Reva. 2016. *Coercive Concern: Nationalism, Liberalism, and the Schooling of Muslim Youth*. Stanford: Stanford University Press.

Jaffe, Rivke, and Anouk de Koning. 2015. *Introducing Urban Anthropology*. London: Routledge.

Jeanes, Ruth. 2011. '"I'm into High Heels and Make up but I Still Love Football": Exploring Gender Identity and Football Participation with Preadolescent Girls'. *Soccer & Society* 12 (3): 402–20. https://doi.org/10.1080/14660970.2011.568107.

Jiwani, Nisara, and Geneviève Rail. 2010. 'Islam, Hijab and Young Shia Muslim Canadian Women's Discursive Constructions of Physical Activity'. *Sociology of Sport Journal* 27 (3): 251–67. https://doi.org/10.1123/ssj.27.3.251.

Jones, Guno. 2014. 'Biology, Culture, "Postcolonial Citizenship" and the Dutch Nation, 1945-2007'. In *Dutch Racism*, edited by Isabel Hoving and Philomena Essed, 315–36. Amsterdam: Rodopi.

de Jong, Jan Dirk. 2007. *Kapot Moeilijk: Een Etnografi sch Onderzoek Naar Opvallend Delinquent Groupsgedrag van 'Marokkaanse' Jongens*. Amsterdam: Aksant.

Karsten, Lia. 2003. 'Children's Use of Public SpJace: The Gendered World of the Playground'. *Childhood* 10 (4): 457–73. https://doi.org/10.1177/0907568203104005.

Kay, Tess. 2006. 'Daughters of Islam: Family Influences on Muslim Young Women's Participation in Sport'. *International Review for the Sociology of Sport* 41 (3–4): 357–73. https://doi.org/10.1177/1012690207077705.

Klein Kranenburg, Diederick Johannes. 2013. *'Samen Voor Ons Eigen': De Geschiedenis van Een Nederlandse Volksbuurt: De Haagse Schilderswijk 1920–1985*. Leiden: Uitgeverij Verloren.

KNVB. 2009. 'Tijd Voor Sport: Werven En Behouden (Allochtone) Meisjes'. Zeist: KNVB.

KNVB. 2014. 'Werving En Behoud van Meidenvoetbal'. Zeist: KNVB.

de Koning, Anouk. 2013. 'Creating an Exceptional Problem Neighbourhood: Media, Policy, and Amsterdam's "Notorious" Diamantbuurt'. *Etnofoor* 25 (2): 13–30. Available online: https://www.jstor.org/stable/43264018.

de Koning, Anouk. 2015a. 'Citizenship Agendas for the Abject: The Production of Distrust in Amsterdam's Youth and Security Domain'. *Citizenship Studies* 19 (2): 155–68. https://doi.org/10.1080/13621 025.2015.1005 947.

de Koning, Anouk. 2015b. '"This Neighbourhood Deserves an Espresso Bar Too": Neoliberalism, Racialization, and Urban Policy'. *Antipode* 47 (5): 1203–23. https://doi.org/10.1111/anti.12150.

de Koning, Anouk. 2016. 'Tracing Anxious Politics in Amsterdam'. *Patterns of Prejudice* 50 (2): 109–28. https://doi.org/10.1080/00313 22X.2016.1161 387.

de Koning, Martijn. 2008. *Zoeken Naar Een 'zuivere' Islam: Geloofsbeleving En Identiteitsvorming van Jonge Marokkaans-Nederlandse Moslims*. Amsterdam: Uitgeverij Bert Bakker.

de, Koning, Martijn. 2012. 'Moslims Tellen: Reflectie Op Onderzoek Naar Islam, Moslims En Secularisering in Nederland'. In *Moslim in Nederland* 2012, edited by Mieke Maliepaard and Mérove Gijsberts, 160–8. Den Haag: Sociaal en Cultureel Planbureau.

de Koning, Martijn. 2016. 'You Need to Present a Counter-Message'. *Journal of Muslims in Europe* 5 (2): 170–89. https://doi.org/10.1163/22117 954-12341 325.

de Koning, Martijn, Joas Wagemakers and Carmen Becker. 2014. *Salafi sme: Utopische Idealen in Een Weerbarstige Praktijk*. Almere: Parthenon.

Krouwel, André, Nanne Boonstra, Jan Willem Duyvendak and Lex Veldboer. 2006. 'A Good Sport? Research into the Capacity of Recreational Sport to Integrate Dutch Minorities'. *International Review for the Sociology of Sport* 41 (2): 165–80. https://doi.org/10.1177/1012690206075419.

Lammers, Dick, and Wouter Reith. 2014. 'Jongeren in de Schilderswijk'. In *De Maakbare Stad. Rondkijken in Den Haag. Haagse Sociale En Culturele Verkenningen 3*, edited by Vincent Smit, 23–31. Den Haag: Lectoraat Grootstedelijke Ontwikkeling, De Haagse Hogeschool.

Lazar, Sian. 2014. 'Citizenship'. In *A Companion to Urban Anthropology*, edited by Donald M. Nonini, 65–82. Chichester: Wiley Blackwell.

van der Leun, Joanne. 2005. 'Naast Elkaar En Langs Elkaar Heen: De Bewoners van Het Haagse Hobbemaplein'. In *Cultuur En Migratie in Nederland. Veranderingen van Het Alledaagse 1950–2000*, edited by Isabel Hoving, Hester Dibbits and Marlou Schrover, 303–14. Den Haag: Sdu Uitgevers.

Liberatore, Giulia. 2017. *Somali, Muslim, British: Striving in Securitized Britain*. London: Bloomsbury.

Lindner, Lucia. 2002. *Ruimtelijke Segregatie van Afkomstgroepen in Den Haag. Wiens Keuze?* Den Haag: Bureau Discriminatiezaken.

Lockwood, Penelope. 2006. '"Someone like Me Can Be Successful": Do College Students Need Same-Gender Role Models?' *Psychology of Women Quarterly* 30 (1): 36–46. https://doi.org/10.1111/j.1471-6402.2006.00260.x.

Long, Jonathan, and Karl Spracklen, eds. 2011. *Sport and Challenges to Racism*. Basingstoke: Palgrave Macmillan.

Lorde, Audre. 2007. *Sister Outsider: Essays and Speeches*. Berkeley: Crossing Press.

Mahmood, Saba. 2005. *Politics of Piety: The Islamic Revival and the Feminist Subject*. Princeton: Princeton University Press.

Marchetti, Sabrina. 2016. 'Resentment at the Heart of Europe: Narratives by Afro-Surinamese Postcolonial Migrant Women in the Netherlands'. In *Postcolonial Transitions in Europe: Contexts, Practices and Politics*, edited by Sandra Ponzanesi and Gianmaria Colpani, 133–47. London: Rowman & Littlefield International.

Markula, Pirkko, and Richard Pringle. 2006. *Foucault, Sport and Exercise. Power, Knowledge and Transforming the Self*. London: Routledge.

Martin, Karin A. 1998. 'Becoming a Gendered Body: Practices of Preschools'. *American Sociological Review* 63 (4): 494–511. https://doi.org/10.2307/2657264.

Martin, Karin A. 1996. *Puberty, Sexuality, and the Self*. New York: Routledge.

Martineau, Erin M. 2006. '"Too Much Tolerance": Hang-around Youth, Public Space, and the Problem of Freedom in the Netherlands." PhD thesis, The City University of New York.

Masquelier, Adeline, and Benjamin F. Soares, eds. 2016. *Muslim Youth and the 9/11 Generation*. Santa Fe: School for Advanced Research.

Massey, Doreen. 1994. *Space, Place, and Gender*. Minneapolis: University of Minnesota Press.

McCall, Leslie. 2005. 'The Complexity of Intersectionality'. *Signs* 30 (3): 1771–1800. https://doi.org/10.1086/426800.

McClintock, Anne. 1995. *Imperial Leather: Race, Gender and Sexuality in the Colonial Contest*. New York: Routledge.

McDonald, Mary G. 2014. 'Mapping Intersectionality and Whiteness: Troubling Gender and Sexuality in Sport Studies'. In *Routledge Handbook of Sport, Gender and Sexuality*, edited by Jennifer Hargreaves and Eric Anderson, 151–9. London: Routledge.

Mepschen, Paul. 2016. 'The Culturalization of Everyday Life: Authochtony in Amsterdam New West'. In *The Culturalization of Citizenship. Belonging and Polarization in a Globalizing World*, edited by Jan Willem Duyvendak, Peter Geschiere and Evelien Tonkens, 73–96. Basingstoke: Palgrave Macmillan.

Mepschen, Paul, Jan Willem Duyvendak and Evelien H. Tonkens. 2010. 'Sexual Politics, Orientalism and Multicultural Citizenship in the Netherlands'. *Sociology* 44 (5): 962–79. https://doi.org/10.1177/0038038510375740.

Mercer, Kobena. 2017. 'Introduction'. In *The Fateful Triangle: Race, Ethnicity, Nation*, edited by Kobena Mercer and Stuart Hall, 1–30. London: Harvard University Press.

Modest, Wayne, and Anouk de Koning. 2016. 'Anxious Politics in the European City: An Introduction'. *Patterns of Prejudice* 50 (2): 97–108. https://doi.org/10.1080/0031322X.2016.1161384.

Mohanty, Chandra Talpade. 1988. 'Under Western Eyes: Feminist Scholarship and Colonial Discourses'. *Feminist Review* 30: 61–88. https://doi.org/10.2307/1395054.

Moors, Annelies. 2009. 'The Dutch and the Face-Veil: The Politics of Discomfort'. *Social Anthropology* 17 (4): 393–408. https://doi.org/10.1111/j.1469-8676.2009.00084.x.

Moors, Annelies, and Ruba Salih. 2009. '"Muslim Women" in Europe: Secular Normativities, Bodily Performances and Multiple Publics'. *Social Anthropology* 17 (4): 375–8. https://doi.org/10.1111/j.1469-8676.2009.00090.x.

Mora, Richard. 2012. '"Do It for All Your Pubic Hairs!": Latino Boys, Masculinity, and Puberty'. *Gender & Society* 26 (3): 433–60. https://doi.org/10.1177/0891243212440502.

Morris, Edward W. 2005. '"Tuck in That Shirt!" Race, Class, Gender, and Discipline in an Urban School'. *Sociological Perspectives* 48 (1): 25–48. https://doi.org/10.1525/sop.2005.48.1.25.

Narayan, Kirin. 1993. 'How Native Is a "Native" Anthropologist?' *American Anthropologist* 95 (3): 671–86. https://doi.org/10.1525/aa.1993.95.3.02a00070.

Nyhagen, Line, and Beatrice Halsaa. 2016. *Religion, Gender and Citizenship: Women of Faith, Gender Equality and Feminism*. New York: Palgrave Macmillan.

Oosterbaan, Martijn. 2014. 'Public Religion and Urban Space in Europe'. *Social & Cultural Geography* 15 (6): 591–602. https://doi.org/10.1080/14649365.2014.922605.

Ortner, Sherry B. 1974. 'Is Female to Male as Nature Is to Culture?' In *Woman, Culture and Society*, edited by Michelle Z. Rosaldo and Louise Lamphere, 68–87. Stanford: Stanford University Press.

Ortner, Sherry B., and Harriet Whitehead, eds. 1981. *Sexual Meanings: The Cultural Construction of Gender and Sexuality*. Cambridge: Cambridge University Press.

Pfister, Gertrud. 2010. 'Outsiders: Muslim Women and Olympic Games – Barriers and Opportunities'. *International Journal of the History of Sport* 27 (16–18): 2925–57. https://doi.org/10.1080/09523367.2010.508291.

Piela, Anna. 2017. 'How Do Muslim Women Who Wear the Niqab Interact with Others Online? A Case Study of a Profile on a Photo-Sharing Website'. *New Media & Society* 19 (1): 67–80. https://doi.org/10.1177/1461444816649919.

Postma, Annemarie. 2019. *Samen Sterk: Het Geheim van de Oranjeleeuwinnen*. Amsterdam: Atlas Contact.

Prange, Martine, and Martijn Oosterbaan, eds. 2017. *Vrouwenvoetbal in Nederland: Spiegel En Katalysator van Maatschappelijke Verandering*. Utrecht: Klement.

Pringle, Richard. 2014. 'Foucauldian Examinations of Sport, Gender and Sexuality'. In *Routledge Handbook of Sport, Gender and Sexuality*, edited by Jennifer Hargreaves and Eric Anderson, 397–405. New York: Routledge.

Prins, Baukje. 2002. 'The Nerve to Break Taboos: New Realism in the Dutch Discourse on Multiculturalism'. *Journal of International Migration and Integration* 3 (3–4): 363–79. https://doi.org/10.1007/s12134-002-1020-9.

Prouse, Carolyn. 2015. 'Harnessing the Hijab: The Emergence of the Muslim Female Footballer through International Sport Governance'. *Gender, Place and Culture* 22 (1): 20–36. https://doi.org/10.1080/0966369X.2013.832664.

Puwar, Nirmal. 2004. *Space Invaders: Race, Gender and Bodies Out of Place*. Oxford: Berg.

Ramji, Hasmita. 2007. 'Dynamics of Religion and Gender amongst Young British Muslims'. *Sociology* 41 (6): 1171–89. https://doi.org/10.1177/0038038507084832.

Rana, Jasmijn. 2014. 'Producing Healthy Citizens Encouraging Participation in Ladies-Only Kickboxing'. *Etnofoor* 26 (2): 33–48. https://www.jstor.org/stable/43264058.

Rana, Jasmijn. 2018. 'Ladies- Only! Empowerment and Comfort in Gender- Segregated Kickboxing in the Netherlands'. In *Race, Gender and Sport: The Politics of Ethnic "Other" Girls and Women*, edited by Aarti Ratna and Samaya Farooq Samie, 148–68. London: Routledge.

Ratna, Aarti. 2011. '"Who Wants to Make Aloo Gobi When You Can Bend It like Beckham?" British Asian Females and Their Racialised Experiences of Gender and Identity in Women's Football'. *Soccer & Society* 12 (3): 382–401. https://doi.org/10.1080/14660970.2011.568105.

Ratna, Aarti. 2014. 'British Asian Female Footballers: Intersections of Identity'. In *Routledge Handbook of Sport, Gender and Sexuality*, edited by Jennifer Hargreaves and Eric Anderson, 160–8. London: Routledge.

Ratna, Aarti, and Samaya Farooq Samie, eds. 2018. *Race, Gender and Sport: The Politics of Ethnic 'Other' Girls and Women*. London: Routledge. https://doi.org/10.4324/9781315637051.

Renold, Emma. 1997. '"All They've Got on Their Brains Is Football." Sport, Masculinity and the Gendered Practices of Playground Relations'. *Sport, Education and Society* 2 (1): 5–23. https://doi.org/10.1080/1357332970020101.

Renold, Emma. 2003. '"If You Don't Kiss Me, You're Dumped": Boys, Boyfriends and Heterosexualised Masculinities in the Primary School'. *Educational Review* 55 (2): 179–94. https://doi.org/10.1080/0013191032000072218.

Renold, Emma. 2005. *Girls, Boys and Junior Sexualities*. London: RoutledgeFalmer.

Rich, Adrienne. 1980. 'Compulsory Heterosexuality and Lesbian Existence'. *Signs: Journal of Women in Culture and Society* 5 (4): 631–60. https://doi.org/10.1086/493756.

Romijn, David, and Agnes Elling. 2017. 'Vrouwenvoetbal Is de Snelst Groeiende Sport': Over Ontwikkelingen in Deelname van Meisjes- En Vrouwenvoetbal. Utrecht: Mulier Instituut.

Rosaldo, Michelle Z. 1980. 'The Use and Abuse of Anthropology: Reflections on Feminism and Cross-Cultural Understanding'. *Signs: Journal of Women in Culture and Society* 5 (3): 389–417. https://doi.org/10.1086/493727.

de Ruiter, Frank. 2013. 'Panna's En Akka's: Laat Je Voeten Spreken'. MA dissertation, University of Amsterdam. Available online: https://scripties.uba.uva.nl/download?fid=612 801.

Ryan, Louise, and Elena Vacchelli. 2013. '"Mothering through Islam": Narratives of Religious Identity in London'. *Religion and Gender* 3 (1): 90–107. https://doi.org/10.18352/rg.8421.

Samie, Samaya Farooq. 2013. 'Hetero-Sexy Self/Body Work and Basketball: The Invisible Sporting Women of British Pakistani Muslim Heritage'. *South Asian Popular Culture* 11 (3): 257–70. https://doi.org/10.1080/14746689.2013.820480.

Samie, Samaya Farooq. 2018. 'De/Colonising "Sporting Muslim Women": Post-Colonial Feminist Reflections on the Dominant Portrayal of Sporting Muslim Women in Academic Research, Public Forums and Mediated Representations'. In *Race, Gender and Sport: The Politics of Ethnic 'Other' Girls and Women*, edited by Aarti Ratna and Samaya Farooq Samie, 35–62. London: Routledge.

Samie, Samaya Farooq, and Kim Toffoletti. 2018. 'Postfeminist Paradoxes and Cultural Difference: Unpacking Media Representations of American Muslim Sportswomen Ibtihaj and Dalilah Muhammad'. In *New Sporting Femininities: Embodied Politics in Postfeminist Times*, edited by Kim Toffoletti, Holly Thorpe and Jessica Francombe-Webb, 87–110. Cham: Palgrave Macmillan.

Sawyer, R. Keith. 2002. 'The New Anthropology of Children, Play, and Games'. *Reviews in Anthropology* 31 (2): 147–64. https://doi.org/10.1080/00988150212940.

Scheffer, Paul. 2000. 'Het Multiculturele Drama'. *NRC*, 29 January. Available online: https://retro.nrc.nl/W2/Lab/Multicultureel/scheffer.html.

Schielke, Samuli. 2009. 'Being Good in Ramadan: Ambivalence, Fragmentation, and the Moral Self in the Lives of Young Egyptians'. *Journal of the Royal Anthropological Institute* 15 (2009): 24–40. Available online: https://www.jstor.org/stable/20527687.

Schielke, Samuli. 2010. 'Second Thoughts about the Anthropology of Islam, or How to Make Sense of Grand Schemes in Everyday Life'. *ZMO Working Papers* 2: 1–16. https://d-nb.info/1019243724/34.

Schielke, Samuli, and Liza Debevec, eds. 2012. *Ordinary Lives and Grand Schemes: An Anthropology of Everyday Religion*. New York: Berghahn Books.

Schippers, Edith. 2016. 'De Paradox van de Vrijheid'. Elsevier/HJ Schoo-lezing 05-09-2016. Avalable online: https://www.ewmagazine.nl/nederland/achtergrond/2016/09/hj-schoo-lezing-edith-schippers-de-paradox-van-de-vrijheid-353734/.

Schmeets, Hans. 2014. *De Religieuze Kaart van Nederland, 2010–2013*. Den Haag: Centraal Bureau voor de Statistiek.

Schmeets, Hans. 2016. *De Religieuze Kaart van Nederland, 2010–2015*. Den Haag: Centraal Bureau voor de Statistiek.

SCP and CBS. 2014. 'Armoedesignalement 2014'. Den Haag: Sociaal en Cultureel Planbureau | Centraal Bureau voor de Statistiek.

Scraton, Sheila, Jayne Caudwell and Samantha Holland. 2005. '"Bend It like Patel" Centring "Race", Ethnicity and Gender in Feminist Analysis of Women's Football in England'. *International Review for the Sociology of Sport* 40 (1): 71–88. https://doi.org/10.1136/bmj.39538.455891.59.

Scraton, Sheila, K. Fasting, G. Pfister and A. Bunuel. 1999. 'It's Still a Man's Game? The Experiences of Top-Level European Women Footballers'. *International Review for the Sociology of Sport* 34 (2): 99–112. https://doi.org/10.1177/101269099034002001.

Sehlikoglu, Sertaç. 2018. 'Revisited: Muslim Women's Agency and Feminist Anthropology of the Middle East'. *Contemporary Islam* 12 (1): 73–92. https://doi.org/10.1007/s11562-017-0404-8.

Selby, Jennifer A. 2011. 'French Secularism as a "Guarantor" of Women's Rights? Muslim Women and Gender Politics in a Parisian Banlieue'. *Culture & Religion* 12 (4): 441–62. https://doi.org/10.1080/14755610.2011.633536.

Siebelink, Jeroen. 2016a. *Het Meisje Centraal*. Zeist: KNVB.

Siebelink, Jeroen. 2016b. *Werving & Behoud: Allemaal Uitblinkende Meiden – Deel 2*. Zeist: KNVB.

Silverstein, Paul A. 2000. 'Sporting Faith: Islam, Soccer, and the French Nation-State'. *Social Text* 18 (4): 25–53. https://doi.org/10.1215/01642472-18-4_65-25.

Silverstein, Paul A. 2002. 'Stadium Politics: Sport, Islam and Amazigh Consciousness in France and North Africa'. In *With God on Their Side: Sport in the Service of Religion*, edited by Tara Magdalinski and Timothy J. L. Chandler, 37–55. London: Routledge.

Silverstein, Paul A. 2005. 'Immigrant Racialization and the New Savage Slot: Race, Migration, and Immigration in the New Europe'. *Annual Review of Anthropology* 34: 363–84. https://doi.org/10.1146/annurev.anthro.34.081804.120338.

Silverstein, Paul A. 2008. 'Thin Lines on the Pavement. The Racialization and Spatialization of Violence in Postcolonial (Sub)Urban France'. In *Gendering Urban Space in the Middle East, South Asia, and Africa*, edited by Martina Rieker and Kamran Asdar Ali, 169–205. New York: Palgrave Macmillan.

Singh, Jakeet. 2015. 'Religious Agency and the Limits of Intersectionality'. *Hypatia* 30 (4): 657–74. https://doi.org/10.1111/hypa.12182.

Smiet, Katrine. 2014. 'Post/Secular Truths: Sojourner Truth and the Intersections of Gender, Race and Religion'. *European Journal of Women's Studies* 22 (1): 7–21. https://doi.org/10.1177/1350506814544914.

Smit, Vincent. 2014. 'Schilderswijk, Wonen En Ontspanning'. In *De Maakbare Stad. Rondkijken in Den Haag. Haagse Sociale En Culturele Verkenningen 3*, edited by Vincent Smit, 38–49. Den Haag: Lectoraat Grootstedelijke Ontwikkeling, De Haagse Hogeschool.

Smith, Joy L. 2014. 'The Dutch Carnivalesque: Blackface, Play, and Zwarte Piet'. In *Dutch Racism*, edited by Philomena Essed and Isabel Hoving, 219–38. Leiden: Rodopi | Brill.

Spaaij, Ramón. 2009. 'Sport as a Vehicle for Social Mobility and Regulation of Disadvantaged Urban Youth Lessons from Rotterdam'. *International Review for the Sociology of Sport* 44 (2–3): 247–64. https://doi.org/10.1177/1012690209338415.

van Sterkenburg, Jacco. 2011. 'Thinking 'Race'and Ethnicity in (Dutch) Sports Policy and-Research'. In *Sport and Challenges to Racism*, edited by Jonathan Long and Karl Spracklen, 19–34. Basingstoke: Palgrave Macmillan.

Stolcke, Verena. 1993. 'Is Sex to Gender as Race Is to Ethnicity?' In *Gendered Anthropology*, edited by Teresa del Valle, 17–37. London: Routledge.

Stoler, Ann Laura. 2002. *Carnal Knowledge and Imperial Power: Race and the Intimate in Colonial Rule*. Oakland: University of California Press.

Stoler, Ann Laura. 2016. *Duress: Imperial Durabilities in Our Times*. Durham: Duke University Press.

Sunier, Thijl. 2009. 'Response to Heiko Henkel'. *Social Anthropology* 17 (4): 473–5. https://doi.org/10.1111/j.1469-8676.2009.00086_2.x.

Sunier, Thijl. 2012. 'Beyond the Domestication of Islam in Europe: A Reflection on Past and Future Research on Islam in European Societies'. *Journal of Muslims in Europe* 1 (2): 189–208. https://doi.org/10.1163/22117954-12341236.

Swain, Jon. 2000. '"The Money's Good, the Fame's Good, the Girls Are Good": The Role of Playground Football in the Construction of Young Boys' Masculinity in a Junior School'. *British Journal of Sociology of Education* 21 (1): 95–109. https://doi.org/10.1080/01425690095180.

Swain, Jon. 2003. 'How Young Schoolboys Become Somebody: The Role of the Body in the Construction of Masculinity.'' *British Journal of Sociology of Education* 24 (3): 299–314. https://doi.org/10.1080/01425690301890.

Tamimi Arab, Pooyan. 2014. 'Amplifying Islam: Pluralism, Secularism, and Religious Sounds in The Netherlands'. PhD thesis, Utrecht University.

Testa, Alberto, and Mahfoud Amara, eds. 2016. *Sport in Islam and in Muslim Communities*. London: Routledge. https://doi.org/10.4324/9781315745480.

Thangaraj, Stanley. 2015. *Desi Hoop Dreams: Pickup Basketball and the Making of Asian American Masculinity*. New York: New York University Press.

Thorne, Barrie. 1993. *Gender Play: Girls and Boys at School*. New Brunswick: Rutgers University Press.

Thorpe, Holly, Lyndsay M. C. Hayhurst and Megan Chawansky. 2018. 'The Girl Effect and 'Positive' Representations of Sporting Girls of the Global South: Social Media Portrayals of Afghan Girls on Skateboards'. In *New Sporting Femininities: Embodied Politics in Postfeminist Times*, edited by Kim Toffoletti, Holly Thorpe and Jessica Francombe-Webb, 299–323. Cham: Palgrave Macmillan.

Tilman, Rosa, and Jacco van Sterkenburg. 2017. 'Vrouwenvoetbal, Gender En Media: Een Receptieonderzoek Naar Betekenisgeving Aan Gender in

Vrouwenvoetbal Op Televisie'. In *Vrouwenvoetbal in Nederland: Spiegel En Katalysator van Maatschappelijke Verandering*, edited by Martine Prange and Martijn Oosterbaan, 237–62. Utrecht: Klement.

Toffoletti, Kim, and Catherine Palmer. 2017. 'New Approaches for Studies of Muslim Women and Sport'. *International Review for the Sociology of Sport* 52 (2): 146–63. https://doi.org/10.1177/1012690215589326.

Toffoletti, Kim, Holly Thorpe and Jessica Francombe-Webb. 2018. *New Sporting Femininities: Embodied Politics in Postfeminist Times*. Cham: Palgrave Macmillan.

Tonkens, Evelien. 2014. 'Misverstanden over de Participatiesamenleving'. *Sociale Vraagstukken*, 24 July 2014. Available online: https://www.socialevraagstukken.nl/misverstanden-over-de-participatiesamenleving/.

Valentine, Gill. 2007. 'Theorizing and Researching Intersectionality: A Challenge for Feminist Geography'. *The Professional Geographer* 59 (1): 10–21. https://doi.org/10.1111/j.1467-9272.2007.00587.x.

van der Veer, Peter. 2002. 'The Netherlands and Islam'. *ISIM Newsletter* 9: 7–8.

Vermeulen, Jeroen, and Paul Verweel. 2009. 'Participation in Sport: Bonding and Bridging as Identity Work'. *Sport in Society* 12 (9): 1206–19. https://doi.org/10.1080/17430430903137886.

Verweij, Arjen. 2014. 'Concentratiewijken: Springplank of Getto?' In *Soort Zoekt Soort. Clustering En Sociaal-Economische Scheidslijnen in Nederland*, edited by Jessie Bakens, Henri L.F. de Groot, Peter Mulder and Cees-Jan Pen, 95–104. Den Haag: Platform31.

Vescio, Johanna, Kerrie Wilde and Janice J. Crosswhite. 2005. 'Profiling Sport Role Models to Enhance Initiatives for Adolescent Girls in Physical Education and Sport'. *European Physical Education Review* 11 (2): 153–70. https://doi.org/10.1177/1356336X05052894.

VROM/WWI. 2007. *Integratienota 2007–2011: Zorg Dat Je Erbij Hoort!* Den Haag: Ministerie van VROM/WWI.

VWS. 2005. 'Nota Tijd Voor Sport'. Den Haag: Tweede Kamer, vergaderjaar 2004–2005, 30 234, nr. 2.

VWS. 2006. *Programma Meedoen Allochtone Jeugd Door Sport 2006–2010*. Den Haag: Ministerie van Volksgezondheid, Welzijn, en Sport.

Walseth, Kristin, and Kari Fasting. 2003. 'Islam's View on Physical Activity and Sport: Egyptian Women Interpreting Islam'. *International Review for the Sociology of Sport* 38 (1): 45–60. https://doi.org/10.1177/10126902030381003.

Water, Sebastiaan van de. 2013. 'Panna Behoort Tot Cultureel Erfgoed'. *Het Parool*, 15 June. Available online: https://imagineic.nl/content/uploads/2020/01/Panna-behoort-tot-cultureel-erfgoed-Parool-15-juni-2013.pdf.

Watson, Beccy, and Aarti Ratna. 2011. 'Bollywood in the Park: Thinking Intersectionally about Public Leisure Space'. *Leisure/Loisir* 35 (1): 71–86. https://doi.org/10.1080/14927713.2011.549198.

Wekker, Gloria. 2002. 'Nesten Bouwen Op Een Winderige Plek. Denken over Gender En Etniciteit in Nederland'. *Tijdschrift Voor Genderstudies* 3: 24–33.

Wekker, Gloria. 2016. *White Innocence: Paradoxes of Colonialism and Race*. Durham: Duke University Press.

Wekker, Gloria, and Helma Lutz. 2001. 'Een Hoogvlakte Met Koude Winden: De Geschiedenis van Het Gender- En Etniciteitsdenken in Nederland'. In *Caleidoscopische Visies. De Zwarte, Migranten- En Vluchtelingenvrouwen Beweging in Nederland*, edited by Maayke Botman, Nancy Jouwe and Gloria Wekker, 25–49. Amsterdam: Koninklijk Instituut voor de Tropen.

West, Candace, and Don H. Zimmermann. 1987. 'Doing Gender'. *Gender and Society* 1 (2): 125–51. https://doi.org/10.1177/0891243287001002002.

van der Wilk, Döske L. 2016. 'Van Wie Is Het Plein? Over de (on) Toegankelijkheid van de Openbare Ruimte in Een Gentrificerende Buurt Te Amsterdam'. PhD thesis, University of Amsterdam.

Willemse, Rob. 2013. 'De Bal, De Bal, En Anders Niet'. *Helden Magazine*. Available online: https://imagineic.nl/content/uploads/2020/01/De-bal-en-anders-niets-Helden-magazine.pdf.

Williams, Jean. 2003. *A Game for Rough Girls? A History of Women's Football in Britian*. London: Routledge.

Williams, Jean. 2007. *A Beautiful Game: International Perspectives on Women's Football*. Oxford: Berg.

Woodward, Kath. 2009. *Embodied Sporting Practices: Regulating and Regulatory Bodies*. New York: Palgrave Macmillan.

Young, Iris Marion. 2005. *On Female Body Experience: 'Throwing like a Girl' and Other Essays*. Oxford: Oxford University Press.

Young, Janet A., Caroline M. Symons, Michelle D. Pain, Jack T. Harvey, Rochelle M. Eime, Melinda J. Craike, and Warren R. Payne. 2015. 'Role Models of Australian Female Adolescents: A Longitudinal Study to Inform Programmes Designed to Increase Physical Activity and Sport Participation'. *European Physical Education Review* 21 (4): 451–66. https://doi.org/10.1177/1356336X15579574.

Index

agency
  children's 23
  conceptualizations of 8, 10, 12, 157, 160
  embodied 3, 10, 14, 17, 85, 126, 157, 159
  football and play as 11, 14–16, 157
  Islamic (*see under* Islam)
  secular notion of 10–11, 14
  sources and practices of 11, 14, 18
Azzarito, Laura 6–7, 84, 117–18

belonging
  ethnic and/or racial 30, 41, 115
  local/neighbourhood 44, 53–4, 58, 65–6, 93, 151
  national (*see under* nationalism)
  to public/football spaces 14, 45, 70, 87, 90–1, 99, 149, 151, 154
  religious 25
bodies (*see also* embodying; disciplining)
  athletic 13, 16, 109, 118
  disciplining 113, 119, 127
  female/girls' 70, 82–3, 88, 119, 129, 144
  male 77, 88, 129
  racialized (Muslim) 7, 45, 90–2, 118, 136, 141–3, 153, 155
  secular 13, 92, 136, 139
  segregated 6, 109, 133, 135
  sexed and gendered 7, 45, 81–5, 106–10, 117, 120, 123, 133
  sexualized 146, 88
Bouras, Nadia 38, 39
Bracke, Sarah 5, 10, 14–15, 40, 90, 125–6, 138, 149
Butler, Judith 7, 101, 107, 133, 139
  performativity 16, 80, 84–5, 109–10, 117–18 (*see also* performativity)

Caudwell, Jayne 6–8, 107, 117–18, 133
citizenship (*see also* nationalism)
  culturalization of 17–18, 91, 125–6, 129, 131, 133, 138–44, 149–50, 157
  discipline and 61, 119, 130
  Dutch 3, 37, 41, 49, 149
  embodying 128, 136, 142, 149–50
  as lived practice 18, 150–1
  Muslims and 11–12, 15, 24, 40, 116, 138, 153–4, 160
  sport and 4, 126–9, 131, 136
  whiteness and 26, 59
  youth and 5, 23, 39, 46
class
  and football/sport 43–5, 128, 138
  intersections of 4, 94–5, 118, 143–4, 154
  in the Schilderswijk (*see under* Schilderswijk)
Cruyff court 2, 46
  6 vs 6 competition 19–21, 33, 69–70, 86–9, 91, 126–7, 143

disciplining
  bodies (*see under* bodies)
  self-discipline 7, 117
  via sports 5, 43, 61, 95, 101, 113, 117, 130
  of (racialized) youth 40, 61, 118–19, 129–30, 133, 139, 151
discourses (*see also* citizenship, culturalization of)
  (*see under* ethnicity; gender; integration; Muslim girls; race; Schilderswijk; sexuality)
diversity (*see also* multicultural)
  in backgrounds 2, 25, 49, 94, 134, 137, 159–60
  in neighbourhoods 3, 5, 20, 23, 50–1, 53, 57, 59
  in sport 45, 59, 137–8, 160

Elling, Agnes 2–6, 69, 77, 95, 97–8, 153–4

El-Tayeb, Fatima 5, 42, 44–5, 55, 59, 62, 94, 118–20, 130, 150
   'queering ethnicity' 147–8
emancipation (*see also* citizenship, culturalization of)
   and Muslim girls 2–5, 8, 39, 42, 125, 130, 133, 138–42, 151, 154
   and sport 129, 136
   and whiteness, colonialism 32, 42
   women's and girls' 1, 120, 126, 129, 140, 143
embodying (*see also* bodies)
   agency (*see under* agency)
   citizenship (*see under* citizenship)
   femininity 6, 8, 107, 120, 156
   (Dutch) nationalism 5, 119
   the 'other' 5, 13, 16, 126, 137, 141–2
   practices and play 16, 70, 81–5, 106, 110, 113, 158–60
   sport and football 7, 81, 85, 89, 99–100, 126, 149
   talking and kicking back 15–17
empowerment 5, 7, 14, 19, 27, 32, 85, 129 (*see also* emancipation)
ethnicity
   as category of difference 16, 18, 41, 149, 158
   discourses on 41, 59, 93, 133
   ethnic backgrounds 1, 2, 85, 98, 159
   ethnic-minority 2, 4, 39–40, 77, 94, 126, 153–4 (*see under* discipline)
   ethnic profiling 27–8, 60
   ethnic segregation 137–8
   intersections of 15, 25, 42, 62, 116, 118–19, 134
   and performativity/play 16, 147, 149, 154, 160
   queering (*see under* El-Tayeb, Fatima)
   and researcher positionality 24, 26, 30–2
   in the Schilderswijk (*see under* Schilderswijk)
   and social control 67, 115
   in sports 2, 4, 5, 8, 12, 44–5, 126–7, 129–31, 136, 147–9
ethnography
   data and material 36, 101, 153, 155–6
   feminist 18–19, 22, 29

fieldwork 3, 19, 21, 158
   vignette 27–31, 47–9, 70–1

femininity
   athletic 6–7, 117–18
   bodies (*see under* bodies)
   performativity of 16, 102, 107, 118–20, 156
   in sport/football 6, 18, 74, 78, 84, 86–90, 101
Foucault, Michel 113, 117
football
   club 2–4, 15, 32–4, 43, 46, 59, 61, 76–7, 89, 95, 100, 104, 106, 109, 118, 128, 137–8, 153–4, 159
   grassroots 3, 18–20, 35, 79
   identity 45, 126, 149
   and sports culture 9, 128, 133, 139–40, 146, 156–7 (*see also* street football culture)
   unorganized 4, 61, 128, 153
   women's 1, 6, 8, 15, 19, 72, 95–7, 100, 108, 117, 131, 147–8, 159
football competition
   boys' 76, 81, 88, 92
   Cruyff Court 6 vs 6 (*see under* Cruyff Court)
   Football Girls United 34–6, 46, 58, 64–5, 101–14, 120, 123, 125, 131–3, 137, 144, 146, 153, 155–6
   girls' 3, 5, 10, 17–18, 20, 23, 27, 140, 144
   play and 15, 83, 86
   separation of 6, 134–5
   street 2, 20–1, 33–4, 61, 73, 76–7, 80–2, 92, 95, 127

gender (*see also* citizenship, culturalization of)
   bodies (*see under* bodies)
   differences 5, 80, 82–3
   discourses 18, 86–7, 89, 100, 110, 115
   education 111, 115–16
   in/equality 2, 15, 17, 32–4, 131
   intersections of 3, 8, 12, 20, 25, 31, 42, 44, 50, 116, 143, 146
   norms 6–8, 10, 40, 67, 84–5, 92, 99, 108, 117–20, 124, 144, 156

performativity of 16, 104, 118, 123, 154, 158, 160 (*see under* play)
power relations (*see under* power relations)
in public playgrounds/sport spaces 65, 69–70, 73–6, 80–2, 93, 96, 99, 139, 155
segregation in football 9, 11, 101–4, 107–8, 133–8, 157
stereotypes 78, 85–6, 123, 135, 147–8

heteronormativity 13, 18, 89, 102, 106–8, 113, 117, 120, 159 (*see also* sexuality)
hooks, bell 14

identity (*see under* football; Muslim; nationalism; Schilderswijk; sexuality)
inequality 6, 8, 17, 25, 59, 70, 131, 151
integration (*see also* citizenship, culturalization of)
discourses on 59, 126, 129, 133, 140, 144, 151, 157
of ethnic and religious minorities 2, 20, 43, 51, 77, 125, 133, 142
Ministry of 4, 51, 129
(racialized) politics of 3, 39, 55, 57, 138–40
through sports 5, 42, 61, 119, 126–9, 131
intersectional 3, 8–9, 12–13, 17–18, 26, 70, 73, 90, 105, 117–18, 146, 153, 160 (*see also* class; ethnicity; gender; Islam; race; sexuality)
Islam (*see also* citizenship, culturalization of; Muslim)
and agency 10–12, 159–60
background 5, 25, 126, 149
Islamophobia 8, 26, 42, 147, 149
public and political debates on 40–2, 55–7, 59, 116, 130, 138, 142, 153
racialization of 8, 90
research on 24–5, 158–60
and the Schilderswijk 2, 3, 20, 51, 55, 125, 140, 155
and sport 9, 13–14, 18, 91, 107, 134–46, 154, 156

kicking back 14, 16–18, 85, 99–100, 126, 142, 147–8, 153–60

Koning, Anouk de 2–3, 5, 26, 40–2, 57–63, 90, 93–4, 114, 125, 137, 150, 153–4
Koning, Martijn de 5, 14–15, 24–5, 31, 90

Mahmood, Saba 10, 14
masculinity
performativity of 16, 70, 84, 101–2, 107, 112, 117, 119–20, 154, 156
racialized 7, 93, 118–19, 142
in sport 6, 45–6, 69–70, 75–82, 86–9, 94, 97, 99–100, 103, 117, 133, 137, 153
migration
Moroccan 2, 18, 37–9, 42–3, 49, 153
policies 39, 40, 125, 131
in the Schilderswijk (*see under* Schilderswijk)
multicultural (*see also* diversity)
Dutch society 40, 44
neighbourhood 2, 3, 20, 26, 28, 51, 57, 90, 125, 128, 153
Muslim
backgrounds 2, 8, 10, 25, 31, 85, 96, 116, 132, 139–40, 144
as category 8, 12–14, 18, 24–6, 41, 148–9, 154, 157–60
identity 12, 14
Muslim girls
discourses on 3, 5, 8, 13–16, 85, 101, 125–6, 148–50, 154, 157, 160
emancipation (*see under* emancipation)
stereotypes of 7, 13–15, 25–6, 90, 116, 143, 145, 147–9, 157

nationalism (Dutch) 5, 40, 129–30 (*see also* citizenship)
belonging 16, 53, 55–6, 120, 151
embodying (*see under* embodying)
identity 5, 16, 26, 42, 125, 139, 154, 156
in sport 7–8, 16, 42, 119, 142, 154, 156
neighbourhood
'disadvantaged' 2–4, 43, 50–1, 56–9, 62, 118, 127–8, 130–1, 154–5
diverse (*see under* diversity)
ethnically mixed 23
gendered 66
multicultural (*see under* multicultural)
sport programmes 5

Orange Lionesses
(*Oranjeleeuwinnen*) 1, 159

performativity (*see also* Butler, Judith)
  of femininity (*see under* femininity)
  in football 14, 17–18, 66, 100, 126, 147, 151, 154, 156–60
  of masculinity (*see under* masculinity)
  performance 15, 72–3, 80, 84, 87–9, 102, 135, 140
  of religion 146

play
  creative 'free' 61, 113
  embodied (*see under* embodying)
  ethnicity (*see under* ethnicity)
  football 17–18, 46, 85, 120, 123, 147, 151, 154
  gendered 73–5, 84
  religion 154, 157, 160
  theories of 14–16

power relations 7–9, 73, 120
  gendered 104, 110–13
  racialized 30, 100, 119

Puwar, Nirmal 55, 88–90
  'out of place' 72, 76, 81, 92–3, 110, 116
  space invaders 18, 70, 77, 81, 84–5, 90, 92, 95, 98–100, 156

race 3, 5, 15, 17
  discourses 70, 138
  performativity of 16, 153–4, 158
  racial profiling 28, 60
  racialized (*see under* bodies; disciplining; integration; Islam; masculinity; power relations)
  in sport and football 7–9, 12, 25, 31, 62, 119, 126, 131

Rana, Jasmijn 4, 5, 9, 11, 33, 43, 50–1, 56–7, 59–60, 77, 94, 119, 125, 130–1, 137, 154

Ratna, Aarti 7–10, 70, 90, 93–4, 104, 148

religion (*see under* belonging; integration; performativity; play) (*see also* Islam)

role model 1, 10, 46, 70, 89, 95–100

Samie, Samaya Farooq 6–10, 14, 90, 124, 135, 137–8, 144, 149, 156

Schielke, Samuli 10–12

Schilderswijk (*see also* urban regeneration)
  citizens 56, 60
  and class 18, 31, 50, 52, 54, 57–9, 67, 100, 153
  discourses on 50, 57, 60
  and ethnicity/race 3, 20, 50–1, 53, 55–7, 59–60, 90, 125, 155
  identity 45
  and Islam (*see under* Islam)
  as migration neighbourhood 51–3, 57
  representation of 18, 27, 50, 155
  stereotypes of 27, 51, 64, 146, 155

secular
  agency (*see under* agency)
  bodies (*see under* bodies)
  society 12, 40–1, 101, 130, 140, 144
  sport and football 8–9, 13, 18, 70, 90–3, 99, 119, 138–41, 149, 156, 158

sexuality (*see also* citizenship, culturalization of; heteronormativity)
  sexualized discourses 70, 81–2, 85–7, 89, 108, 144, 156
  equality 2, 17
  heterosexuality 6, 101–2, 107–8, 118–20, 123, 144
  (hetero)sexualizing of athletes 8, 73, 88–9, 112–13, 115, 146, 156
  identity 89, 149, 159
  intersections of 116, 133–4, 137
  and the Muslim 'other' 32, 40–2, 125–6, 129, 136–40, 153
  norms 7–8, 10, 16, 45, 52, 67, 117–20, 124, 138
  performativity of 120
  in public space 80

Silverstein, Paul 5, 41, 60, 90, 119, 127, 129–30, 151

social cohesion 5, 126–7, 131

social justice 19, 101, 104–5, 108, 110

spatial 3, 52, 57, 65, 74, 94, 100, 119
  organisation of sport 58, 78–9, 88, 91, 101, 110, 116–17, 120
  practices 70, 113–14, 124, 133, 137, 160
  segregation 59, 77, 108–9, 123, 138, 156
  space invaders (*see under* Puwar, Nirmal)
  stereotypes (*see under* Muslim girls; gender, Schilderswijk)

street football culture 2, 18, 44–5, 101

talking back 14–16, 110, 142, 148
Turkish-Dutch 2, 26, 35, 51, 97–8, 129

urban regeneration 4, 5, 20, 42, 51, 62

Wekker, Gloria 5, 26, 39–40, 42, 60, 88, 120, 126, 129, 133, 136, 153
white
  Dutch people 55, 59–60, 64, 126, 128–9, 132–3, 137–8, 140, 142–3
  Dutch society 13, 50, 101, 139 (*see also* Wekker, Gloria)
  girls and boys 1, 3, 5, 11, 35, 94, 118–19, 145–6, 148–9
  norms 70, 90, 95, 99, 144
  researcher 24, 26–7, 30–1, 116, 143
  sport professionals 21, 32, 36, 90–3, 96
whiteness 6, 8, 99 (*see under* citizenship; emancipation)

Young, Iris Marion 83–4, 117

www.ingramcontent.com/pod-product-compliance
Lightning Source LLC
Chambersburg PA
CBHW061831300426
44115CB00013B/2333